D'ORCY'S
AIRSHIP MANUAL

D'ORCY'S
AIRSHIP MANUAL

AN INTERNATIONAL REGISTER OF AIRSHIPS WITH A COMPENDIUM OF THE AIRSHIP'S ELEMENTARY MECHANICS

COMPILED AND EDITED
BY
LADISLAS D'ORCY, M.S.A.E.

Reprint of *D'Orcy's Airship Manual Copyright* © 2018 by VertVolta Press

All rights reserved. Published in the United States by VertVolta Press.

No part of this book's design may be reproduced in any manner whatsoever without prior written permission.

Cover design/facsimile formatting: Vladimir Verano, VertVolta Design

Rediscover Edition Introduction © 2018 Vladimir Verano

Portrait image of Ladislas D'Orcy © 2018 Vladimir Verano

'D'Orcy's Airship Manual' by Baron Ladislas Emile D'Orcy was originally published in New York, 1917.

The illustrations for the 1917 edition were drawings by Geo. F. McLaughlin

The photographs for the 1917 edition were from the collection of Mr. Henry Woodhouse

To contact the publisher:
vvdesignpress@gmail.com

First VertVolta Press edition 2013

ISBN: 978-1-60944-083-1

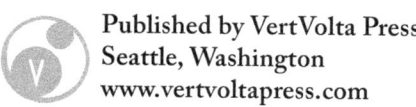

Published by VertVolta Press
Seattle, Washington
www.vertvoltapress.com

*A la Mémoire
des Aérostiers de la Republique
et de ses Alliés
morts pour la
Liberté des Peuples.*

———

*To the Memory
of the Aeronauts of the French Republic
and of her Allies
who died for the
Freedom of the Peoples.*

CONTENTS

		PAGE			PAGE
	INTRODUCTION	1	V	AIRSHIP LOSSES OF THE ALLIES	199
	ELEMENTARY MECHANICS OF THE AIRSHIP	2	VI	GERMANY'S AIRSHIP LOSSES	201
	THE AIRSHIP IN THE GREAT WAR	39	VII	THE GERMAN AIRSHIP RAIDS ON GREAT BRITAIN	205
I	THE WORLD AIRSHIP BUILDERS	51			
II	THE WORLD'S AIRSHIP PRODUCTION	185	VIII	THE COMMERCIAL AIRSHIP FLEETS OF 1914	209
III	THE MILITARY AIRSHIP FLEETS	191	IX	THE WORLD'S AIRSHIP SHEDS	213
IV	COMPARATIVE STRENGTH OF THE MILITARY AIRSHIP FLEETS	197		INDEX	229

Introduction to D'Orcy's Essays . . . Vladimir Verano

X   Essays

Super-Zeppelins

Mastery of the Air vs. the Control of the Sea

On the Threshold of the Flying Age

Is Transport by Air a Succcess?

NOTICE

In compliance with the recommendations of the National Advisory Committee for Aeronautics, all data in *D'Orcy's Airship Manual* are expressed in the metric system. For the convenience of readers unfamiliar with the metric system the approximate equivalents of the metric units employed are herewith given in English units:

1 meter (m.) = $3\frac{1}{3}$ feet.
1 kilometer (km.) = $\frac{3}{5}$ statute mile.
1 cubic meter (cbm. or mc.) = $35\frac{1}{3}$ cubic feet.
1 kilogram (kg.) = $2\frac{1}{5}$ pounds.
1 metric ton = 2,200 pounds.

INTRODUCTION

The present volume is the result of a methodical investigation extending over a period of four years in the course of which many hundreds of English, French, Italian, German and Spanish publications and periodicals dealing with the present status as well as with the early history of airships have carefully been consulted and digested. It has thus become possible to gather under the cover of a handy reference-book a large amount of hitherto widely scattered information which, having mostly been published in foreign languages, was not immediately available to the English speaking public.

The information thus gathered is herewith presented in two parts; one being a compendium of the elementary principles underlying the construction and operation of airships, the other constituting an exhaustive, but tersely worded register of the world's airshipping which furnishes, whenever available, complete data for every airship of 500 cubic meters and over, that has been laid down since 1834. Smaller airships are listed only if they embody unusual features.

It has been attempted to furnish here the most up-to-date information regarding the gigantic fleet of airships built by Germany since the beginning of the Great War, a feature which may, in a certain measure, repay the reader for the utter lack of data on the Allies' recent airship constructions, which had to be withheld for military reasons. A revised and enlarged edition of *D'Orcy's Airship Manual*, in which all the airships built during the Great War will be listed and their features duly discussed, will be issued upon the termination of the war.

Ladislas d'Orcy,
New York City (U. S. A.)

ELEMENTARY MECHANICS OF THE AIRSHIP

Definition and Classification.—The airship belongs, with its immediate forerunner, the free balloon, to the family of *static aircraft*.

Static aircraft derive their sustentation from a hull which is filled with a gas lighter than air; free balloons and airships consequently float in the atmosphere, like ships float on the sea, by virtue of buoyancy.

The airship's sustentation is, unlike that of the aeroplane, independent of forward motion, in other words, the airship can stay aloft without expending engine power, in which case it drifts with the prevailing wind like a free balloon.

The airship is the outcome of a century-long endeavor to endow the free balloon with independent velocity whereby it would be able to navigate the atmosphere regardless of winds in any direction desired; hence the now little used terms of "navigable" and "dirigible balloon" under which the airship first became known.

The very nature of the airship's sustentation, which permits to assimilate the airship to the ship of the sea, sufficiently justifies the retention of the term "airship" and the condemnation of the term "dirigible," the customary abbreviation of "dirigible balloon," which may reasonably be applied to the aeroplane too, since it fails to specify the type of aircraft it is supposed to describe.

The hitherto customary division of airships into the rigid, semi-rigid, and non-rigid types, which was based on primitive and now obsolescent conceptions, has been found totally inadequate to express the features of novel sub-types which have more recently been produced; it has therefore been deemed advisable to adopt a new nomenclature, based on the constructional features of the hull which alone permit fundamental differentiation.

Whereas every airship hull presents to the relative wind an essentially rigid body, it follows that the term "rigid" cannot logically be applied to one particular airship type, the same argument barring also the terms "semi-rigid" and "non-rigid." Consequently all airships in which the shape of the hull is rendered permanent by means of a rigid structure, the hull frame, are here termed *structure airships*, whereas all those in which the shape of the hull is maintained through internal pressure are here listed as *pressure airships*.

Structure Airships.—The fundamental principles of the structure airship were first laid down in a patent taken out in 1873 by the Alsatian engineer Joseph Spiess. Twenty years later David Schwarz of Zagreb (Croatia) built at Petrograd a structure airship which was the earliest representative of its kind, but it was a failure. Shortly afterwards Count Ferdinand von Zeppelin, a German cavalry general, emulated Schwarz, whose patents he had purchased, and eventually succeeded in developing by gradual improvement of design the highly efficient modern structure airship. Structure airships are characterized by a rigid hull frame generally built up of longitudinal girders which are connected at intervals by polygonal ties; the resulting framework is covered with a waterproof, but non-gas-tight, fabric skin. On Zeppelin airships every second tie is braced athwartships by a radial wire truss resembling the spokes of a bicycle wheel, through the hub of which a steel hawser runs from stem to stern. Both the hawser and the radial truss wires are fitted with turnbuckles whereby the whole framework may be tightened up when required. The radial, or tie, trusses form the compartments in which from 18 to 24 individual gas-cells are housed; the cells are drum-shaped and are fitted with an inflation appendix and a relief-valve. Owing to the constancy of displacement realized by the hull frame, no deformation will occur through a contraction of the hydrogen, whereas an expansion of the gas will be promptly relieved by the automatic and manually operated valves; but as the latter process may create an explosive mixture between the gas-cells and the outer cover, it is necessary to keep this space constantly ventilated by forced draught, the escaping hydrogen being expelled through shafts leading to the roof. These shafts are fitted with automatic valves which can also be manually controlled.

As a further measure of precaution recent Zeppelin airships have the lower half of the outer skin treated with a gas-proof varnish to prevent its penetration by the heavy and impure gas collecting in the bottom of the gas-cells, which on coming in contact with the engine exhaust might set the vessel on fire.

The portions of the hull which are in the immediate neighborhood of the propellers are protected against possible injury from this source by a plating of veneer.

It has been reported that on the latest Zeppelin airships the gas-cells are connected with a storage tank whither the expanding hydrogen escapes under rising pressure through automatic valves and whence it can be pumped back into the gas-cells when the hydrogen contracts. Whatever truth there be in this so far unverified statement, it is obvious that such a storage tank would greatly obviate the structure airships' great drawback of losing gas and consequently lift in the process of regulating variations of gas-pressure. A similar arrangement incidentally existed on the first Schütte-Lanz airship, where the excess of gas generated by rising pressure was forced by means of a centrifugal pump into two gas-cells which remained empty at sea-level pressure. This system enabled the airship to reach an altitude of 2,000 meters without any loss of gas.

The Hull Frame.—The material employed in the construction of hull frames is either a zinc aluminum alloy or wood. The former is used in Zeppelin airships in the shape of triangular lattice girders, whereas in the Schütte-Lanz airships laminated wood girders are employed. The wooden girders of the Spiess airship were of tubular form, built in halves and glued together.

The longitudinals and polygonals of Zeppelin airships are built up of punch-pressed corner-rails and X-pieces; they are riveted together so as to form triangular girders. The only authoritative statement regarding the strength and weight of these girders is one by Count Zeppelin to the effect that on his first airship " the aluminum which served as the material of construction had a specific weight of 2.7 kg. and a tensile strength of 33 kg. per square meter of surface. The frames proper (longitudinals) were built of angle and T-bars and the bracing girders (polygonals) of angle bars. The weight of these frames, as applied to the construction, was 0.9 and 1.8 kg. per meter length, this being equivalent to 0.516 kg. per cubic meter of volume." On the Zeppelin airship *Sachsen*, built in 1913, the adoption of an aluminum alloy of greater tensile strength and the use of triangular girders resulted in a considerable increase in strength, while the weight per meter of length was reduced by 0.13 kg.

On the first Schütte-Lanz airship the hull frame consisted of a closely meshed lattice-work of laminated wood girders, spirally wound and diagonally

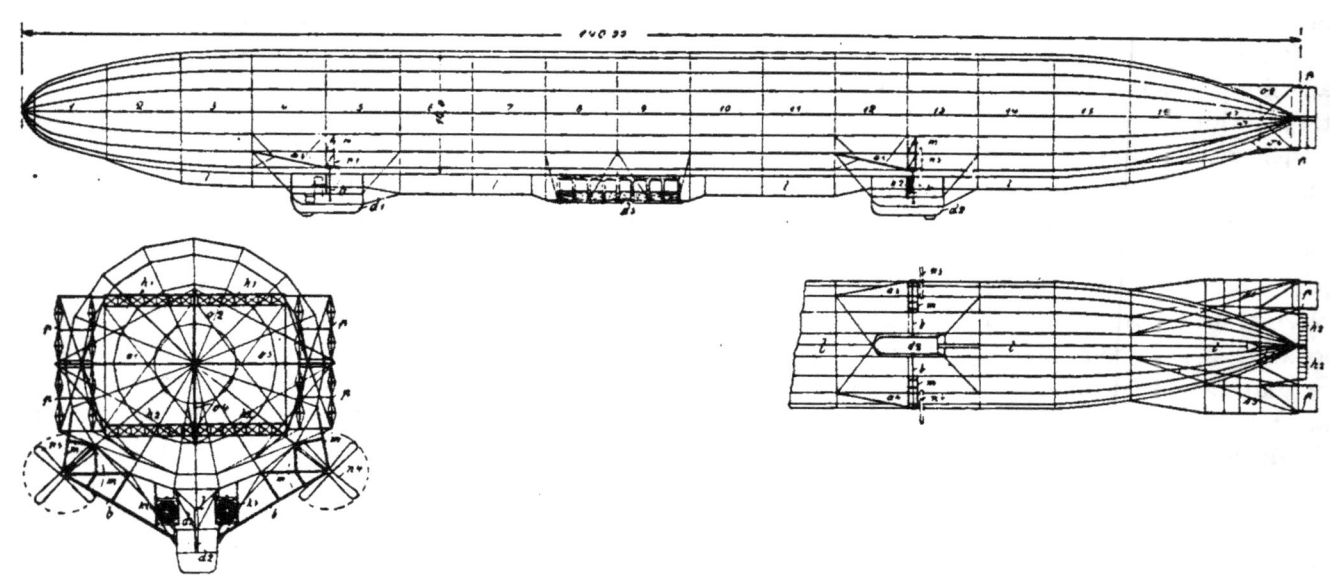

DIAGRAM OF AN 18,000 CBM. ZEPPELIN AIRSHIP, THE *SCHWABEN* (STRUCTURE TYPE).

1–17 gas cells; a_1–a_4 propeller stays; b transmission shaft; d_1 forward car; d_2 after car; d_3 cabin car; h_1, h_2 elevators k_1, k_2, k_3 radiators. l gangway; m propeller outrigger; n_1–n_4 propellers; o_1–o_3 horizontal planes; o_2 vertical plane; p rudder.

crossed, which were kept under tension by circular ties and an elaborate steel wire trussing. This framework possessed a certain amount of springiness which constituted a valuable asset in the case of a rough landing; unfortunately the time and cost of production of this hull proved to be so great that it had to be abandoned on later ships for the Zeppelin type of construction, though the material remained the same.

Hull Shapes.—One of the most important items of hull design is that of the shape, for this determines the amount of air resistance that must be overcome, the most favorable shape being obviously the one which affords the greatest power economy and develops the least stresses while the airship is under way. The first requirement is primarily one of general efficiency, since the saving of one horse-power reduces, on the average, the dead and live loads (weight of engine, fuel, oil, and cooling water) by 3 kg. per hour of operation. The saving thus effected may advantageously be turned into an increase of fuel, ballast, etc., and is therefore of considerable interest to the airship-builder.

The stresses developed by an airship hull in its progress through the air are of two kinds: *compression* on the bow through impact resistance, and *tension* on the sides and on the stern through frictional resistance and suction, respectively. On structure airships these stresses are, on account of the rigid hull frame, only of relative importance, namely, in so far as they are accompanied by parasite resistance which decreases the power efficiency and by a certain wear of the outer cover. Their value is, nevertheless, considerable enough, for the impact resistance of an airship travelling at a speed of 90 kilometers per hour represents a pressure of 75 kg. per square meter of projected area, that is the area of the cross-section at the master-diameter.

On pressure airships, where the hull retains its shape exclusively through internal pressure, the question of using a hull of "streamline" shape—that is, of easy penetration—is, on the contrary, one of primary importance. According to M. Eiffel, the air resistance which a pressure airship develops in her progress through the air causes a deformation in the hull whereby its volume may increase by as much as 10 per cent. of its displacement. Since to the strain caused by this deformation, which tends to weaken the envelope, must be added those created by the excess of internal pressure as well as by the considerable bending moment existing in all pressure airships (except in those of the tension truss type), it follows that the design of pressure

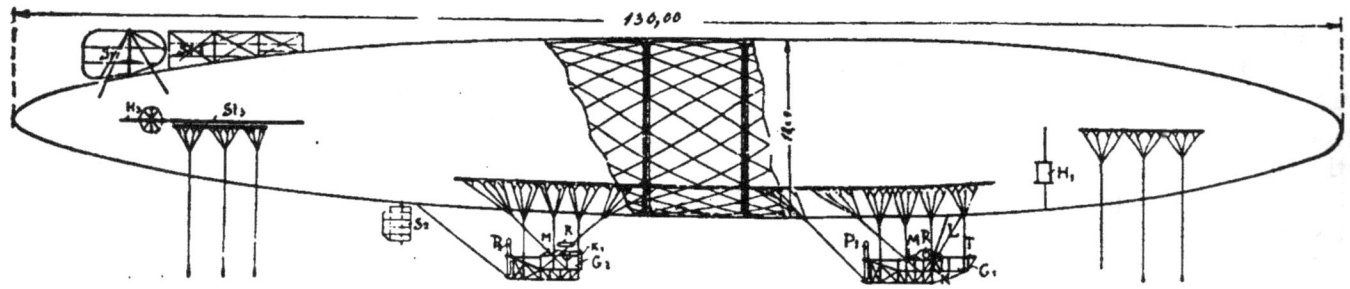

DIAGRAM OF A 19,000 CBM. SCHÜTTE-LANZ AIRSHIP, THE *S. L. I.* (STRUCTURE TYPE).

G_1 forward car; G_2 after car; P_1, P_2 propellers; H_1 forward elevator; H_2 after elevator; St_1, St_2 stabilizer planes; S_1, S_2 rudders.

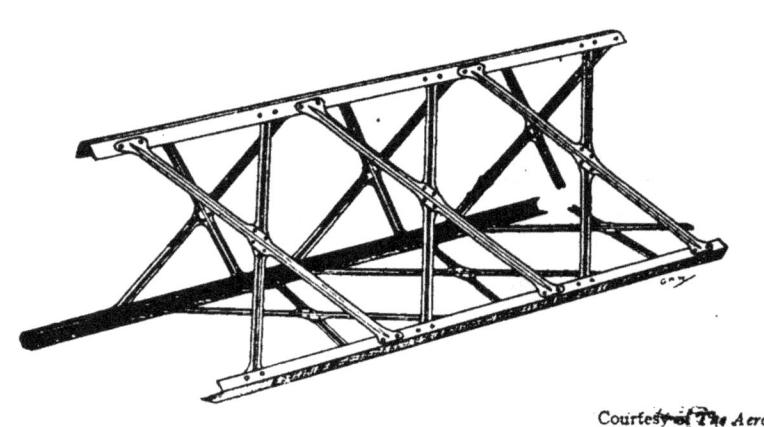

SPECIMEN OF A ZEPPELIN LATTICE-GIRDER.

airship hulls should closely follow the best results arrived at through laboratory research work.

Aerodynamic Notes on Hulls.—A certain divergence of views exists regarding the best streamline shape for airship hulls. In principle the most efficient shape appears to be one elliptical, six diameters long, with the master-diameter at about from 30 to 40 per cent. of the length aft of the nose, the bow being somewhat blunter than the stern. This shape is the one proposed by the British and French laboratories; the German laboratory suggests a similar shape except for the stern, which should taper off to a sharp point. The principle of the dissymmetrical shape of hull was first laid down by the Frenchman Jullien, who built in 1850 an airship model of such shape; it was later taken up and further developed by Captain Renard of the French Army Engineers, who built the celebrated airship *La France*. Nowadays this shape is used on all but the Zeppelin airships, where the prevalent reason for building the hull straight-sided for three-quarters of its length seems to be facility of construction. Standardization of parts used in the construction of the hull frame thus becomes perfectly feasible for Zeppelin airships, a feature well nigh impossible to achieve were all the longitudinals of different curvature and all polygonals of different diameter, as would be the case in a true streamline shape of hull.

Besides reducing the air resistance to be overcome the dissymmetrical, fish-shaped hull has the property of endowing the airship with a certain amount of "weathercock stability" which means that the vessel will tend to always turn into the wind, unless otherwise directed. This feature is very important, because a solid of revolution which progresses in the direction of its longitudinal axis is in a state of indifferent equilibrium, that is to say, the slightest inclination of the axis suffices to produce a turning couple which may cause the airship to assume a vertical position relative to the ground.

Nevertheless, the fish-shaped hull, even when combined with fin surfaces abaft, can check longitudinal instability only up to a certain speed, called the *critical speed*, which varies according to the radius of curvature of the hull and the angle of inclination to the horizontal.

Pressure Airships.—The principal feature which distinguishes pressure airships from structure airships is that in the former the hull retains its shape through the agency of internal pressure, which must exceed the atmospheric pressure, and not by means of a hull frame.

The theory of the pressure airship was first enunciated in a memorandum which General Meusnier submitted in 1784 to the French Academy of Sciences and in which he incorporated a very comprehensive design of a pressure airship. "The Meusnier design was indeed a creation of fundamental importance which, for want of engine power, had to wait upwards of a century before it could be practically employed." (Zahm.)

The first pressure airship that navigated—under limited control—the air was built in 1852 by Henri Giffard, the inventor of the steam-injector. This steam propelled airship was followed in 1884 by Captain Renard's electrically driven *La France* which was the first airship to make a return voyage against a moderate wind. The advent of the internal combustion engine completed the pressure airship's conquest of the aerial ocean in 1902 when Henri Juillot produced the gasoline driven *Lebaudy*.

The Ballonnet.—Excess of pressure is generated on most pressure airships by means of one or more *ballonnets*, or bladders, which are located in the bottom of the hull and can be inflated with air through a fan-blower. A contraction of the gas and the resulting loss of volume and deformation of the hull are thus compensated for by an expansion of the ballonnet; on the contrary, an expansion of the gas beyond a certain limit (generally 30 mm. of water) will open the ballonnet valves and relieve the pressure without loss of gas, through the only escape of air. Should, however, the pressure still rise in spite of the open ballonnet valves the pressure within the hull will be relieved by the automatic gas valves which are generally timed to open at 35-40 mm. of water.

Both gas and air valves are of the spring-loaded type. Some airships are provided with gas valves both on the top and on the bottom of the hull in which case the upper ones act as safety valves while the lower ones serve as manoeuvre valves. This system permits to expel the heavy, impure gas collecting in the bottom of the hull, thus saving the pure gas for further service.

Since the very existence of a pressure airship is dependent upon ability to maintain the shape of the hull regardless of variations of atmospheric pressure and temperature, it follows that both the ballonnet and the relief-valves must have a sufficient capacity effectively to compensate sudden changes of buoyancy. For this reason it is also customary to employ on modern airships an auxiliary engine for actuating the ballonnet-blower, thus making the latter independent of a possible breakdown of the main power plant.

THE WOODEN LATTICE-GIRDER FRAME OF THE SCHÜTTE-LANZ AIRSHIP S. L. I.

The ballonnet was invented in 1872 by the French naval architect Dupuy de Lôme, although its invention is generally accredited to General Meusnier. The latter proposed on the contrary to maintain the tautness of the hull by means of a *double skin*, the internal acting as a gas-container while the external skin would be nothing but a protective cover. The continuous air space between the two skins would not only allow its being inflated at the excess of pressure required, but would also give the gas-container an efficient insulation against variations of temperature.

This over-a-century-old idea has lately been embodied with marked success in the Forlanini type of airships. There the gas container is suitably trussed to the outer cover so that both will maintain their correct relative position. Excess of pressure within the air space is generated in two ways. When the airship is under way an intake valve fitted to the nose of the hull admits and distributes the on-rushing air to the air space whence it escapes through a relief valve mounted on the stern, the amount of internal pressure being regulated by the greater or lesser aperture of the relief valve. Thanks to this arrangement the air circulates all the time around the gas-container and effectively prevents the leaking hydrogen from creating an explosive mixture. When the engines are stopped excess of pressure is generated in the usual way, that is, by means of a fan-blower.

Rubberized Fabric.—The considerable stresses to which the hull of pressure airships is subjected have brought about the adoption of rubberized fabric of high tensile strength. On Parseval airships of over 8,000 cubic meter volume the fabric is tested to withstand a pressure of 2 metric tons per square meter of surface. For this purpose *diagonal doubling* is resorted to, which consists in building up the fabric of two or three layers, the threads of which diagonally oppose each other.

To counteract the destructive influence of sunlight on rubberized fabric the latter is generally treated on the outside with chrome yellow or aluminum paint. Hence the yellow or silvery color of most airship hulls.

Airships whose outer cover is made of rubberized fabric are subject to danger of fire from self-electrification because this material quickly becomes electrified in dry air. "When rolled up or creased in any way it rustles and gives out electric sparks, the latter being clearly visible in the dark." (Moedebeck.)

This danger is particularly characteristic of pressure airships where insufficient tautness of the rubberized envelope and gas leakage may combine to cause disastrous results. On structure airships this danger is greatly lessened by the use of non-rubberized fabric in the outer cover.

To prevent self-electrification airship fabrics built up of several layers of diagonally doubled and specially gummed and varnished silk have more recently been used to good effect.

"Gas Tightness" of Fabrics.—The rubberized fabric used in airship hulls is theoretically gas-tight; in practice, however, as hydrogen absorbs the air and diffuses through osmosis, allowance must be made for a daily leakage of from one half to one per cent. of the volume. The only really gas-tight material is gold-beater's skin, which is used in the gas-cells of Zeppelin airships; unfortunately this material has a low tensile strength and is, furthermore, not as impervious against water as it is against gas so that it cannot be employed to advantage in the construction of pressure hulls. On structure airships, where there is an outer cover to protect the gas-cells against the weather, the use of gold-beater's skin is, on the contrary, very satisfactory, although its cost is very high.

The Ripping Panel.—All pressure airships are provided with a *ripping panel* whereby the hull can almost instantly be deflated, should the wind prove too strong to permit mooring in the open.

The ripping panel, of which there may be several on a large airship, consists of a strip of rubberized fabric which is applied over a vertical seam in the hull. It is operated by a ripping cord which its bright red color easily distinguishes from the rest of the operating cords.

The system of construction of structure airships obviously prohibits the use of a ripping panel.

The Understructure of Pressure Airships.—The understructure of an airship is the part situated underneath the hull proper, which affords accommodation for the machinery (engines, transmission, propellers, fuel, oil, and water-tanks, dynamo, ballonet-blower, etc.) and the crew.

The machinery and crew are housed on most pressure airships in one or more cars which are *suspended* from the hull by means of rigging guys, whereas on most structure airships the cars are *rigidly connected* with the hull frame.

According to their system of suspension, pressure airships may be divided into the following subtypes:

(1) The *girderless* type, in which the load, represented by a *short car*, is directly distributed over the hull by means of steel cables ending at the top in crow's feet of flax rope, which are toggled to a *rigging band* of canvas, sewn upon the bottom of the

hull. The rigging band may further be strengthened by canvas belts passing around the hull. This type was originated by Major von Parseval.

(2) The *car-girder* type, originated by the late Colonel Renard, in which the load is distributed over the hull by means of a *trellis girder*, extending up to two thirds the length of the hull, which is suspended by a rigging similar to the one above described, although the rigging band may be omitted. Only part of the girder is fitted as a car proper in this case, the great length of the girder serving primarily to reduce the bending moment. A divergent application of this principle consists in fitting a short car with fore-and-aft outriggers, which serve the same purpose as a trellis girder, with a considerable saving of weight, however.

(3) The *keel-girder* type, in which the load, represented by a *short car*, is distributed over the hull by means of a *girder*, attached to the bottom of the hull, from which the car is suspended. There exist many divergent applications of the keel-girder principle.

On the original keel-girder airship, the *Lebaudy*, designed by the eminent French aeronautic expert, M. Henri Juillot, the girder consisted of an oval platform of steel tubing which was built into the underside of the hull and held in place by internal crow's feet. On a later ship, the *Morning Post*, the girder was long and narrow, built in two pieces, hinged and suspended a short distance from the hull. The Gross-Basenach airships (Prussian Army Airship Works) are built on the same principle.

The considerable head-resistance such a suspension generates led Italian airship-builders to seek and find a different solution of the problem. In the Italian Army airships, designed by Captains Crocco and Ricaldoni, the so-called "girder" is nothing but a Gall's chain of considerable proportions, which is inserted between two layers of fabric on the bottom of the hull. Thanks to its being articulated, this girder closely follows the hull's curvature, allowing for longitudinal, but not for lateral, play. It realizes a method of suspension which gives for the same amount of air resistance a better distribution of load than the girderless type of airship, which it outwardly resembles.

On all the foregoing keel-girder airships the car is suspended a considerable distance below the hull by a rigging of steel cables.

The minimum of air resistance not only for the keel-girder type, but for any pressure airship as well, is attained on the Forlanini airships. There the cable rigging is entirely done away with, for the car is closely adherent to the hull. The keel-girder, to

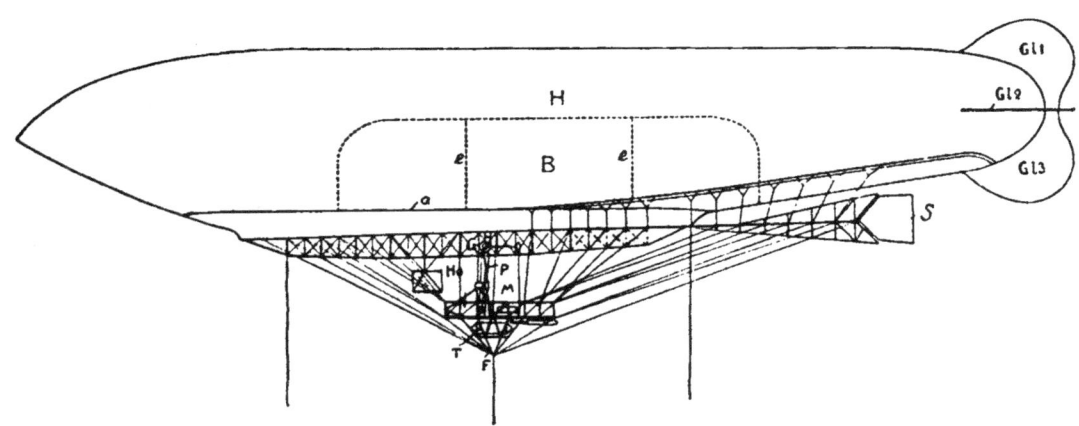

DIAGRAM OF THE 7,000 CBM. LEBAUDY AIRSHIP *CAPITAINE-MARCHAL* (KEEL-GIRDER, PRESSURE TYPE).

H gas container; B ballonnet; C girder; M car; P air discharge pipe; Ho elevator; T fuel tank; F landing pyramid; S rudder; Gl_{1-3} stabilizer planes; e ballonnet partitions.

which the car is rigidly connected, consists of a triangular lattice-work of steel tubing which follows the curvature of the hull's underside from stem to stern. The front end serves to stiffen the nose and holds the air intake valve in place; the rear end carries the steering group. This girder, which is entirely rigid, is inserted into a longitudinal slot provided in the hull and is supported by a crow's feet rigging from a suspension band which is situated in the centre-line of the hull.

(4) The *tension-truss* type, created by the Spanish engineer Leonardo Torrès-Quevedo, in which the load is distributed over a hull of trefoil section by means of a flexible truss contained within and a cable rigging attached thereto.

The tension truss consists of three cables, running from bow to stern, which are carried in fabric pockets sewn to the hull at the intersection lines of the three lobes, and are trussed to one another by flax ropes and fabric strips. When the hull is under pressure, the truss is under tension and acts as a perfectly rigid girder, which distributes the load of the car or cars uniformly over the entire hull. The car is hung to this girder by a limited number of cables, the crow's feet of which are toggled within the hull to the lower sides of the triangular girder. Thanks to this feature, not only is the air resistance reduced to a great extent, but large airships of this type can be kept rigid when under way with an excess of pressure of only 15 mm. of water, whereas all other pressure airships require an average pressure of from 25 to 30 mm. of water.

It is obvious that, since the load is evenly distributed over the hull, each portion of buoyancy carrying a proportionate amount of load, the bending moment will come very near being nil, which is the ideal condition sought. Furthermore, owing to the much lower internal pressure required, the hull is subjected to stresses and strains of much smaller value than on other pressure airships; consequently the life of the hull is increased, and lighter fabric can be used in its manufacture.

The only apparent drawback of the "polylobe" hull is that the surface area exposed to the relative wind is greater than for a hull of circular cross-section, so that the skin friction is proportionately increased.

The Understructure of Zeppelins.—The above considerations hold true to an even greater extent in the case of structure airships. There the hull frame forms a permanently rigid girder over which the loads can more uniformly be distributed than over a pressure hull. One can dismiss with a few words the Schütte-Lanz type, in which the hull carries the cars on a cable suspension, since it embodies one great drawback of pressure airships the avoidance of which should be and is one of the principal points in favor of true structure airships. This drawback is the position of the propellers, which are, except in the case of the Forlanini airships, applied too far beneath the centre of resistance. As a consequence, airships of the suspended-car type have a tendency to drag the hull behind, thus causing disturbing couples, which must constantly be corrected by the control organs.

On true structure airships, such as the Zeppelin, the cars are rigidly connected with the hull and at but a little distance, so that the propulsive apparatus can furnish its maximum of efficiency. Prior to the Great War the Zeppelin airships had a V-shaped keel protruding from underneath the hull, which formed the vessel's backbone and was fitted as a gangway affording passage between the engine cars. In the gangway there were the fuel- and oil-tanks, which fed the Maybach engines, these driving two sets of twin-screws stayed on outriggers. In the middle the gangway flared out and formed a spacious compartment which served on passenger airships as a cabin-car, seating twenty-four; on military airships the compartment was divided into a wardroom for the convenience of the officers, quarters fitted with hammocks for the crew, a wireless room, and a photographic cabinet. Lavatories were provided on both types of airships.

A lookout post, permitting astronomical observation as well as the mounting of aeroplane-defense guns, was provided on the top of the hull, near the bow. This platform, about three meters square and provided with a hand-rail, communicated with the forward car by means of a stairway which was inclosed in a shaft of aluminum plating and led right through the hull between two gas-cells.

On the latest known type of Zeppelin various alterations are embodied in the understructure. The V-shaped keel no longer protrudes from the hull; the bottom is flat, and the gangway is built up within the hull in the form of an inverted V. Obviously a corresponding portion of the drum-shaped gas-cells is cut away. The cars number four and are arranged crosswise: the fore and aft cars are coaxial, the remaining two cars, nicknamed "power-eggs," being mounted amidships right and left of the hull. The classic double twin-screw drive of ante-bellum Zeppelins is displaced by four pusher-screws, of which there is one on each car, each being driven through a clutch and change-speed gear by a 240 h.p. Maybach engine. The after car houses, however, two more such engines, which drive through bevel gear shafts a pair of twin-screws stayed on outriggers.

The cars are built up of lattice girders similar to those used in the hull frame, and are covered with corrugated aluminum sheeting 2 mm. thick.

The forward car comprises three compartments; the one foremost serves as a chart-room and commander's cabin, next to which comes a small wireless room, the rear compartment constituting the first engine-room. The "power-eggs" and the after car serve chiefly as engine-rooms; the after car may also afford quarters for the crew.

There are two gun emplacements on the roof, one, near the bow, mounting two 12 mm. guns on collapsible tripods and affording to each gun an arc of fire of 180 degrees from the center line, and one near the stern, aft of the rudder, mounting a Maxim. Six more guns of this type are mounted on the cars; namely, two each on the fore and aft cars, and one each on the "power-eggs." Sixty bombs are carried amidships on two racks situated underneath the gangway. The bombs are released by an electromagnetic gear from a switchboard in the chart-room. The release device can also be worked by hand, though in either case a sliding shutter must first be opened to allow the bombs to drop.

Stability, Trim, and Steering.—An airship is, when in motion, subject to rotation around three axes, *transverse*, *vertical*, and *longitudinal*, which cause the airship to assume oscillating movements. These are, respectively, *rolling*, *yawing* and *pitching* and in order to keep an airship to a true course it is necessary to possess means with which to check these oscillations.

Rolling is automatically checked on all airships by having the load underneath the lift, thus placing the centre of gravity below the centre of buoyancy.

Yawing is counterbalanced on all modern airships by means of vertical fins, and pitching by means of horizontal fins. It is customary to mount these fins directly on the hull, near the stern, or a little distance below it so as to bring them in line with, and a great distance from, the centre of resistance. In this respect structure airships possess a distinct advantage over pressure airships in that the fins may be rigidly mounted on the hull frame, whereas on a pressure hull the fins must be stayed by an elaborate truss, which is furthermore dependent for its rigidity upon the hull's ability to maintain its shape. This is why on most keel-girder airships the keel-girder extends far back along the hull and carries the stabilizing fins, a solution which must unreservedly be preferred to that, customary

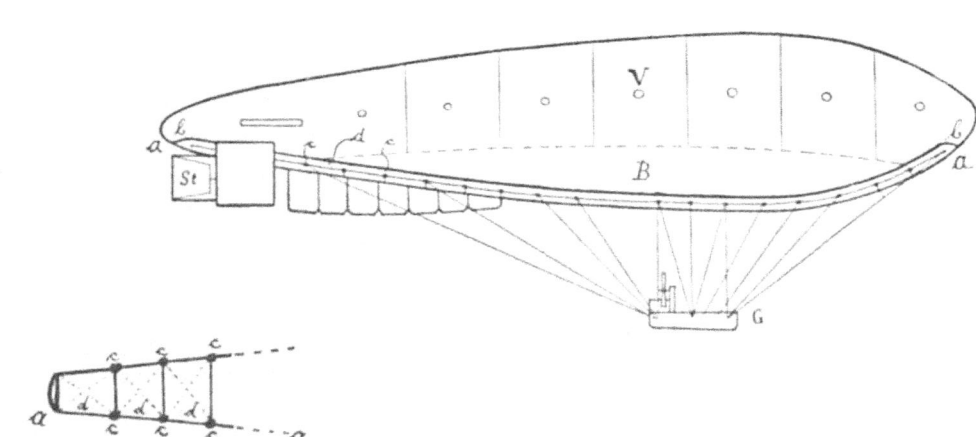

DIAGRAM OF THE *P.* TYPE AIRSHIPS OF THE ITALIAN ARMY AIRCRAFT WORKS (KEEL-GIRDER PRESSURE TYPE).

V gas valve; B ballonnet; G car; St stabilizer and rudder; aa articulated keel-girder, carried in pocket bb; cc keel-girder links.
In the left-hand corner a plan view of part of the keel-girder.

on car-girder airships, of mounting the fins on the end of the girder a considerable distance below the hull.

The tendency in fin design is at present toward simplification, such as is displayed by the cross-shaped fins, which are gradually displacing the multiplane and cellular fins of the last few years and the inflated fins of still-earlier days. The *raison d'être* of the latter was chiefly their ability to lift their own weight; inflated fins did not, however, prove of efficient action and greatly increased the air resistance.

The steering of an airship in the horizontal plane —that is, sidewise—is effected by means of a rudder similar to that used on ships. This rudder is generally of the balanced type, to facilitate manual control, and is mounted in the wake of the vertical fin. In some cases multiplane rudders are employed. Steering sidewise may also be assisted by swivelling-screws.

Steering, in the vertical plane—that is, up and down—is effected in a great variety of ways. An airship can ascend through purely statical means, like a spherical balloon, by jettisoning ballast; but this manœuvre is never made use of alone, because it is slow and involves much loss of ballast. The proper way for an airship to ascend is to alter its trim, whereby the bow will point upward, so that the pull of the air-screws will be applied at an angle to the horizontal. It is true that the latter object may be attained without change of trim by means of swivelling screws, which can be inclined at the angle desired; but this kind of ascent is highly inefficient, because it increases to an appreciable extent the projected area of the hull relative to the line of flight, thus creating additional air resistance.

Changes of trim can be effected by static or dynamic means, or by a combination of both. Static control of trim may be attained through a shifting of the centre of buoyancy or of the centre of gravity. In the first case the hull is provided with two ballonnets which can respectively be pumped full of air; thus, for ascending the rear ballonnet is pumped full and the front ballonnet emptied, and vice-versa. The difference between the specific weights of hydrogen and air causes—in the ascent—the centre of buoyancy to move forward, which in its turn raises the nose of the airship. This is the system employed on the Parseval and Gross-Basenach airships; it is worth noting that on both types additional trim control is secured by a simultaneous shifting of the centre of gravity. On the Parseval airships this is effected by the car itself, which can move back and forth a distance of 0.75 m., owing to the car's main stays passing under rollers. This fore-and-aft motion is limited by appropriate anchor-stays. On the Gross-Basenach airships the centre of gravity is displaced by trimming-tanks, which are filled and emptied by compressed air. The double-ballonnet system, besides being of very efficient action, has the further advantage of affording means for checking the disequilibrating moments which the sudden surging of hydrogen toward the high side may generate. Additional means for checking this tendency are found on most pressure airships in the form of fabric partitions.

The trim can also be controlled by dynamic means through the use of lifting planes (elevators) which raise or depress the airship's nose by virtue of the pressure onrushing air exerts upon them. This system is principally employed on structure airships where the under side of the hull affords a considerable amount of lifting surface when inclined to the line of flight. On a 20 ton Zeppelin airship 2 tons may thus be added to the static lift, in which case the airship is, at the moment of starting, actually *heavier than air*.

On the Zeppelin airships the action of the lifting planes is seconded by static trim control. Prior to the war this was effected by a shifting of the center of gravity. For this purpose the gangway of the early Zeppelins was fitted with a track on which a small lorrie carrying tools and spare parts could be moved back and forth. This primitive system was discarded in 1909 in favor of water-ballast trim, the water being carried in rubber bags which were suspended in the gangway. On the latest known Zeppelins the trim appears to be also controlled by a displacement of the center of buoyancy, each gas-cell being provided with a ballonnet whereby the volume of gas can be increased or reduced at will. Since the low tensile strength of gold-beaters' skin, which is the material used in the gas-cells, does not permit the storage of hydrogen under pressure, all excess or deficiency of gas is regulated by the aforementioned compensating tank (see p. 4). This system, which is nothing but an application of Parseval's double-ballonnet system to the cellular construction, appears on the main as very efficient, for the ascensional speed of the latest Zeppelins is given by Swiss publications as being a thousand meters in three minutes, two thousand meters in eight minutes, and three thousand meters in fifteen minutes.

Volume, Displacement and Lift.—It has been said before that an airship floats in the aerial ocean, as ships float on the sea, by virtue of buoyancy. A clear comprehension of the laws of the

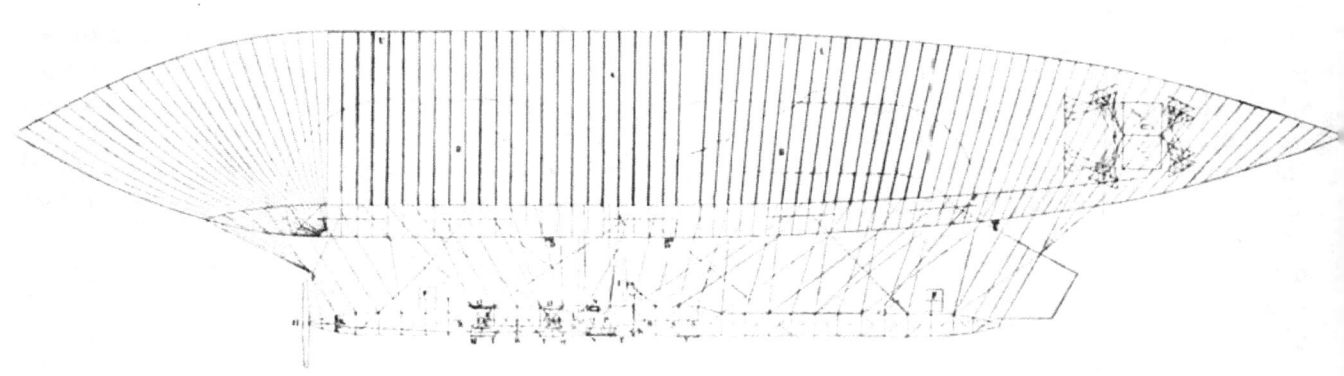

DIAGRAM OF THE 9,000 CBM. ASTRA AIRSHIP *ADJUDANT-RÉAU* (CAR-GIRDER PRESSURE TYPE).

A envelope; B ballonnet; C stabilizer planes; D air valve; E gas valve; F elevator; H tractor screw; I side propeller; K transmission; M engine; N fuel tank; O oil tank; P chart room; Q instrument board; R engine room; S passenger compartment; T landing carriage; U ripping panel.

atmosphere is absolutely essential for understanding and comparing airship performances. It will therefore repay the reader to read the present chapter in its entirety.

At normal barometric pressure (760 mm.) and 0° Centigrade 1 cubic meter (cbm.) of air weighs 1.293 kg.; an airship of 6,000 cbm. volume displaces consequently (6000×1.293=) 7758 kg. of air, or, roughly, 7.8 metric tons. This tonnage, called the normal displacement of an airship, affords the most convenient means of comparison between airships, because it is applicable to both the metric and English systems of measurement, and also because it permits the use of small values. The latter advantage is particularly striking in the English measures, where an airship of 6,000 cbm. volume, which is a small vessel, is expressed in the imposing form of 211,800 cubic feet.

Under the above-mentioned normal atmospheric conditions 1 cbm. of pure hydrogen weighs 0.090 kg.; that is, approximately 1.2 kg. less than an equal volume of air. For practical purposes the latter figure should, however, be reduced to 1.1 kg., because hydrogen cannot be produced in a totally pure state, and also on account of the partial deterioration (diffusion) of this gas under the influence of the air.

The difference between the weights of equal volumes of air and hydrogen generates an equivalent lifting force which is caused by the upward pressure the displaced air exerts upon the hydrogen. It follows from the foregoing that 1 cbm. of commercial hydrogen possesses a normal lifting force, or "lift," of 1.1 kg. An airship of 6,000 cbm. volume has thus a normal lift of 6,600 kg., or 6.6 tons. By subtracting the lift of an airship from its displacement we obtain the weight of the hydrogen contained in the hull. In the case of the above airship we have:

Displacement..................7.8 tons
Lift........................6.6 tons
―――――
Weight of hydrogen........1.2 tons

Coal-gas, which is currently used for inflating free balloons, is much cheaper and much less inflammable than hydrogen. It is, nevertheless, but little employed in airships, on account of its greater weight and obviously lesser lift. Coal-gas weighs, according to its degree of purity, from 0.520 to 0.650 kg. per cubic meter.

It is customary to express the degree of purity of a gas in terms of specific weight. In that case the normal weight of 1 cbm. of air is assumed to be the unit in terms of which the weight of the gas is expressed. Thus, for instance, a specific weight of 0.15 means that a given volume of gas is 0.15 times heavier than an equal volume of air. Its actual weight is therefore $0.15 \times 1.293 = 0.1935$ kg., and its lift $1.293 \times 0.1935 = 1.0995$ kg., or approximately 1.1 kg. per cubic meter.

The lift of an airship, as obtained by subtracting the weight of the contained hydrogen from that of the displaced air, gives the maximum weight an airship can lift for a given volume. The *gross lift*, therefore, comprises the weights of the hull, the understructure, the machinery, and the equipment. The difference between these weights and the total lift gives the *useful load*, which is made up of the fuel supply, the crew, and the military or commercial load.

The Static Attitude of Airships.—The lift of an airship may be considerably influenced by variations of atmospheric pressure and temperature; hence all statistics of airships are based upon normal displacement and normal lift; that is, at 760 mm. barometric pressure and 0° Centigrade.

Whenever the altitude above sea-level increases by 80 meters, the atmospheric pressure decreases by one per cent. The corresponding expansion of the air results in a decrease of the air's density whereby its ability to exert lift is proportionately lessened. But since hydrogen expands under the decreased atmospheric pressure in the same proportion as air, it follows that the lessened density of the air will be compensated for by an increased volume of hydrogen. Consequently an airship does not lose any lift upon ascending as long as the gas is able to expand within the hull.

The expansion of the gas within the hull is, however, necessarily limited by structural considerations. The low tensile strength of balloon fabrics, which is the logical outcome of the well-known weight-saving tendency applied to all aircraft, makes it imperative to prevent the hull from being subjected to considerable internal pressure, such as would arise through the expansion of the gas were the hull a totally sealed gas-container. This is why the gas-containing portions of all airships are provided with relief valves, which automatically open when the internal pressure reaches the safety limit.

Such being the case, it becomes obvious that if an airship is to reach a certain level without loss of lift, it must be only partly inflated at sea-level. This initial deficiency of lift relative to the maximum lift afforded by full volume must be compensated for, upon ascending, by throwing off an equivalent amount of ballast.

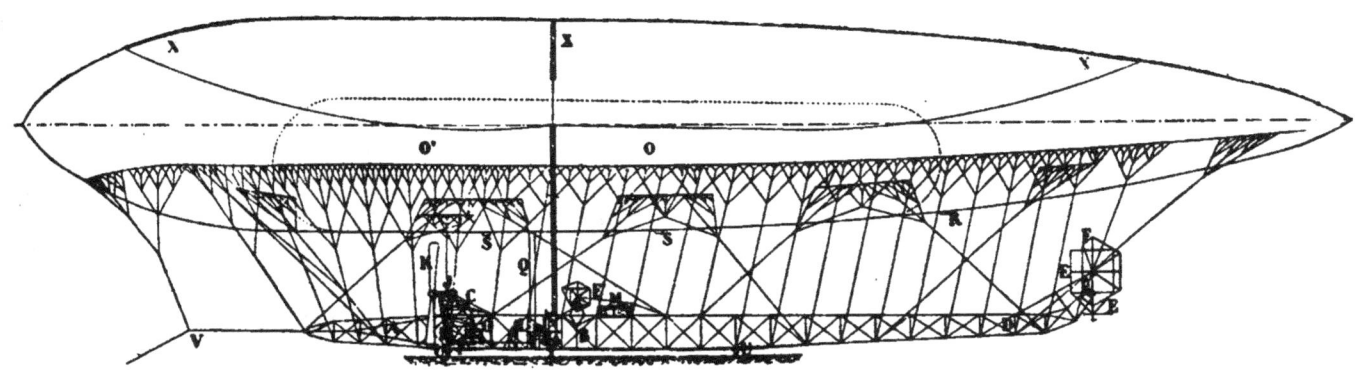

DIAGRAM OF THE 9,000 CBM. CLÉMENT-BAYARD AIRSHIP *DUPUY-DE-LÔME* (CAR-GIRDER PRESSURE TYPE).

ABD car-girder; C propeller outriggers; E elevator; F rudder; G engine; H clutch; I spring suspension of engine; J transmission; K propeller; L radiator; M fuel tank; N pilot stand; OO' ballonnets; P fan-blower; Q air discharge pipe; R gas valve; SS' air valves; U bumping bag; V mooring point; XXX ripping panels.

The allowance for lift deficiency due to partial inflation greatly varies according to the type of airships. On structure airships the considerable weight of the hull frame generally limits the allowance for gas expansion to ten per cent. of the gas-cells' volume, a fact which eloquently demonstrates the need of large displacements for making structure airships efficient.

The absence of a hull frame enables pressure airships, on the contrary, to embody a much greater allowance for gas expansion, the capacity of the ballonnet often attaining thirty-three per cent. that of the envelope. Since pressure airships are dependent upon internal pressure for the maintenance of their shape, variations of gas pressure being regulated by the ballonnet (see p. 7), it follows that the capacity of the latter determines the allowance for gas expansion and consequently the attainable altitude. It should be clearly understood that the ballonnet is nothing but a compensating device for variable gas volumes, which endows the pressure airship with constant displacement up to the ballonnet's capacity of contraction or expansion. Structure airships can, on the other hand, do without a ballonnet, because the greater or lesser inflation of the gas-cells does not affect the airship's displacement; the latter is, indeed, invariably constant, since it is determined by the volume of the outer cover, which is kept rigid by the hull frame.

It has been said before that an airship loses in theory one per cent. of its lift whenever the altitude above sea-level increases by 80 meters; in practice, however, the stretch of the fabric and the not wholly isothermic expansion of the gas lower this ratio to such extent that one may assume the gas to expand one per cent. of its volume for every ascent of 100 meters. Thus, or instance, an airship which is ninety-seven per cent. inflated at sea-level can reach an altitude of 300 m. without loss of gas, provided the temperature of the air remains constant; but if it ascends to the 500 m. level, then the airship loses through the relief valves two per cent. of its lift, which must be compensated for by releasing ballast of equivalent weight. On descending from 500 m. to 300 m. altitude, the airship loses once more two per cent. of its lift; for, the gas having contracted in the descent, the gas container will be only 98 per cent. inflated. The resulting lift deficiency of two per cent. must again be equalized by releasing ballast, unless it be balanced by an expenditure of fuel. The above example is drawn from the operation of commercial Zeppelin airships, which were normally navigating at the 300 m. level.

Variations of the hydrogen's density are, owing to the small specific weight of that gas, of so little magnitude that it is customary to disregard their influence upon the static attitude of airships.

Variations of barometric pressure affect the operation of airships in a way similar to those of atmospheric pressure. A 10 millimeters drop of the barometer corresponds approximately to an ascent of 100 m., and consequently to an expansion of the gas of one per cent. its volume, and vice versa. In practice it is, however, difficult to distinguish the influence of atmospheric pressure due to altitude from that of barometric pressure due to meteorological phenomena, since both kinds of pressure variations are recorded on airships by the self-same instrument; namely, the barometer.

The static attitude of airships is furthermore affected by the temperature of the gas and that of the atmosphere.

A rise of the gas temperature decreases the density of the gas and increases its volume. As a consequence, the gas weighs less and proportionately lifts more. Whenever the gas temperature rises 3° Centigrade, the lift of an airship increases by one per cent. of its volume, and vice versa.

As an example, if means were provided on the above-discussed commercial Zeppelin wherewith to raise the gas temperature 6° Centigrade while the vessel descends from 500 m. to 300 m. altitude, it is obvious that no additional loss of lift would be incurred, since the previous loss of gas would be compensated for by a greater expansion of gas. On the other hand, if the gas temperature of this airship should rise 6° Centigrade at sea-level, then the maximum altitude the vessel could reach without loss of gas would be reduced to 100 m., because at sea-level the hydrogen would fill ninety-nine per cent. of the gas-cells' capacity.

If the temperature of the atmosphere rises, the corresponding decrease of density and increase of the air's volume decreases the air's specific weight, and consequently its ability to exert upward pressure upon a gas the specific weight of which remained stationary. A rise of 3° Centigrade in the temperature of the atmosphere decreases the lift of an airship by one per cent. of its volume, and vice versa.

The altitude to which a ninety-seven per cent. inflated airship can normally ascend, as above explained, would thus be raised by 100 meters should the atmospheric temperature drop 3° Centigrade.

The foregoing considerations amply illustrate the magnitude of the losses of lift an airship may undergo at high altitudes or in a hot climate.

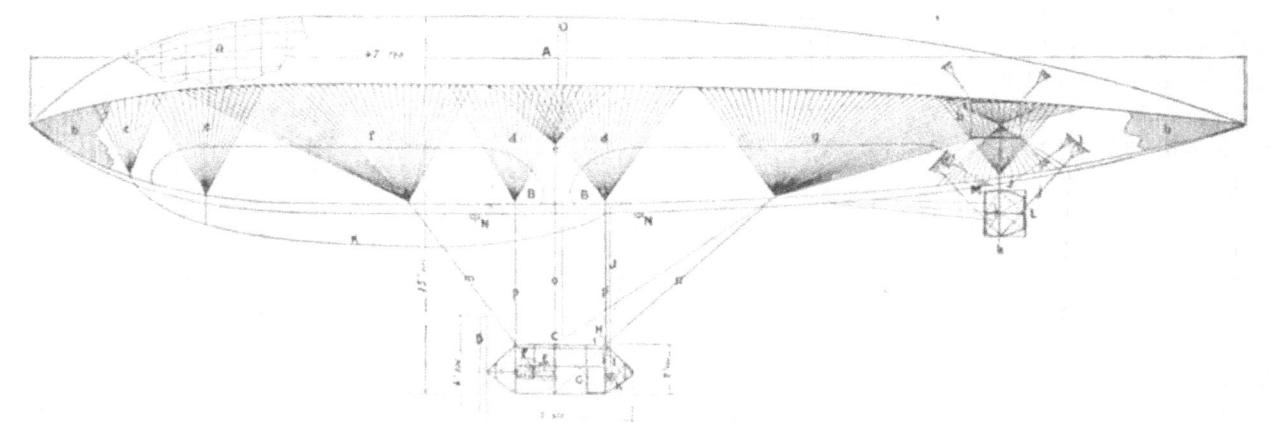

DIAGRAM OF A TENSION-TRUSS PRESSURE AIRSHIP, THE *ASTRA-TORRÈS I*.

A envelope; BB ballonnets; C car; D propeller; E engine; F transmission; G fuel tank; H oil tank; I, K ballonnet blower; J air pipe; L rudder; M elevator; N, N ballonnet valves; O ripping panel.

a airship fabric; bb rope girder; c, d, e, f, g, h, i crow's feet; jj rudder truss guys; k truss terminal; l truss hem; m, n, o, p rigging guys.

For instance, an airship which is ninety-five per cent. inflated at sea-level pressure loses, on reaching an altitude of 3,000 metres, and through the sole agency of decreased atmospheric pressure, 25 per cent. of its lifting force. This comes to say that a 24 ton Zeppelin lifts at said altitude only 18 tons, which is 6 tons less than the vessel weighed, fully loaded, at the moment of starting. As the useful load (weight of fuel, ballast, armament, and crew) of a Zeppelin amounts to one third its total weight when fully loaded, a 24 ton vessel should be able to lift a useful load of 8 tons, which may be apportioned as follows:

Fuel for 20 hours (600 h.p.)	3 tons
Crew of 14	1 ton
Armament	1 ton
Ballast	3 tons
Total	8 tons

In view of the foregoing table it would at first sight seem that to reach an altitude of 3,000 meters a Zeppelin would not only have to jettison all of her ballast, but to exhaust her fuel supply as well, so that on reaching the desired altitude she would actually find herself adrift, deprived of means to progress and to control her altitude. Such would indeed be the case were the airship trying to reach said level fully loaded, and were she not endowed with dynamic lift. In practice a Zeppelin of the military (22,000 cbm.) type built prior to the Great War could reach an altitude of 3,000 m. and still retain a sufficient reserve of fuel and ballast by making up the 6 tons of lift deficiency partly by dynamic lift (2 tons) and partly by burning fuel and releasing ballast. An altitude of 3,000 meters, which could safely be reached after 12 or 14 hours of navigation, represents, nevertheless, for such a vessel the ultimate limit—*the roof*, as the French say.

With the development of anti-aircraft defense, this level has proved inadequate even relatively to safeguard an airship against high-angle guns and aeroplanes; so the Germans were compelled, if they were to continue using Zeppelins, greatly to increase the latter's ascensional power.

Advices from neutral sources state that the Zeppelins of the latest known type, built in 1916, displace 54,000 cbm., furnishing a total lifting force of about 60 tons, two thirds of which are taken up by the weight of the hull, the machinery, and the armament. Consequently 20 tons remain available to lift the crew, the fuel-supply, and the ballast. The "roof" is variously estimated as being between 3,500 and 4,500 meters. The remains of the *L. 33*, which was brought down fairly intact in England,

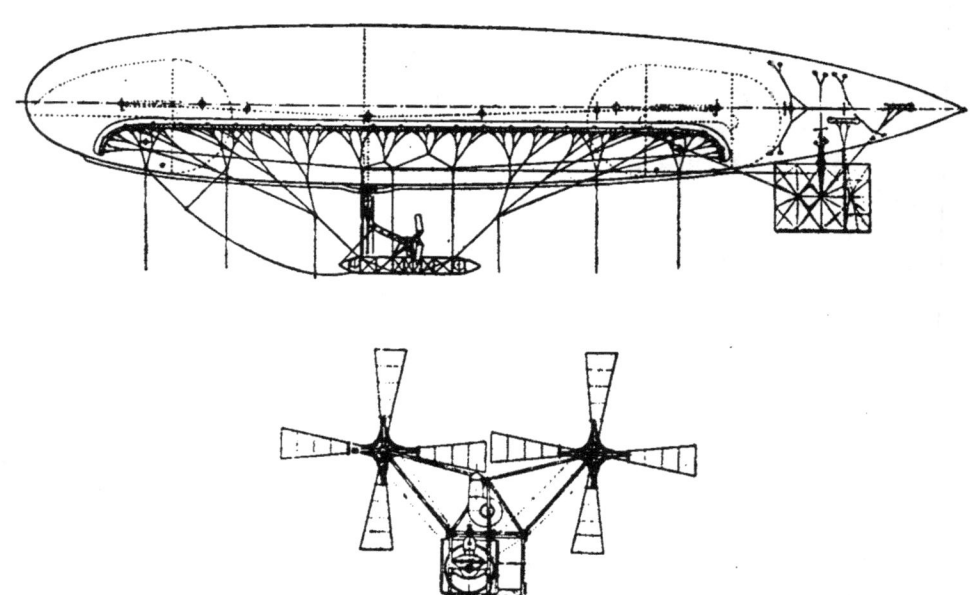

DIAGRAM OF AN 8,000 CBM. PARSEVAL AIRSHIP, THE *GRIFF* (GIRDERLESS PRESSURE TYPE).

as well as observation by Allied aviators confirm the above data; indeed, Zeppelins engaged by Allied aviators at a 3,000 m. level have frequently *climbed out of range,* and the *L. 39,* which was shot down at Compiègne, was caught by the French gunners at an altitude of 3,500 meters.

Now, assuming such a vessel to be fuelled for 20 hours at full speed, the following apportionment of the useful load might be established.

Fuel for 20 hours	7½ tons
Crew of 22	1½ tons
Ballast	11 tons
Total	20 tons

The loss of buoyancy of a 60 ton airship is 18 tons at 3,500 m. altitude and 24 tons at 4,500 m., or 30 and 40 per cent. of the total lift, respectively, always assuming a 95 per cent. inflation. This means that even supposing the dynamic lift amounts to 6 tons—a rather optimistic estimate—a 4,500 m. level can be reached only when the airship has nearly exhausted her fuel- and ballast-supply.

Advantages and Drawbacks of Structure and Pressure Airships.—Structure airships possess the following advantages and drawbacks over pressure airships:

(1) Constancy of displacement due to a rigid framework, which maintains the hull's shape and prevents its deformation through a breakdown of the ballonnet-blower or impact resistance. Drawback: the airship cannot be deflated on landing in the teeth of a storm; it is also likely to be damaged in a rough landing through impact with the ground.

(2) Cellular construction, subdividing the lifting force into individual gas-chambers, much of which may be pierced without depriving the airship of considerable lifting force. Furthermore the size of an airship can easily be enlarged by increasing the number of compartments.

(3) Double skin, affording protection against weather to the gas-chambers which can therefore be made of highly gas-tight gold-beater's skin. The outer cover also insulates the gas-cells to a certain extent against sudden variations of temperature. Drawback: the leakage of hydrogen may create a detonating mixture between the outer cover and the gas-cells. This can, however, be prevented by efficient ventilation.

(4) Possibility of greatly increasing the all-round efficiency of airships by increasing their size, because in a structure airship the weight of the hull and understructure increases in a less proportion than the lift. The lift of an airship increases as the length multiplied by the square of the beam. In

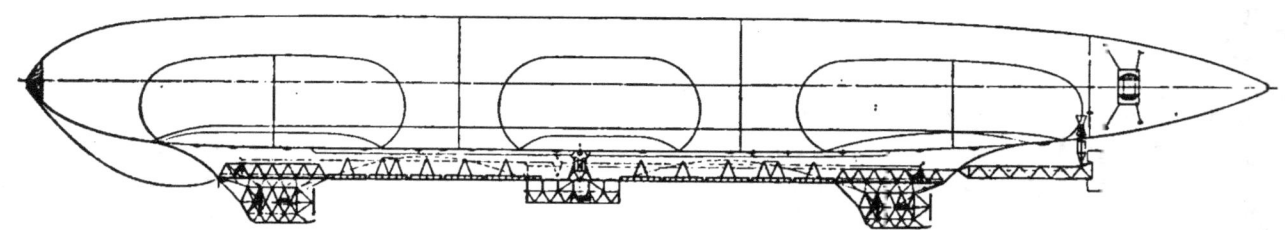

DIAGRAM OF THE 13,000 CBM. SIEMENS-SCHUCKERT AIRSHIP *S. S. I* (GIRDERLESS PRESSURE TYPE; RIGGING BAND REINFORCED BY A FLEXIBLE KEEL OF FABRIC STRIPS).

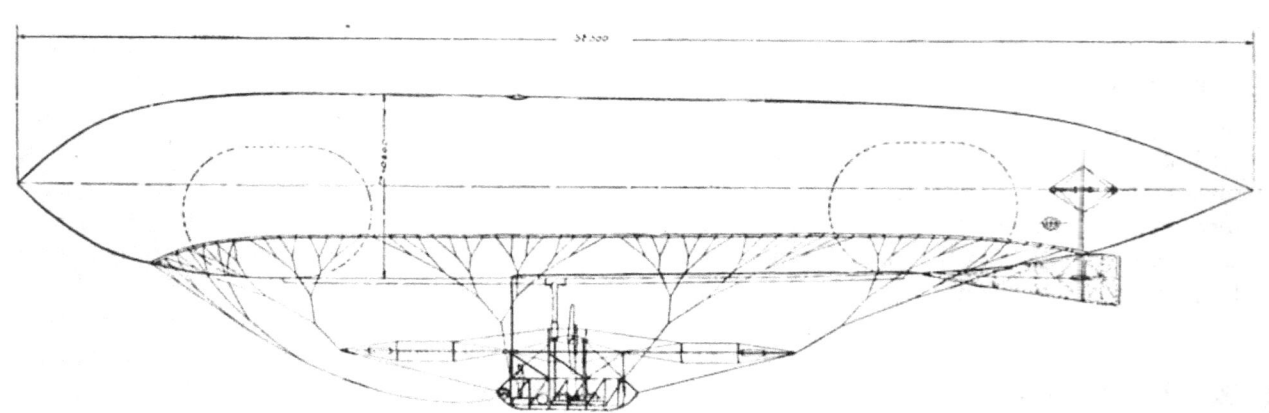

DIAGRAM OF THE 3,600 CBM. KOERTING AIRSHIP *M. III* (CAR-GIRDER PRESSURE TYPE; OUTRIGGER SUSPENSION).

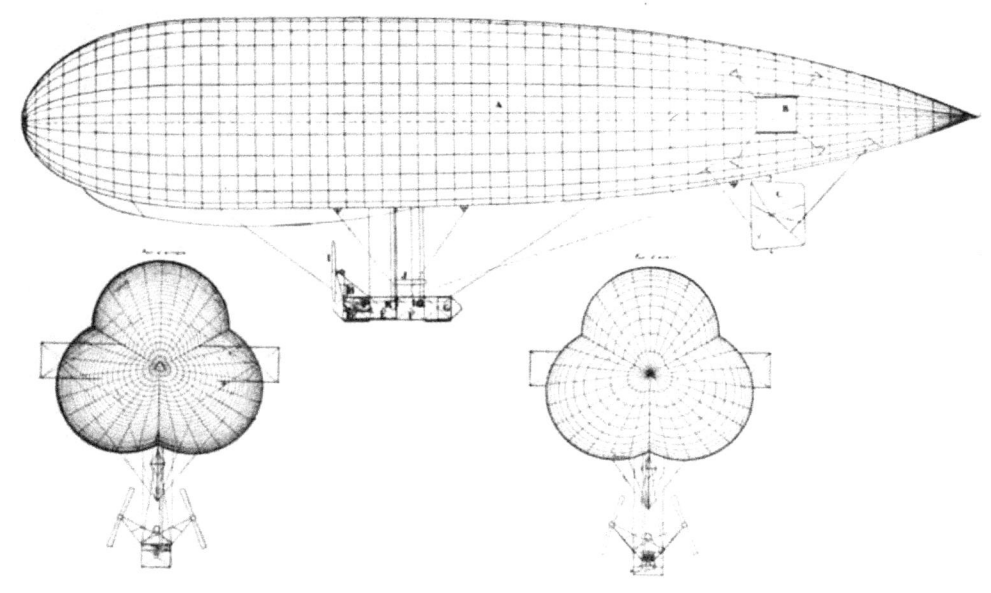

DIAGRAM OF A 7,500 CBM. ASTRA-TORRÈS AIRSHIP (TENSION-TRUSS PRESSURE TYPE).
A envelope; B stabilizer planes; C rudder; D engine; E pilot stand; F passenger compartment; G fuel tank; H propeller stays; I propeller.

other words, by doubling the linear dimensions of an airship the resulting lift will be eight times as great. In a structure airship the weight of the hull and understructure will increase nearly in the same proportion as the lift, because the dimensions of the framework and the thickness of the fabric must proportionately be increased; but on pressure airships the weight of the hull or envelope must increase at a greater rate, because of the additional thickness of material required to withstand the increased internal pressure. It follows that by increasing the linear dimensions of airships a size will be reached where the useful load of a structure airship will equal that of a pressure airship and whence the rate of increase will grow in favor of the former. The pressure airship here considered is one of the tension-truss type, which has a very low or virtually no bending moment. This is an important point, because the bending moment increases as the weight multiplied by the length of the hull, which is to say that by doubling the linear dimensions of an airship the bending moment will be sixteen times as great. This consideration alone should be a convincing argument in favor of limiting the size of pressure airships in which the load is not uniformly distributed over the hull. On a properly designed airship the weights should be so distributed that the bending moment be virtually nil. If such be the case,—and this is more easily attained on structure airships than on pressure airships,—the weight of the hull and understructure will increase at a rate much nearer to the linear dimensions than to their square. The result would obviously constitute a net gain in useful load. At present the useful load of the most efficient pressure airships, those of the Astra-Torrès system, varies between 45 and 50 per cent. of the total weight, whereas a Zeppelin airship carries only about 33 per cent. of useful load:

Apportionment of Useful Load
on a 23,000 cbm. Astra-Torrès airship.*
Crew of 18, equipment, etc............ 2,040 kgs.
Fuel, oil and water for a 20 hour flight. 4,400 kgs.
Armament........................... 600 kgs.
Ballast............................. 5,060 kgs.
    Total................12,100 kgs

Apportionment of Useful Load
on a projected 22,000 cbm. Parseval airship.*
Crew of 15........................... 1,200 kgs.
Equipment, search-light, etc.......... 140 kgs.
Radio and cabinet.................... 250 kgs.
Fuel, oil, and water for a 20 hour flight. 3,600 kgs.
Armament........................... 500 kgs.
Ballast............................. 2,310 kgs.
    Total................... 8,000 kgs.

*From official sources.

Airship Harbors and Mooring Stations.—The operation of airships necessitates the establishment of specially adapted airship harbors, fitted with sheds, repair works and hydrogen plants, where airships can find shelter in case of bad weather and hydrogen for refilling their gas-chambers, and where minor repairs can be effected.

Prior to the war, Germany's airship harbors had come to be known as models of their kind. Experience, dearly bought by a score of disasters to Zeppelin airships, taught the Germans so to build airship sheds that their entrance would lay in the direction of the prevailing winds. Where the winds are apt to change their direction suddenly, such as on the seashore, elaborate and very costly revolving sheds were provided, which could be turned into the prevailing wind, thus enabling an airship always to enter the shed with a head wind. The possibility of an airship being caught in a side wind and thrown against the shed, where she would break her back, was thus greatly obviated. The landing was further facilitated by electric- or gasoline-driven lorries running on tracks, which extended a whole airship length in front of the shed; on landing, an airship would throw her handling guys, which would be fastened on the lorries, and be promptly towed into the shed.

The organization of docking facilities for airships was undertaken in Germany not only by the military and naval authorities, but also by municipalities and private concerns, thus giving an admirable example of progressive foresight. Mooring stations, where an airship could weather a storm in the open, were also provided in large numbers.

The British Navy has evolved a particularly promising mooring mast, which permits an airship to put its nose into a revolving cup wherefrom it can swing freely and follow the direction of the prevailing wind. This system has proven very satisfactory in practice because it lessens the risk of a downward air current throwing the airship against the ground.

Where no such nose-cup is available a simple mast will answer the purpose, provided the airship is fitted on the nose with a mooring attachment. On structure airships as well as on the pressure airships of the Astra-Torrès and Forlanini types the forward end of the hull frame or of the truss girder gives a solid mooring point wherefrom all traction is evenly distributed over the hull. On the girderless Parseval airships the nose is reinforced by an internal metal cup.

An interesting type of airship shed is that presumably adopted by the German Navy for the airship harbor of Heligoland, which is made to open sidewise, like a mouth, and receives an airship from above. The considerable cost involved in the construction of modern airship sheds seems to point to the ultimate adaptation of natural resources, such as deeply cut valleys, for airship harbors.

The Future of the Airship.—The question is often asked, and it is quite pertinent in view of the stupendous development of the latter day aeroplane—"What is the airship's future?"

To the military aspects of this query the reader may find a rather exhaustive reply in a subsequent review of the services the airship has rendered in the Great War and the functions it may fulfill in the near future.

There nevertheless remains the commercial side of the problem to be answered.

Aeroplane constructors—who are the natural adversaries of the airship—point with a pride not illegitimate to the considerable velocities dynamic aircraft have attained of late, and which is double that of the swiftest airship, as an argument against the latter's commercial future. Further emphasis appears to be given this argument by the recent successful development of large weight-carrying aeroplanes.

Without going into a detailed discussion of these claims one might remark that whereas the safety of the passengers is quite an interesting item in public transportation the airship appears on the main to fulfill this condition to a far greater degree than the aeroplane, since the airship is capable of staying aloft regardless of engine failure, a thing the aeroplane cannot and, probably, will not do for some time to come. This feature, which enables the airship to outride a storm if a landing proves impracticable, should eventually prove a valuable asset for oversea voyages where the matter of alighting on the sea during a storm appears all but a pleasant prospective.

And, finally, it should be remembered that the development of the airship has by no means kept pace with that of the aeroplane, this being mainly due to the important expenditure involved in the construction of airships.

Nothing could better illustrate this fact than the humorous zoological parallel one of the cleverest contemporary writers on aeronautics, C. G. Grey, editor of the London *Aeroplane*, has drawn between the airship and the aeroplane, and the mammoth and the dog, respectively.

"The mammoth, breeding once in ten years or so, and running a hundred years or more to the

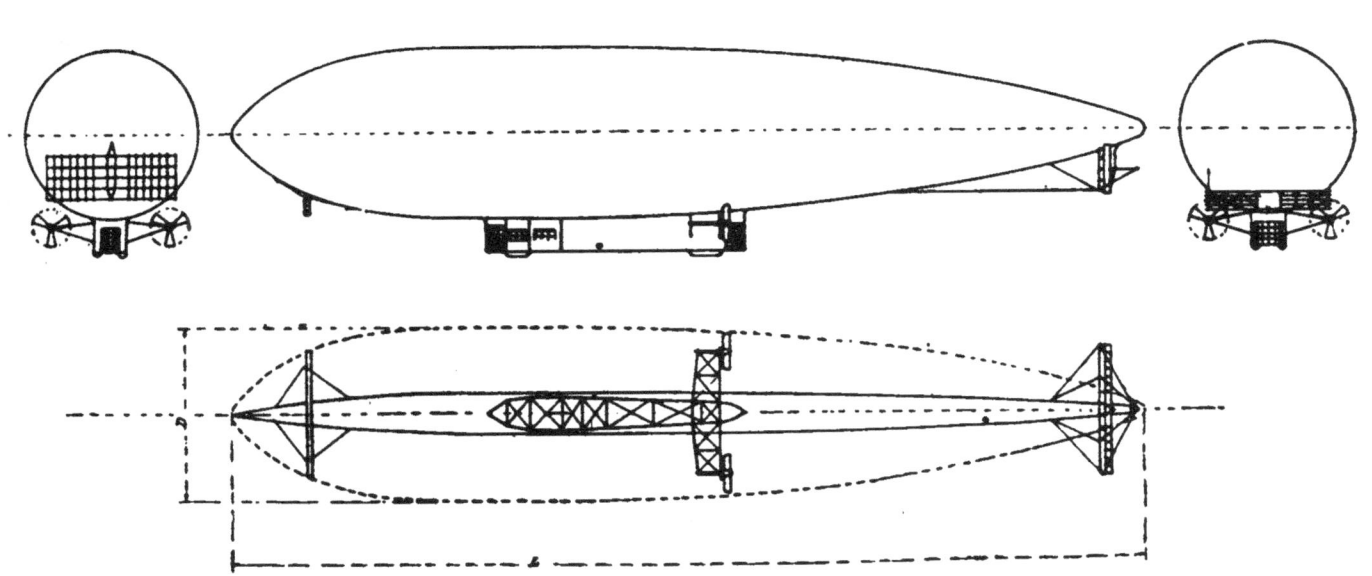

DIAGRAM OF A 15,000 CBM. FORLANINI AIRSHIP (KEEL-GIRDER PRESSURE TYPE)

generation, has developed no further than the elephant, who is an unfinished sort of job at his best, whereas the dog, breeding two or three times a year, and averaging about seven or eight years to the generation, is a very highly developed animal, and is, incidentally, capable of scaring the life out of an elephant."

As a conclusion, one may safely assume that whatever the ultimate issue between the airship and aeroplane be, the immediate future, that is, the *post-bellum* period, will see the aerial ocean filled with a respectable number of passenger and pleasure airships, not to speak of those devoted to military pursuits.

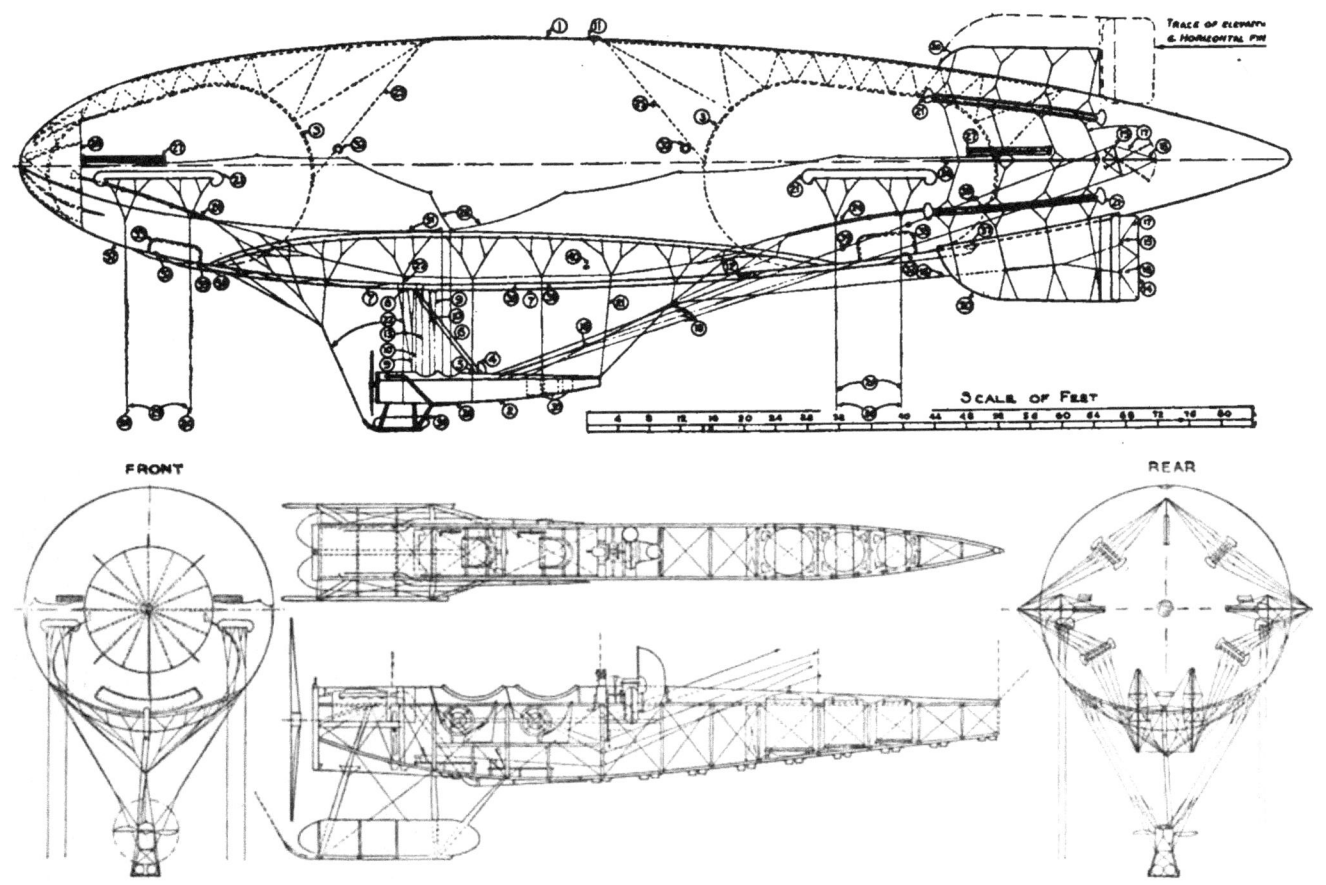

DIAGRAM OF THE 2,200 CBM. SCOUT AIRSHIPS OF THE U. S. NAVY.

1 envelope; 2 car; 3 ballonnet; 4 blower intake pipe; 5 blower engine; 6 main air discharge pipe; 7 air pipe to ballonnet; 8 air manifold; 9 operating cord of ballonnet exhaust valve; 10 operating cord of butterfly valve; 11 pressure relief valve; 12 gas control valve; 13 operating cord of gas control valve; 14 twin-rudders; 15 king-post; 16 steering gear leads; 17 bracing wire; 18 elevator; 19 elevator leads; 20 stabilizing planes; 21 double patch; 22 suspension; 23 rigging (or belly-) band; 24 webbing; 25 ballonnet suspension; 26 nose reinforcement; 27 ripping panel; 28 ripping cord; 29 grab ropes; 30 weights; 31 mooring rope; 32 sight holes; 33 patch for removing ballonnet; 34 kapok floats; 35 fuel tanks; 36 exhaust silencer; 37 trimming tanks; 38 operating cords for trimming tanks; 39 guides for operating cords; 40 filling hole and doubling patch.

THE AIRSHIP IN THE GREAT WAR

The Ante-bellum Airship Programs.—A large weight-carrying capacity, permitting to carry fuel for long cruises or powerful explosives in the form of bombs or torpedoes for shorter raids; the possibility of drifting noiselessly with the wind and of hovering over a given point for observation or attack; the steady gun-platform afforded by the great buoyancy; and, finally, the possibility of sending as well as receiving wireless messages—all these seem to outline the large structure airship as the capital fighting craft of the air.

Such was, prior to the war, Germany's conception of the military airship, and her determined effort to become supreme in the air by just such a fleet materialized in 1913 in a building program which provided for the construction, within four years, of thirty airships for service with the Army and ten airships for service with the Navy. The Army airships were to form five squadrons, the Navy airships two squadrons; means for establishing an adequate number of airship harbors was also provided in the expenditure. The naval expenditure was apportioned as follows:

Construction of 10 airships........$2,750,000
Construction of airship harbors......$3,500,000
Maintenance of *matériel*.............$2,500,000
                                     ―――――――
    Total...................$8,750,000

It is worth noting that all the naval airships and the greater part of the army airships of this program were to be of the structure type (Zeppelin or Schütte-Lanz) and of the largest size (24 tons and over). Cleared for action, these airships would possess an endurance of from 1,600 to 1,750 kilometres; carry one ton of munitions with which to supply their bomb tubes and machine guns; ballast enabling them to reach, partly lightened by fuel consumption, an altitude of 2,500 metres; and wireless apparatus having a range of 300 kilometres in daytime. Provision was also made in the program for the automatic replacement of airships lost through accident or having reached the age limit of four years.

When the war broke out three ships of the 1913 program had been commissioned, and eight more Zeppelins, not to count minor units, were available from previous programs. Of the Allied countries, France possessed the largest and most efficient airship fleet; unfortunately, all but one of her vessels were of the pressure type, of medium size, and slow speed, and consequently devoid of a great cruising radius. The only structure airship was, furthermore, an experimental vessel. There was, to be sure, a building program, dating from 1912, which was to provide seven large pressure airships (of 25 tons and over) to the Army; but none of these vessels was commissioned in August, 1914, and no allowance had been made for naval airships.

In Great Britain the situation was still worse, for the airship fleet was nearer *to be* than *in being*. Prior to 1914 the Army possessed a few airships, and these were very small and short-ranged vessels indeed; the Navy had no airships at all, if one excepts the experimental structure airship ordered in 1910 from Messrs. Vickers, Sons and Maxim, which proved a failure, and was therefore never commissioned. The rebirth, or, rather, the creation of Great Britain's airship fleet dates from Mr. Winston Churchill's arrival at the Admiralty in 1913. At the instance of this far-seeing minister the still serviceable Army airships were placed under control of the Navy, and orders were passed for the construction of two large structure airships and ten medium-sized pressure airships. On war being declared, two of the latter were available for service.

In Italy conditions paralleled those of France. A few excellent pressure airships of medium size were in commission, and four capital airships of the largest size (from 25 to 40 tons) were building or projected. As to the Russian airship fleet, it was chiefly remarkable for its heterogeneous *matériel*, hailing from Russian, French, and German yards; its personnel possessed, in contradistinction to the aforenamed fleets, only the rudiments of training and little practical experience. Austria had no airship fleet.

Early Airship Operations in the Great War.— The foregoing picture of Europe's airship situation in the summer of 1914 is indicative of the overwhelming potential means the Hun possessed for strategical reconnaissance in those terrible first few weeks of the war when his hordes were overrunning heroic Belgium and the northern *départements* of France. As a means of quickly gaining and reporting information about the movement of troops, munition columns, etc., the Zeppelin proved a matchless instrument to which the German Army must owe many a success. The smooth working of the Zeppelin fleet was further facilitated by a total lack of any efficient Allied anti-airship defense system. Anti-aircraft guns, and principally range-finders, were still in their infancy; and destroyer-aeroplanes, which were to blow up the airships with incendiary bombs or darts, existed mainly in popular fancy.

Germany's naval airships proved equally formidable, for though little has come to be known about their reconnaissance work, one of them was "iron-crossed" for "coöperation with a submarine in a successful attack on three British armored cruisers," as the Berlin version runs. The exploit referred to was the sinking of H. M. ships *Hogue*, *Aboukir*, and *Cressy* by the German submarine *U. 9*. In view of the undoubted military achievements of the Zeppelin it seems pitiable that its record should have been soiled from the very beginning of the war by the despicable practice of terrorizing peaceful populations through an indiscriminate destruction of lives and homes. The practice of dropping bombs on undefended towns and villages, which from sporadic attempts gradually developed into a highly systematized policy, cannot be qualified but as piracy and murder, and it is to be hoped that its perpetrators will not escape just chastisement when the Allied High Court assembles to pass upon such and similar acts committed in the name of German *Kultur*.

The losses incurred by the German airship fleet in the early part of the war, chiefly in the first nine months, were considerable. Some vessels were shot down, others were captured on their moorings, still others were destroyed by storms; but nearly all were lost through reckless handling by officers unfamiliar with war-time conditions or willing to take risks.

Within the limitations imposed upon it by a peculiar building policy the "old" French airship fleet gave an excellent account of itself. Nothing could better illustrate the intrinsic value of the Gallic *matériel* than the exploit of a three and one-half year old Army airship, the *Adjudant-Vincenot*, which raised, only one month before the war, the world's endurance record for airships to thirty-six hours, thus beating the record previously established by a brand-new naval Zeppelin.

Besides effecting numerous strategical reconnaissances of considerable value in the early "mobile warfare" which came to an end with the Battle of the Marne and the "race to the sea," French airships also made a number of offensive raids on German communication lines, dépots, and encampments. Most of these incursions were made at night, for the French quickly realized the great vulnerability of airships in daylight, when the huge hulls form an appreciably large target; whereas by night an airship must first be discovered before she can be fired at.

The British used their few airships to good effect in patrolling the Channel, thus affording their troop-ships efficient protection against surprise attacks by submarines. In this function airships have proved very efficient fleet auxiliaries, for their cone of vision increases in proportion to their elevation, and extends, furthermore, on clear days a goodly depth into the sea. It is true that with a choppy sea the range of deep-sea vision stops at the surface; but since a submarine cannot fire a torpedo without showing her periscope, it is obvious that the airship has still the better of it. By combining the deep-sea vision obtained from the car of an airship with the weight-carrying capacity and the variation of speed afforded by these craft, it should be possible to develop a submarine-chaser airship which would rid the seas of their terror by attacking the submarine with bombs or torpedoes. The question of accurately hitting the target would resolve itself into that of developing appropriate bomb-tubes and range-finders, a problem which is bound to be solved sooner or later. The British and French navies now possess a large number of such submarine scouts,—termed *Blimps* in the Royal Naval Air Service,—and they are used very extensively in connection with harbor and coast patrol work, although their offensive value is still a matter of conjecture. The United States Navy will soon have such airships, an order for sixteen *Blimps* having been awarded several manufacturers in 1917.

Resuming the review of the first year of airship operations, it can be said to have been characterized by strategical and tactical reconnaissances and by coast patrol work. Offensive actions were of a sporadic nature and more or less of an experimental sort.

The German Airship Offensive.—The summer of 1915 saw the opening of Germany's long-heralded grand airship campaign against the British Isles, and the novel warfare thus launched gave the world the first intimation of the offensive power of capital airships. The main purpose of this cam-

THE STERN OF THE 19,000 CBM. SCHÜTTE-LANZ AIRSHIP *S. L. I.* THE ELLIPSOIDAL SHAPE OF THE HULL IS NOTEWORTHY.

paign was to be, in the opinion of authoritative German writers on military subjects, the gradual destruction of London and the consequent wearing down of Great Britain's nerve-centres.

To quote Captain Persius, the German naval writer, "the chief use and object of the airship attacks on England consists in damaging military means and power of our most dangerous enemy. The idea of what are military forces is not a narrow one. Not only may bombs be thrown upon fortified places, war-ships, and workshops for making shells and ammunition of all kinds, in order to destroy them, but they are also intended to destroy places of economic importance which, if they remain untouched, would add more or less to England's power to continue the war. To the economic places which are looked upon as proper objects for bombs, such as railway docks and wharves, may be added coal and oil depots, electricity- and gas-works, buildings which serve for meteorological purposes when they are in military hands, such, for instance, as Greenwich Observatory. All these are valuable targets, and the list could be continued."

Strategical considerations such as the above were surely in no mean way responsible for the launching of Germany's airship offensive against Great Britain; one might nevertheless point out that by that time the Western front had become a very much alive barrier of highly efficient anti-aircraft guns and battle-aeroplanes which threatened to greatly curtail, f not altogether to stop, the Zeppelin's career of overland scout. And Germany so well realized this changed condition that most of her Army airships were sent to the Eastern front, where the Russians' little developed anti-airship defense system proved no match for them.

Contrary to all expectations, and to inspired German press reports, the Zeppelin offensive did not start with a concerted attack in fleet formation. Instead of such a bold stroke, the Germans indulged for months in experimental raids on English coast towns, so that by the time London was actually attacked enough time had elapsed to enable the English to work out the rudiments of a defense system which practical experience, gained in successive raids, gradually brought to the highest point of perfection.

In the meantime the airship offensive proceeded month after month, claiming an ever-increasing toll of human lives and wrecked homes. For it is remarkable how ludicrously small an amount of strictly military damage the Hun airships were able to cause, notwithstanding highly colored semi-official German reports to the contrary effect; and

THE STERN OF THE 20,000 CBM. VICKERS AIRSHIP *No. 1* (OR *MAYFLY*) AFTER THE VESSEL BROKE HER BACK.

military damage consisted mainly of delays in railway and harbor traffic, the stationing in England of anti-aircraft guns and aeroplanes which could otherwise be sent to the front and, lastly, general inconvenience resulting from darkened cities. The measure of turning out all lights on an impending Zeppelin raid, which was first applied in London, proved a fairly good stratagem for misleading the raiders as to their whereabouts, since most of the incursions took place on dark, moonless nights; and gradually the more important manufacturing and shipping towns of England were darkened in their turn. To complete these measures of safety, the names of places raided by airships were strictly withheld by the censor, thus depriving the enemy of all useful information.

For a whole year the Zeppelin raids continued without showing signs of abatement, although a few airships had been destroyed on their homeward voyage through being intercepted by British aviators stationed on the Continent. Still, this was not quite a satisfactory defense system, since it punished the Hun only after he had accomplished his purpose. On their part, the German Admiralty seemed in no way satisfied with the results achieved by their airships, for in the spring of 1916 orders were given to the Zeppelin factories for the construction of a number of vessels twice the size of those laid down in 1914, and with which a decisive stroke was to be made against London.

The stroke totally miscarried, for the Zeppelin raids which began toward the end of August, 1916, ended for the enemy in an unparalleled series of disasters. Three airships of the largest size were brought down by anti-aircraft guns and aviators in September, and one in October, all around London; and when, discouraged by so grievous losses, the Germans in the following month sent an airship squadron against the Eastern Counties, which they believed to be less well protected, British aviators added to their bag of airships two more Zeppelins, which they sent in flames into the sea. Tacit admission of the failure of German's second airship campaign against Great Britain may be found in the following comment by the above-quoted Captain Persius: "It would be premature to express any decided hope as to whether airships can be of any decisive influence upon the conduct of the war." And as if the German Admiralty wanted to confirm this opinion, extended Zeppelin raids on Great Britain came to an abrupt end with the disastrous autumn campaign of 1916.

During the first six months of 1917 only two isolated incursions of Zeppelins took place, one in

March and one in June, and each was marked by the destruction of one of the enemy airships.

Capital Airships as Naval Scouts.—The recent failure of capital airships to act as weapons of offense, as well as the growing difficulty attending to their employment for strategical reconnaissance over 'and, appears to limit their rôle to that of serving as naval scouts.

It was Sir Percy Scott who first directed the attention of naval authorities toward this aspect of the Zeppelin's potentiality when he wrote, in 1909, the following prophetic words: "In gaining information of the locality, strength and disposition of the enemy's fleet and so unmask his strategy . . . an airship's services would be invaluable, for it might not be possible to obtain the information in any other way."

The large structure airship is truly an invaluable super-scout in naval operations, for its combined range of vision, speed, and cruising radius make it by far superior to any vessel afloat. Kite-balloons, carried on mother-ships, are of considerable value in spotting targets otherwise invisible to the gunners, but they are poor substitutes for long-range airships, whose speed and movements are independent of naval vessels, whereas kite-balloons are moored to their carriers and therefore entirely dependent on the latter's speed. Nor can the present day seaplane be employed for cruising out to sea with a fleet, because (1) its range is still very limited and amounts in the best case to only one fourth that of a capital airship; (2) it cannot vary its speed or remain motionless in the air, and these requirements are often desirable for accurate observation; and (3) it can neither start from, nor alight on, a really rough sea, where it could otherwise be refuelled from a tender.

Against the above drawbacks of the kite-balloon and the seaplane the modern structure airship presents the following advantages: (1) It can reduce its speed or altogether stop its engines and hover over a given place on a windless day, or else drift with a favorable wind, thus saving fuel; (2) its large cruising radius, which for a well-designed 60 ton vessel should amount to from 2,500 to 3,000 kilometres, provided only defensive armament, such as machine-guns, is carried; (3) the possibility of refuelling the airship from a tender at sea by means of a charging-pipe operated by compressed air—the hydrogen could be renewed in the same way—(4) it can operate by night as well as by day. The last, and not the least, argument in favor of the use of airships as naval scouts is their much lesser vulnerability over the seas than over land. Over land

TOP—THE MOORING MAST OF THE ROYAL NAVAL AIR SERVICE—AIRSHIP LEAVING A SHED; *BOTTOM*—INFLATION OF AN AIRSHIP FROM A FIELD GENERATOR—AIRSHIP WEIGHTED DOWN IN A SHED.

an airship runs the ever-present risk of being hit by an anti-aircraft gun, which may be masked by a bush, a tree, or any natural or artificial shelter and is therefore invisible from above; but on the sea a gun means a ship, and a ship can be detected, from an airship navigating at an elevation of 1,500 metres, in a radius of 100 kilometres, provided the weather is clear. And since the range of vision afforded from the top of a surface ship but seldom reaches 30 kilometres, it is obvious that an airship can leisurely reconnoiter an enemy squadron without even being seen by the latter. Surprise encounters may naturally occur between airships and surface vessels, more specially if one of them suddenly emerges from a cloud or fog-bank; but losses have to be expected in warfare. Furthermore, in the above contingency an airship, with her greatly superior speed, could in most cases successfully outrun a surface vessel.

The Great War has fully demonstrated the value of capital airships in naval reconnaissance work, for the strategical advantage possessed by the German fleet in various actions fought in the North Sea must almost entirely be attributed to the clever reconnoitering effected by Zeppelin flotillas. The element of surprise was thus in favor of the German battle-cruiser squadron when it raided Yarmouth, Scarborough, and Lowestoft, because it could ascertain the whereabouts of the British battle-cruisers by a squadron of far-flung Zeppelins, which would report every British move by wireless. In the Battle of Jutland the participation of Zeppelins enabled the German High Sea Fleet nearly to overwhelm Admiral Beatty's battle-cruiser squadron in the first phase of the engagement, and to break off the action after the British Grand Fleet had arrived on the scene in full force, thus turning an impending disaster into a fairly balanced draw.

One may also assume that the repeated slipping of the British blockade by German commerce-destroyers, such as the *Möwe* and the *Seeadler*, has been made possible to a great extent, if not wholly, by intelligent coöperation with Zeppelins.

How decisive the foregoing considerations are is best illustrated by the establishment, in 1917, of a joint board of officers of the United States Navy and Army, which has been ordered to lay down the plans for the first American capital airships. Not wanting to lag behind, the Japanese Navy decided at about the same time to lay down a 20-ton airship of the structure type.

Germany's Airship Production.—Although Germany's war-time output of airships is shrouded, like all production of war *matériel*, by the veil of military secrecy, it is assumed on good authority that the Friedrichshafen and Potsdam works of the Zeppelin Company are equipped to turn out one complete airship in three weeks' time. This rapid rate of construction is made possible by laying down several airships at a time, as well as by a strict standardization of the pieces which make up the hull frame, the understructure, etc. The Friedrichshafen works appear to mainly build the larger naval airships, while the army is kept supplied by the Potsdam branch.

Little is known regarding the activity of the Schütte-Lanz Works; information from neutral sources places their recent rate of production at one airship every month, although their earlier output seems to have been considerably slower. It also appears that since 1916 the Schütte-Lanz works are exclusively building airships of the Zeppelin type.

Knowing the approximate rate of construction of the Hun's principal airship works, that is, those where capital airships are built, it appears little difficult to figure out Germany's total production of capital airships during the war, provided the rate of output has remained the same.

While the following table does not claim to be strictly accurate in regard to the apportionment of airship constructions to single yards, the yearly output since August 1st, 1914, as well as the grand total herewith given, may eventually be found to have missed the mark by little. Confirmation of this view may be found in a Swiss report announcing the launching, in February, 1916, of the *LZ. 95*, that is, the ninety-fifth Zeppelin of current series, which number includes twenty-five airships built prior to the war.

Works	1914	1915	1916	Total
Friedrichshafen..	7	17	17	41
Potsdam.......	7	17	17	41
Rheinau.......	5	12	12	29
Total.......	19	46	46	111

It may be noted that the above table extends only over the period ending with December 31st, 1916. The reason for this is to be found in reports stating that the General Staff of the German Army decided in January, 1917, to discontinue the use of structure airships. If this report proves true,—and there are good reasons to believe that it will,—then Germany's production of capital airships will have suffered an obvious reduction, for the Navy will henceforth be its sole customer until such day when the construction of passenger-airships can once more be taken up.

I. THE WORLD'S AIRSHIP BUILDERS

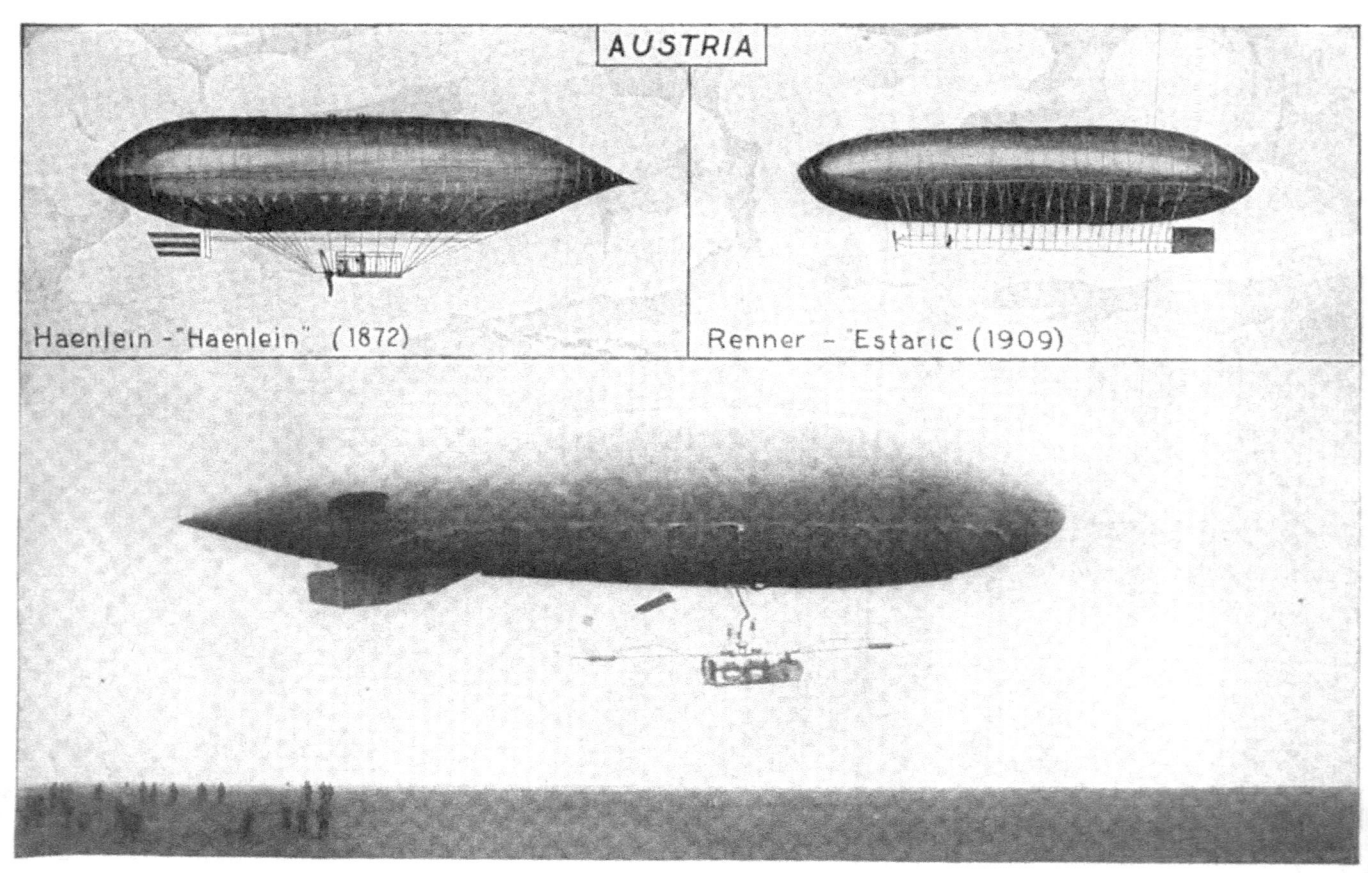

THE *M. III* (1911).

AUSTRIA

Boemches (Captain F.), Vienna.—Builder of a pressure airship of the car-girder type. Girder consisting of a short car fitted with bow-outrigger only. Trim controlled by lifting planes and compensating ballonets.

Works No.	Name Trials	Length (m)	Beam (m)	Volume (mc)	Power (h.p.)	Speed (km)	Notes
1	Boemches (1912)	57	9	2,750	72	40	Experimental airship.—Two Koerting engines; twin-screws. The airship did not prove satisfactory on her trials and was dismantled the following year. (Photo wanted.)

Haenlein (Paul), Vienna.—Builder of a pressure airship of the keel-girder type. Trim controlled by ballast.

Works No.	Name Trials	Length (m)	Beam (m)	Volume (mc)	Power (h.p.)	Speed (km)	Notes
1	Haenlein (December, 1872)	50.4	9.2	2,400	3	4.5	Experimental airship.—One Lenoir gas engine fed by the foal-gas contained in the hull; one pusher-screw. The trials disclosed the inadequacy of the power-plant, which barely enabled the airship to make any headway.

Koerting (Maschinenbau A. G.), Vienna.—Builders of a pressure airship of the car-girder type. Girder consisting of a short car with two outriggers. Trim controlled by two compensating ballonets and trimming tanks, the latter being operated by compressed air.

Works No.	Name Trials	Length (m)	Beam (m)	Volume (mc)	Power (h.p.)	Speed (km)	Notes
1	M. III. (January, 1911)	68	10.5	3,600	150	49	Austrian Army airship.—Two Koerting engines; twin-screws. Ballonets. 900 mc. A fairly successful vessel. Was accidentally destroyed on June 20th, 1914, over Schwechat (near Vienna) through being rammed by a military aeroplane. The crews of both aircraft perished.

THE *AUSTRIA* (1911).

AUSTRIA—Continued

Motor-Luftfahrzeug Gesellschaft, Vienna.—Builders of pressure airships to various designs.

Works No.	Name Trials	Length (m)	Beam (m)	Volume (mc)	Power (h.p.)	Speed (km)	Notes
1	M. I. (November, 1909)	50	8.6	2,450	100	44	Austrian Army airship.—Built to the designs of the Luftfahrzeug Gesellschaft (Parseval's patents). Girderless, pressure type. Trim controlled by two compensating ballonets and self-shifting car. Ballonets: 400 mc. One Austro-Daimler engine; one pusher-screw. Best endurance: 200 km. in 7 hrs. Dismantled in 1913.
2	M. II. (May, 1910)	70	10.9	4,800	130	45	Austrian Army airship.—Built to the designs of Messrs. Lebaudy Frères. Keel-girder pressure type. Trim controlled by lifting planes. Ballonet: 1,300 mc. One Austro-Daimler engine; twin-screws. Designed endurance: 10 hrs. Best altitude: 1,350 m. Dismantled in 1913.

Renner (A. & J.), Gratz.—Builders of a pressure airship of the car-girder type. Trim controlled by ballast.

Works No.	Name Trials	Length (m)	Beam (m)	Volume (mc)	Power (h.p.)	Speed (km)	Notes
1	Estaric (July, 1909)	32	6	700	40	35	Exhibition airship.—One Puch engine; one tractor-screw. Was wrecked by the storm on Nov. 28th, 1910, while landing.

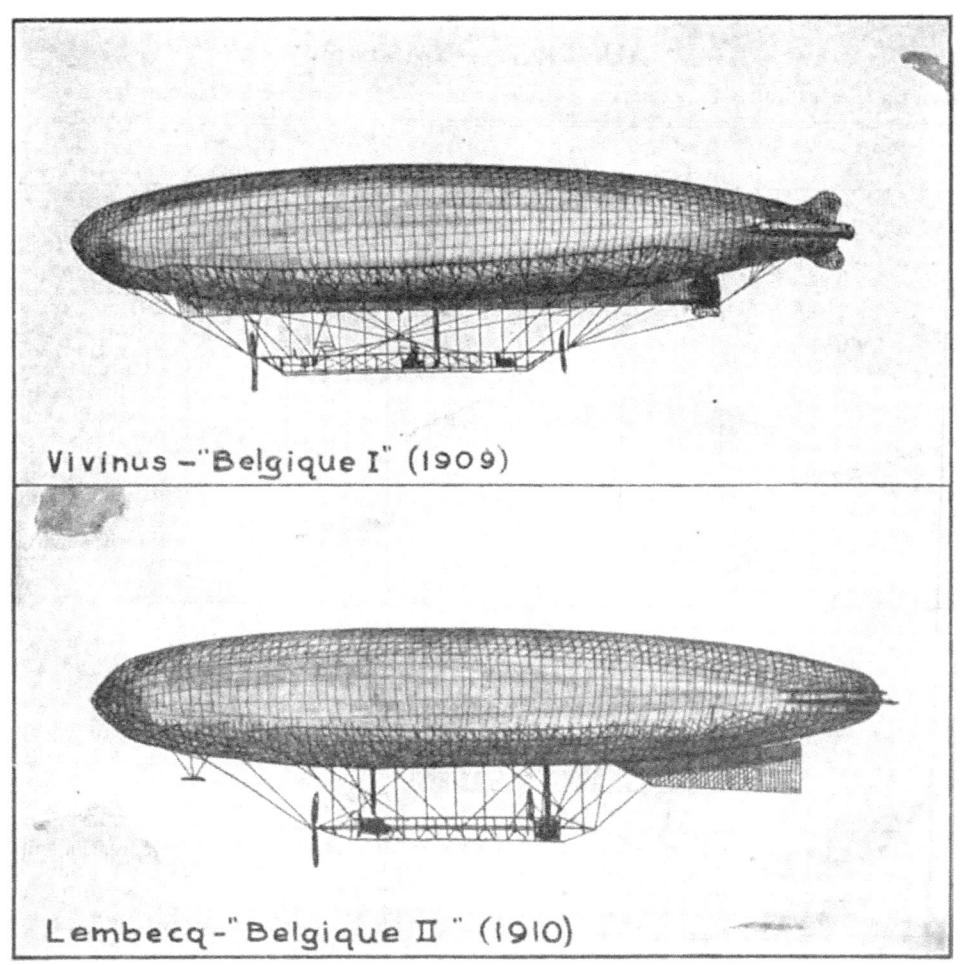

AUSTRIA—Continued

Stagl & Mannsbarth, Vienna.—Builders of a pressure airship of the car-girder type. Trim controlled by lifting planes, swivelling screws and compensating ballonets. Four compartments.

Works No.	Name Trials	Length (m)	Beam (m)	Volume (mc)	Power (h.p.)	Speed (km)	Notes
1	Austria (1911)	91	13.2	8,150	260	65	Experimental airship.—Four ballonets: 2,500 mc. Two Austro-Daimler engines; two pairs of twin-screws and two swivelling screws, one fore and one abaft. Best endurance: 8¼ hrs. Dismantled in 1914 and sold at auction.

BELGIUM

Vivinus Works, Brussels.—Builders, to M. L. Godard's designs, of a pressure airship of the keel-girder type. Godard hull. Trim controlled by lifting planes.

Works No.	Name Trials	Length (m)	Beam (m)	Volume (mc)	Power (h.p.)	Speed (km)	Notes
1	La Belgique (June, 1909)	54.8	9.8	2,700	100	39	Excursion airship of Messrs. Goldschmidt and Solvay of Brussels.—Ballonet: 625 mc. Two Vivinus engines; one tractor and one pusher screws. Best endurance: 2¾ hrs.
1a	La Belgique II (April, 1910)	65	11	4,000	120	43	Re-built to M. Goldschmidt's designs by the Lembecq Works of Brussels. Car-girder type. Ballonet, heated by engine, 800 mc. One Germain engine; one tractor-screw. Was presented by her owners to the Belgian Army in Sept., 1910; was again re-built and fitted with a hull made by Zodiac and with trimming tanks.
1b	La Belgique III (May, 1914)	63	11	4,200	120	52	Training airship, Belgian Army. Ballonets: 1,000 mc. Designed endurance: 10 hrs.

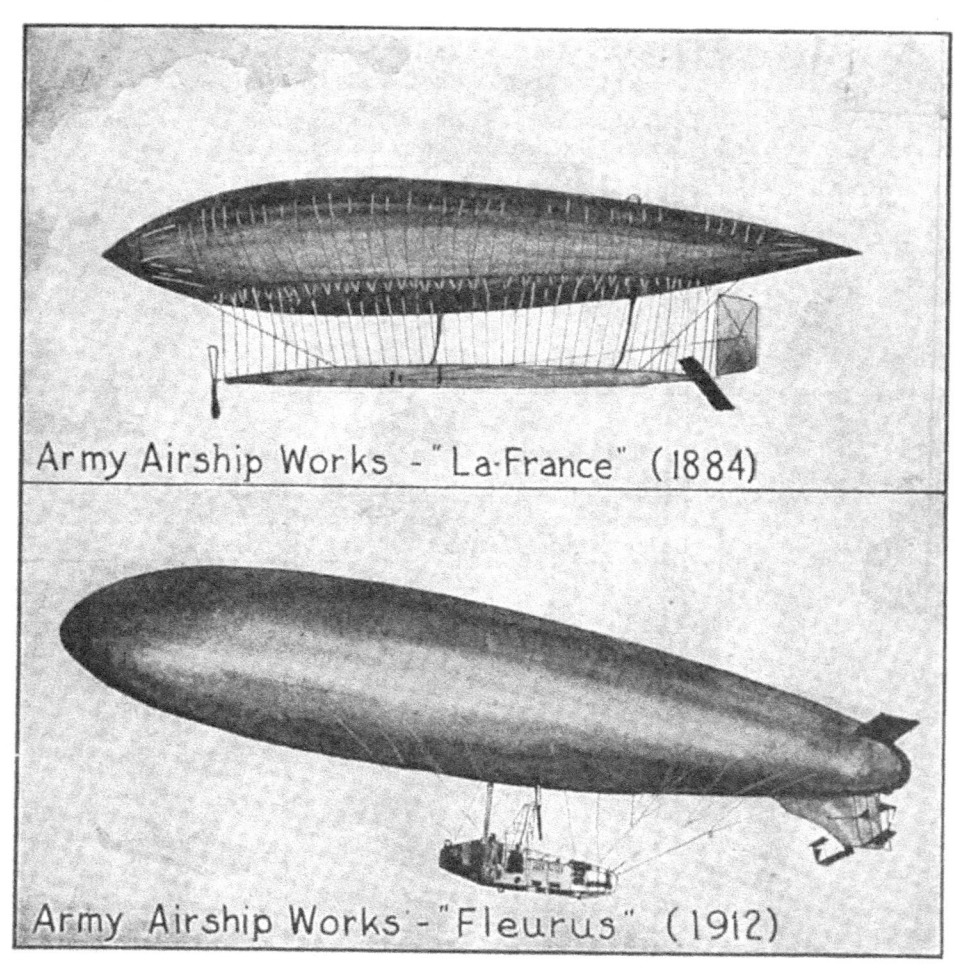

Army Airship Works - "La-France" (1884)

Army Airship Works - "Fleurus" (1912)

BRAZIL

Patrocinio (José de), Sao Paulo.—Builder of a pressure airship of the keel-girder type. Carton-Lachambre hull. Trim controlled by lifting screws.

Works No.	Name Trials	Length (m)	Beam (m)	Volume (mc)	Power (h.p.)	Speed (km)	Notes
1	Santa Cruz (1903)	45	21	3,900	40		Experimental airship.—One Buchet engine. On the trials the airship failed to leave the ground and was eventually broken up.

DENMARK

An airship, named **Fionia**, was tested near Copenhagen, in June, 1912. (Photo or sketch and data wanted.)

FRANCE

Army Airship Works, Chalais-Meudon (Seine-et-Oise).—Builders of airships to various designs.

Works No.	Name Trials	Length (m)	Beam (m)	Volume (mc)	Power (h.p.)	Speed (km)	Notes
1	La France (August, 1884)	50.4	8.4	1,864	9	23	Experimental airship, built to the designs of Captain (later Colonel) Renard and Lieut. Krebs. Car-girder, pressure type; ballonet, 438 mc. First airship to be fitted with an elevator. One Gramme electric battery-motor; one tractor-screw. Made seven trips in all and returned five times to her starting place, thus solving the problem of airship navigation. Best endurance: 1 hour in a closed circuit.

THE CAR OF THE *FLEURUS*.

FRANCE—Continued

Works No.	Name Trials	Length (m)	Beam (m)	Volume (mc)	Power (h.p.)	Speed (km)	Notes
2	Général Meusnier	70	9	3,400	45		Experimental airship, built to the designs of Col. Ch. Renard and his brother, Commandant P. Renard. Car-girder, pressure type. One gasoline engine; one tractor-screw. Owing to the unreliability of the engine the airship, though completed in 1893, could not be tested and was eventually dismantled.
3	Fleurus (November, 1912)	77	13	6,850	160	60	French Army airship.—Built to the designs of Capt. Lenoir. Girderless pressure type. Two Clément-Bayard engines; twin-screws. Best endurance: 680 km. in 15 h. 30'. Named after the battle in which the first military use was made of a balloon (June 26th, 1794). The *Fleurus* made in the early part of the war numerous gallant raids on German R. R. junctions.
4	(Building)	110	15	17,000	1,200	80	French Army airship.—Two Dansette-Gillet engines. (The herewith given data are unconfirmed, being based on Weyer's Taschenbuch.)

"Astra" (Société de Constructions aéronautiques), Billancourt (Seine).—Builders of pressure airships to the designs of Messrs. Edouard Surcouf and Henri Kapferer (car-girder type) and to the patents of M. L. Torrès-Quevedo (tension truss type). Trim controlled by lifting planes (Astra type) by ballonets on Astra-Torrès type.

Works No.	Name Trials	Length (m)	Beam (m)	Volume (mc)	Power (h.p.)	Speed (km)	Notes
1							Hull of the *Lebaudy-I*.
2	Ville-de-Paris (November, 1906)	60.4	10.5	3,200	50	36	Excursion airship of M. Henri Deutsch de la Meurthe. Ballonet: 500 mc. One Chenu engine; one

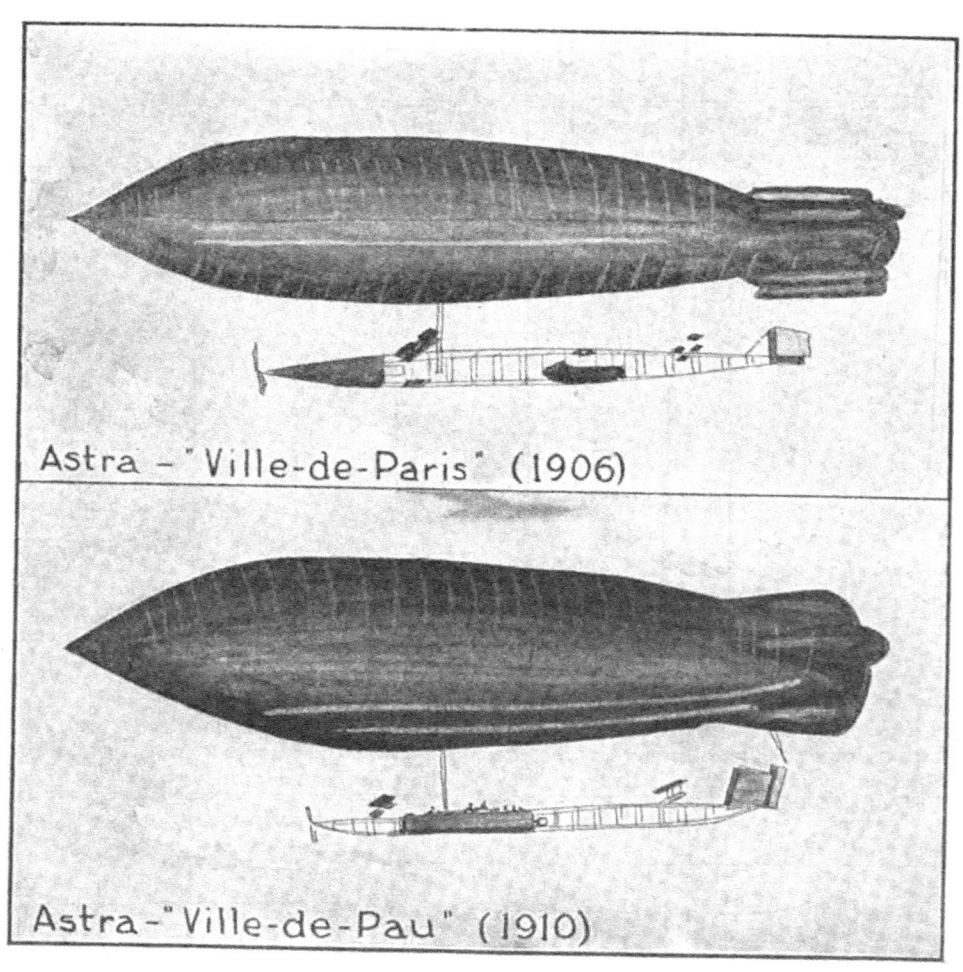

Astra - "Ville-de-Paris" (1906)

Astra - "Ville-de-Pau" (1910)

FRANCE—Continued

Works No.	Name Trials	Length (m)	Beam (m)	Volume (mc)	Power (h.p.)	Speed (km)	Notes
2a	(1909)	66	10.5	3,600	70	44	tractor-screw. Cylindrical fins. Best endurance in 1908: 260 km. (Paris-Verdun). Presented by her owner to the French Army after the loss of the *Patrie*. Suffered numerous mishaps and was again rebuilt and re-engined. Ballonet: 1,100 mc. One Chenu engine. Served for years as a training airship and was eventually dismantled in 1913.
3	Ville-de-Nancy (June, 1909)	56	10	3,350	80	45	Excursion airship of the Compagnie Générale Transaérienne of Paris. One Renault engine; one tractor-screw. Ballonet: 1,100 mc. Was laid down as *Ville-de-Bordeaux*. Made numerous ascents with passengers.
4	Clément-Bayard I (October, 1908)	56.3	10.6	3,500	105	48	Excursion airship of M. Clément-Bayard. Ballonet: 1,100 mc. One Clément-Bayard engine; one tractor-screw. Best endurance: 200 km. in 4 h. 53 min.; altitude: 1,550 m. On concluding the latter test, on Aug. 23, 1909, the airship fell for lack of ballast into the Seine, but was salvaged, repaired and sold to the Russian Army who re-named her *Berkout*. Dismantled in 1913.
5	Colonel-Renard (July, 1909)	64.7	10.8	4,300	100	50	French Army airship.—Named after the builder of the first successful airship. One Panhard-Levassor engine; one tractor-screw. Ballonet: 1,500 mc. Best endurance: 100 km. in 1½ hrs. Was re-fitted with twin-screws in 1911.

FRONT AND REAR VIEWS OF THE *ASTRA-TORRÈS I* (1911).

FRANCE—Continued

Works No.	Name Trials	Length (m)	Beam (m)	Volume (mc)	Power (h.p.)	Speed (km)	Notes
6	España (October, 1909)	64.7	10.8	4,200	120	50	Spanish Army airship.—Ballonet: 1,500 mc. One Panhard-Levassor engine; one tractor-screw. Best endurance: 250 km. in 5 hrs. Was commissioned but a short time.
7	Ville-de-Pau (April, 1910)	60	12.2	4,475	105	50	Excursion airship of the Compagnie Générale Transaérienne. Ballonet: 1,000 mc. One Clément-Bayard engine; one tractor-screw. Made up to July 31, 1911, 273 trips, aggregating 8,000 km., on which 2,950 passengers were carried, chiefly at Pau and Lucerne. At the latter place the airship was named *Ville-de-Lucerne*. Dismantled in 1912.
8	Ville-de-Bruxelles (July, 1910)	74.5	14.3	8,300	220	52	Excursion airship of the "Avia" Co. of Brussels. Ballonet: 2,460 mc. Two Pipe engines driving one tractor-screw and one pair of twin-screws. First of a new series of Astra airships. Best endurance: 5 hrs. Made numerous trips over Brussels.
9	Astra-Torrès I (March, 1911)	47.7	8.4	1,590	60	53	Experimental airship, the first Astra vessel of the tension-truss type. Ballonet: 500 mc. One Chenu engine driving one tractor-screw. Best endurance: 3¼ hrs. Was destroyed by a fire on Sept. 9th, 1912, in the air-port of Issy.
10	Lieutenant-Chauré (August, 1913)	83.9	14	8,850	240	53	French Army airship. Ballonet: 3,200 mc. Laid down to be of the *Ville-de-Bruxelles* class, was altered during the construction and made similar to *Adjudant-Réau*, the bal-

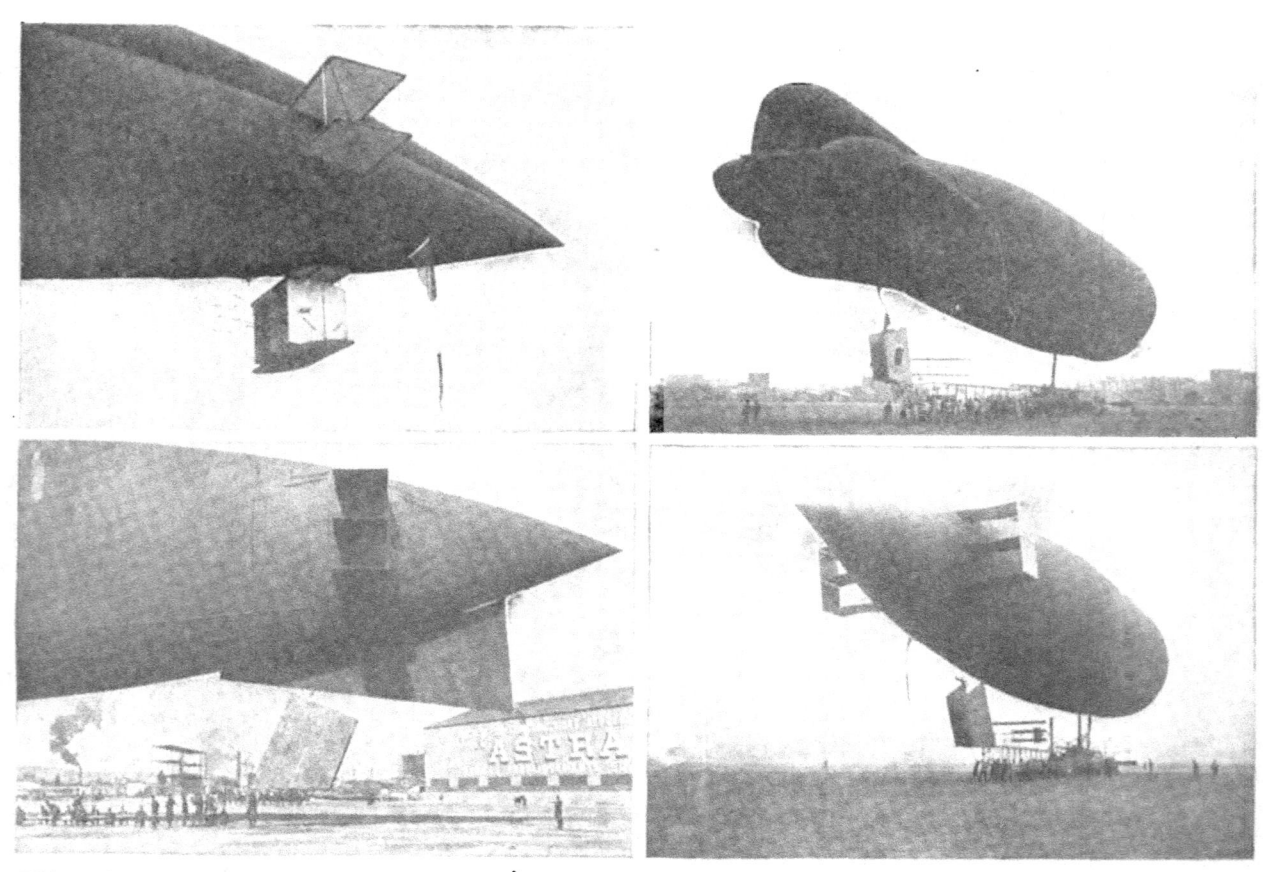

TOP—STERN VIEW OF THE *ASTRA-TORRÈS I* AND THE *VILLE-DE-BRUXELLES*; *BOTTOM*—STERN VIEW OF THE *CONTÉ* AND THE *ADJUDANT-RÉAU*.

FRANCE—Continued

Works No.	Name Trials	Length (m)	Beam (m)	Volume (mc)	Power (h.p.)	Speed (km)	Notes
11	Adjudant-Réau (September, 1911)	86.8	14	8,950	240	55	loon-fins being replaced by stabilizers. Commissioned after much delay. Two Panhard-Levassor engines. French Army airship.—Ballonet: 3,200 mc. Two Brasier engines; one tractor and twin-screws. Best endurance: 917 km. in 21 hrs. 20 min.; altitude: 2,150 m. Trips in 1912 aggregated 3,845 km. and 105 hrs. 39 min. One of the finest airships of her time. Was destroyed by a fire on May 2nd, 1914, in the air-harbour of Verdun.
12	Conté (June, 1912)	65	14	6,650	180	48	French Army airship.—Ballonet: 2,200 mc. Two Chenu engines; twin-screws. Best altitude: 3,050 m. Was damaged by the fire which destroyed the *Astra-Torrès I* and was re-built and fitted with a ballonet of 3,000 mc., larger Chenu engines and a second pair of twin-screws. Best endurance: 700 km. in 16 hrs. Dismantled in 1914.
12a	(1913)	82.5	14	9,100	400	61	
13	(March, 1913)	77.8	14.9	9,800	400	61	Russian Army airship.—Two Chenu engines; twin screws and one tractor-screw. Ballonet: 3,100 mc. Was laid down as an excursion airship for the Compagnie Générale Transaérienne, but was sold to Russia while under construction. Best endurance: 650 km. in 11 hrs.
14	No. 3 (September, 1913)	76.2	13.5	7,360	400	82	British naval airship.—Astra-Torrès type; the fastest vessel of her time. Two Chenu engines; twin-screws. Elevators were altered in 1914.

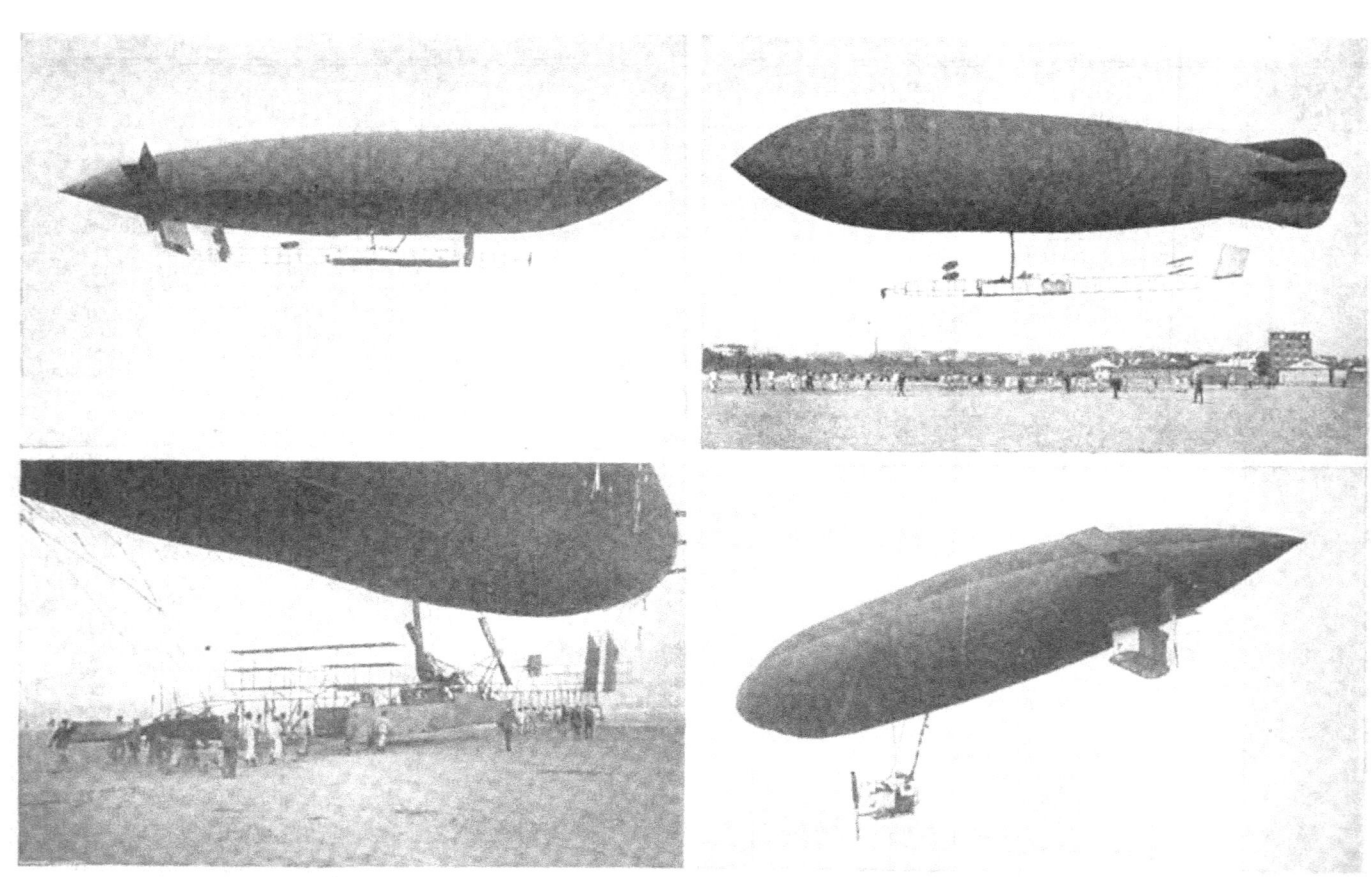

TOP—THE *ADJUDANT-RÉAU* (1911) AND THE *COLONEL-RENARD* (1909); *BOTTOM*—THE CAR OF THE *ADJUDANT-RÉAU* AND THE *ASTRA-TORRÈS I* (1911).

FRANCE—Continued

Works No.	Name Trials	Length (m)	Beam (m)	Volume (mc)	Power (h.p.)	Speed (km)	Notes
15	Pilâtre-de-Rozier (January, 1915)	97	24.5	24,300	1,000	85	French Army airship.—Astra-Torrès type. Two cars. Four Chenu engines, in pairs on each car, driving two pairs of swivelling twin-screws. Four machine-guns on the cars, one on the roof. Designed endurance: 15 hrs. at 2,500 m. and full speed; 30 hrs. at ¾ speed. Wireless carrying 600 km.
16	(1915)	97	24.5	25,000	1,000	85	French Army airship.—*Pilâtre-de-Rozier* class.
17	(Building)	97	24.5	25,000	1,000	85	Russian Army airship.—*Pilâtre-de-Rozier* class.
18	(Building)			10,000	500	85	British naval airship.—Astra-Torrès type. Two Chenu engines; twin-screws.
—	(S. S. type)	53					A certain number of these airships, about which no further data can be given at present on account of the war, have been built and are building for oversea patrol work with the Allied naval forces. In the Royal Naval Air Service these airships are commonly termed "Blimps."

Bot & L'Allemand, Paris.—Builders of a pressure airship of the keel-girder type. Length: 75 m. Was wrecked by a storm in her shed at Verdun on March 1st, 1911. (Data and photo wanted.)

BRITISH S. S. TYPE AIRSHIP [ASTRA] (1915).

FRANCE—Continued

Bradsky (Count Ottokar de), Paris.—Builder of a car-girder pressure airship. Carton-Lachambre hull. Trim controlled by ballast.

Works No.	Name Trials	Length (m)	Beam (m)	Volume (mc)	Power (h.p.)	Speed (km)	Notes
1	Bradsky (October 3rd, 1902)	34	6.3	850	16	30	Experimental airship.—One Buchet engine; one pusher screw and one lifting screw. Primitive construction. The only ascent ended in the car breaking away from the envelope at an altitude of 500 m., killing M. de Bradsky and his engineer, M. Paul Morin.

Carton & Veuve Lachambre, Paris.—Builders of airship hulls and aerostatic matériel.

Clément-Bayard (A.), Levallois (Seine).—Builder of pressure airships of the car-girder type to the designs of M. Sabathier. Trim controlled by lifting planes; on late models also by lifting screws.

Works No.	Name Trials	Length (m)	Beam (m)	Volume (mc)	Power (h.p.)	Speed (km)	Notes
C. B. I.	Clément-Bayard I.						Excursion airship built for M. Clément-Bayard by the "Astra" Works.
C. B. II.	Clément-Bayard II. (June, 1910)	76.5	12.7	6,500	260	52	British Army airship, purchased by a national subscription organized by the London *Daily Mail*. The hull was built by "Astra," the machinery and cars by Clément-Bayard. Ballonet: 2,200 mc. Two engines; twin-screws. After a partial re-construction the airship flew on Oct. 16th, 1910, from Paris to London, covering 390 km. in 6 hrs. with a crew of seven, this being the first airship flight across the Channel.
C. B. IIa.	(September, 1910)	76.5	13.2	7,000	260	52	

TOP—THE *CLÉMENT-BAYARD II* (1910) AND THE *DUPUY-DE-LÔME* (1912); BOTTOM—THE *ADJUDANT-VINCENOT* (1911) AND THE *E. MONTGOLFIER* (1913).

FRANCE—Continued

Works No.	Name Trials	Length (m)	Beam (m)	Volume (mc)	Power (h.p.)	Speed (km)	Notes
C. B. III.	Dupuy-de-Lome (May, 1912)	89	13.5	9,000	260	55	French Army airship.—*C.B.II* type. Two Clément-Bayard engines; twin-screws. Ballonet: 3,000 mc. Best endurance: 800 km. in 19½ hrs. Trips in 1912 aggregated 4,424 km. and 110 hrs. Was accidentally lost in the Great War.
C. B. IV.	Adjudant-Vincenot (June, 1911)	88	13.5	9,000	260	56	French Army airship.—*C.B.II* type. Best endurance: 650 km. in 16¼ hrs. Trips in 1912 aggregated 2,235 km. and 55 hrs. Was re-built to the designs of the *C.B.V.*
	(1913)	91	15	9,600	260	58	Best endurance: 35 hrs. 20 min. During the early part of the war this airship made numerous raids on German communication lines.
C. B. V.	(February, 1913)	86	13.5	9,000	360	60	Russian Army airship.—Two Clément-Bayard engines; twin-screws. Ballonet: 4,500 mc.
C. B. VI.	E. Montgolfier (August, 1913)	73.5	12.2	6,500	180	68	French Army airship.—New type: short car fitted with two outriggers. Ballonet: 2,400 mc. Two Clément-Bayard engines; twin-screws and one lifting screw. Designed endurance: 15 hrs. at 2,000 m. altitude. Armed with two machine guns.
C. B. VII. C. B. VIII.	(1914) (1915)	130	16	21,500	1,400	80	French Army airships.—Four Clément-Bayard engines; two pairs of swivelling twin-screws. One car. Designed endurance: 15 hrs. at full speed and 2,500 m. altitude. Wireless carrying 600 km. Four machine guns on the car; one on the roof, on a platform connected with the car by a shaft.

TOP—THE POWER PLANT AND STEERING GEAR OF THE *ADJUDANT-VINCENOT*; *BOTTOM*—THE CAR OF THE *ADJUDANT-VINCENOT* AND OF THE *E. MONTGOLFIER*.

FRANCE—Continued

Works No.	Name Trials	Length (m)	Beam (m)	Volume (mc)	Power (h.p.)	Speed (km)	Notes
C. B. IX.	(Building)	130	16	21,500	1,400	80	Russian Army airship.—*C.B.VII* type. Since the outbreak of the war a number of airships have been laid down, regarding which no information can be given at present.

Debayeux, Paris.—Builder of a pressure airship. Trim controlled by movable weights.

Works No.	Name Trials	Length (m)	Beam (m)	Volume (mc)	Power (h.p.)	Speed (km)	Notes
1	Debayeux (1878)			3,000	5		Experimental airship.—One Siemens electric battery-motor, driving four paddle wheels. On her trials, at Villeneuve St. Georges, the airship failed to make any headway and proved unmanageable.

De la Vaulx (Count Henri), Paris.—Builder of a spherical airship of 3,400 mc, the *Méditerraneen-II*, which was fitted with a ballonet and a 22 h.p. gasolene engine driving one screw. During the trials, which took place in the summer of 1905 over the Mediterranean Sea, a deviation of 45–50° was obtained. The experiments were then discontinued and an elongated airship was ordered from the Mallet Works. (See Zodiac.)

De Marçay & Kluytemans, Paris.—Builders of a pressure airship of the keel-girder type. Propeller mounted amidships, halving the hull.

Works No.	Name Trials	Length (m)	Beam (m)	Volume (mc)	Power (h.p.)	Speed (km)	Notes
1	De Marçay (1908)	30.5	3.8	340	6		Experimental airship.—The trials were apparently unsuccessful, as nothing has since been heard about this airship.

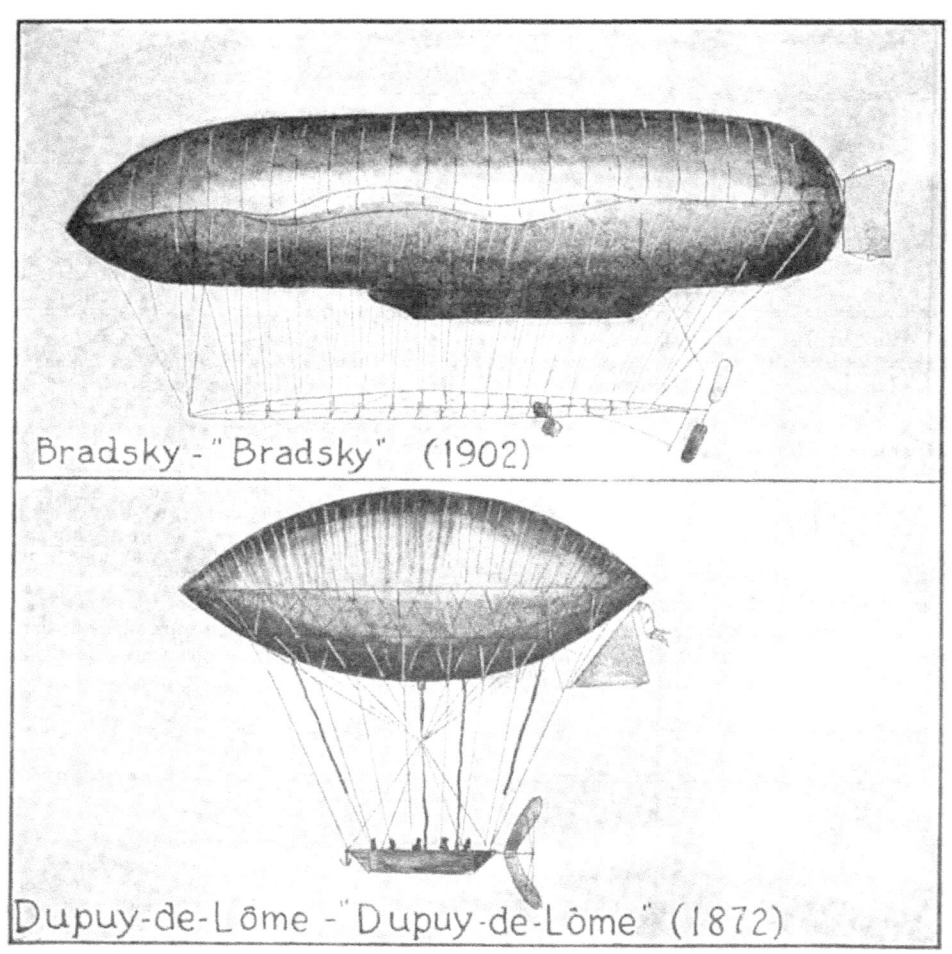

FRANCE—Continued

Dupuy-de-Lôme, Paris.—Builder of a pressure airship of the car-girder type; first airship to be fitted with a ballonet and a non-deformable suspension. Net suspension. Trim controlled by ballast.

Works No.	Name Trials	Length (m)	Beam (m)	Volume (mc)	Power (h.p.)	Speed (km)	Notes
1	Dupuy-de-Lôme (February, 1872)	36.1	14.8	3,450	8 men	8	French government airship, built during the Franco-Prussian war to relieve the besieged garrison of Paris. Completed only after the war. One ballonet: 345 mc. One pusher-screw, actuated by eight men. Made only one ascent, during which the airship was unable to make any headway against a moderate wind, although a deviation of 12° was obtained.

Eubriot, Paris.—Builder of an elongated pressure airship which was tested in October, 1839, in Paris, without giving any results.

François & Contour, Paris.—Builders of a pressure airship of the car-girder type. Carton-Lachambre hull. Trim controlled by lifting planes.

Works No.	Name Trials	Length (m)	Beam (m)	Volume (mc)	Power (h.p.)	Speed (km)	Notes
1	Ville-de-Saint-Mandé (1907)	32.5	10.5	1,850	40	25	Exhibition airship.—One Buchet engine; one tractor-screw. Participated in 1907 at the Saint-Louis (Mo., U. S. A.) airship race.

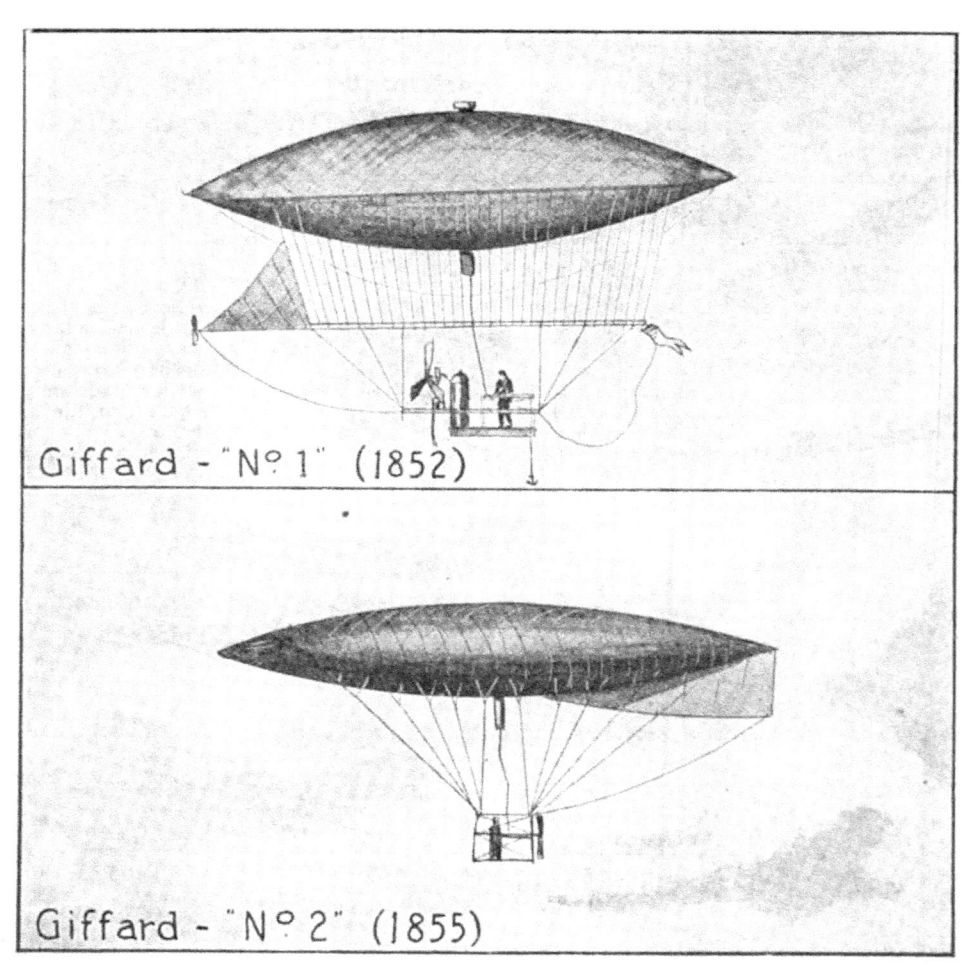

FRANCE—Continued

Giffard (Henri), Paris.—Builder of the first mechanically propelled airships. Keel-girder, pressure type; no ballonet. Steam engines with coke-firing used. Net suspension. Trim controlled by ballast.

Works No.	Name Trials	Length (m)	Beam (m)	Volume (mc)	Power (h.p.)	Speed (km)	Notes
1	Giffard (September 24, 1852)	44	12	2,500	3	12	Experimental airship.—One pusher-screw. At the trials the airship's speed did not prove sufficient to fight the wind although partial control was obtained.
2	Giffard-II. (1855)	72	10	3,200	5	12	Experimental airship.—One pusher-screw. Poor horizontal stability. Made only one ascent; on landing the suspension net slipped off the envelope and the latter burst. None was injured.

Godard (Louis), Paris.—Builder of pressure airships of the keel-girder type. Trim controlled by lifting planes.

Works No.	Name Trials	Length (m)	Beam (m)	Volume (mc)	Power (h.p.)	Speed (km)	Notes
1	America	50.3	16	6,350	60	30	Polar airship of the Wellman Expedition.—One 60 h. p. Clément engine; twin-screws. Designed endurance: 120 hrs.; provisioned for 75 days. Crew of five.
1a	(September, 1907)	56.4	16	7,800	80	30	Re-built and re-engined with one Lorraine-Dietrich engine by the Mallet Works, to the designs of Mr. Vaniman, prior to trials. Provisioned for ten months. Made an ascent of 2 hrs. at Virgo-Bay (Spitzbergen); ran into a snow storm and was damaged on landing.

THE *AMERICA* (1906–08).

FRANCE—Continued

Works No.	Name Trials	Length (m)	Beam (m)	Volume (mc)	Power (h.p.)	Speed (km)	Notes
1b	(August 15th, 1908)	70	16	9,200	160	40	Re-built and fitted with an additional engine (E.N.V.) driving a second pair of twin-screws. Made a trip of 200 km. over the Polar Sea on her first ascent; lost the equilibrator and fell into the sea, but was salvaged and shipped to Atlantic City, N. J., where she was re-fitted for a transatlantic trip, under the direction of Mr. Vaniman, and equipped with a lifeboat and wireless. Left Atlantic City on Oct. 15th, 1910, headed for Europe, with a crew of five. Engine and equilibrator troubles forced the crew to abandon the *America* after a voyage of 70 hrs., when the steamer *Trent* came to their assistance and took them off. Only the lifeboat of the *America* was salvaged.
2	La Belgique						Belgian excursion airship.—Built to M. Godard's designs by the Vivinus Works of Brussels. (See Belgium.)

Lebaudy Frères, Moisson près Mantes (Seine-et-Oise).—Builders of pressure airships of the keel-girder type to the designs of M. Henri Juillot. Keel-girder of steel-tubing, forming a rigid understructure. Trim controlled by lifting planes.

Works No.	Name Trials	Length (m)	Beam (m)	Volume (mc)	Power (h.p.)	Speed (km)	Notes
1	Lebaudy (November, 1902)	56.5	9.8	2,284	40	35	Experimental airship.—Astra hull. One Mercédès engine; twin-screws. Ballonet: 300 mc. Was the first successful modern airship. Best en-

TOP—THE *LEBAUDY* (1902–08) AND THE *PATRIE* (1906); *BOTTOM*—THE *LIBERTÉ* (1909) AND THE *CAPITAINE-MARCHAL* (1911).

FRANCE—Continued

Works No.	Name Trials	Length (m)	Beam (m)	Volume (mc)	Power (h.p.)	Speed (km)	Notes
1a	Lebaudy II. (August, 1904)	56.5	9.8	2,660	40	35	durance: 98 km. in 2¾ hrs. Refitted with a new hull, the airship made 12 ascents but was carried away by the storm on Aug. 28, 1904, and badly damaged. Was repaired and eventually rebuilt. Ballonet: 500 mc. Resumed her ascents, but was again laid up for repairs of her hull, which had been torn by the storm when landing at the Camp de Châlons. Reached on Nov. 10th, 1905, twice in succession an altitude of 1,370 m. Her builders sold the airship to the French Army for the nominal sum of Frs. 80,000 ($16,000) in December, 1905.
1b	Lebaudy III. (July, 1905)	56.5	10	2,950	50	35	
1c	Lebaudy IV. (October, 1908)	61	10.3	3,300	70	40	French Army airship, as rebuilt by the Army Airship Works.—Ballonet: 650 mc. One Panhard-Levassor engine; twin-screws. Best altitude, 1,550 m. (in 1908). Was moored in the open for 17 days in the autumn of 1909. Dismantled in 1912.
2	Patrie (November, 1906)	61	10.3	3,250	60	45	French Army airship.—Ballonet: 650 mc. One Panhard-Levassor engine; twin-screws. Best endurance: 240 km. in 6¼ hrs., after reconstruction. Was carried away by the storm on Nov. 30th, 1907; foundered in the Atlantic.
2a	(November, 1907)	61	10.9	3,650	60	45	
3	République (June, 1908)	61	10.9	3,700	70	50	French Army airship.—Ballonet: 730 mc. One Panhard-Levassor engine; twin-screws. Best endurance

TOP—THE CAR OF THE *LEBAUDY;* *BOTTOM*—THE CAR OF THE *CAPITAINE-MARCHAL.*

FRANCE—Continued

Works No.	Name Trials	Length (m)	Beam (m)	Volume (mc)	Power (h.p.)	Speed (km)	Notes
							(in closed circuit): 210 km. in 7¼ hrs. Was destroyed in mid-air on Aug. 25th, 1909, through the breaking of one screw which burst the hull. The crew of four were killed.
4	Lebedj (ex-Russie) (May, 1909)	61.2	10.9	3,800	70	49	Russian Army airship.—One Panhard-Levassor engine; twin-screws. Ballonet: 900 mc.
5	Liberté (August, 1909)	65	12.5	4,200	120	45	French Army airship, as originally laid down. Was modified, on account of the disaster of the *République*, before being commissioned.
5a	(June, 1910)	84	12.8	7,000	120	53	Two Panhard-Levassor engines; twin-screws. Designed endurance: 8 hrs. Dismantled in 1914.
6	M. II.						Austrian Army airship. Built to Messrs. Lebaudy's designs by the Motor-Luftfahrzeug Gesellschaft of Vienna. (See Austria.)
7	Morning-Post (September, 1910)	103	12	9,800	270	55	British Army airship, purchased by a national subscription started by the London daily *Morning Post*. Ballonet: 2,500 mc. Two Panhard-Levassor engines; twin-screws. On Oct. 26th, 1910, the airship flew from Moisson to Aldershot (370 km. in 5½ hrs.), but was damaged on being berthed. Re-commissioned a few months afterwards, the airship was wrecked through faulty manœuvring on May 4th, 1911, by stranding in some trees.
8	Kretchet						Russian Army airship, built to Messrs. Lebaudy's designs by the Russian Army Airship Works. (See Russia.)

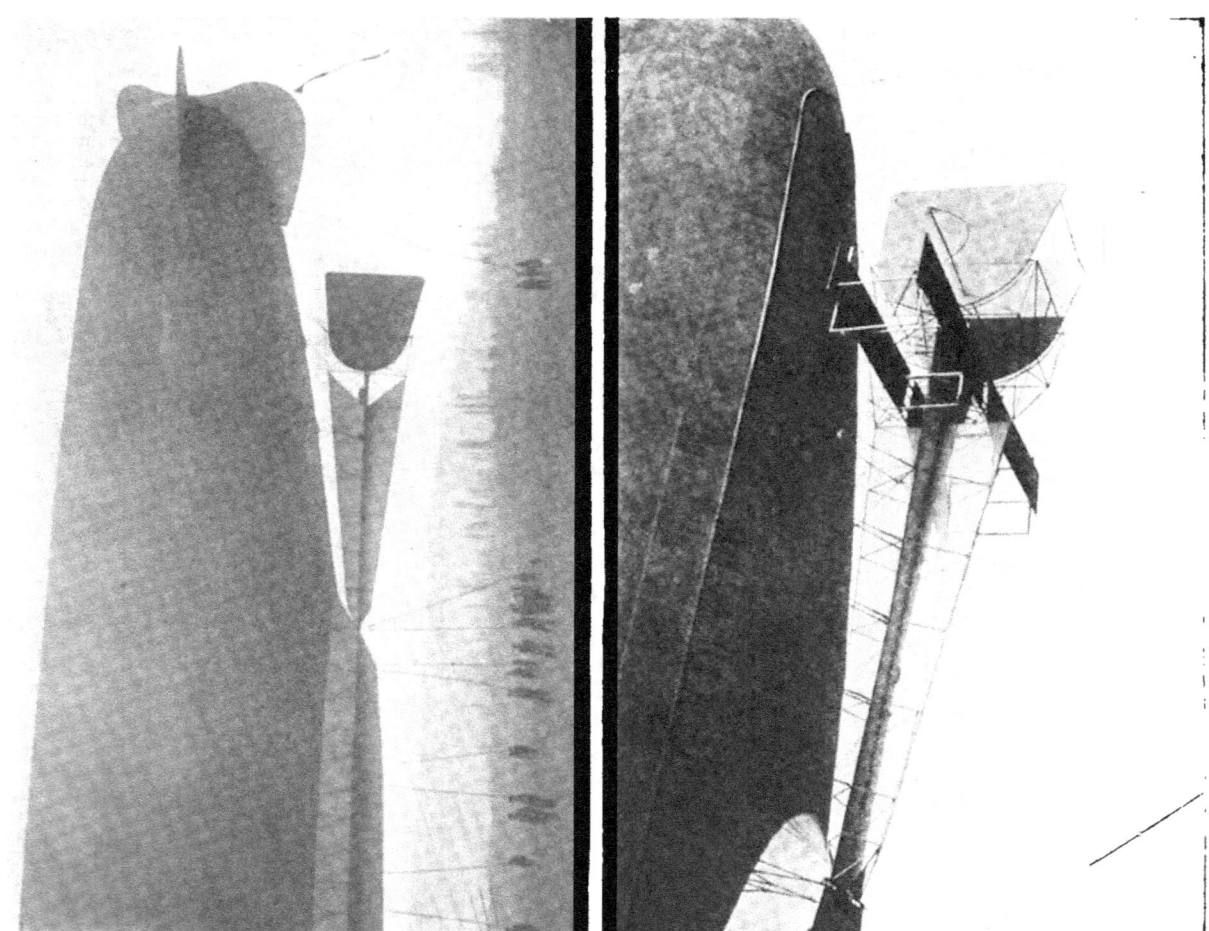

STERN VIEW OF THE *LIBERTÉ* AND OF THE *CAPITAINE-MARCHAL*.

FRANCE—Continued

Works No.	Name Trials	Length (m)	Beam (m)	Volume (mc)	Power (h.p.)	Speed (km)	Notes
9	Capitaine-Marchal (March, 1911)	85	12.8	7,200	160	50	French Army airship.—Two Panhard-Levassor engines; twin-screws. Named after the commander of the ill-fated *République*; presented to the Army by her builders. Designed endurance: 10 hrs. Dismantled in 1914.
10	Lieut. Selle-de-Beauchamp (October, 1911)	89	14.6	10,000	200	55	French Army airship. Two Panhard-Levassor engines; twin-screws. Named after a balloon observation officer of the First French Republic. Designed endurance: 12 hrs. Best altitude: 1,685 m.
11	Tissandier (December, 1914)	140	15.5	28,000	1,350	80	French Army airship. Nine Salmson engines mounted in groups of three on three cars; three sets of triple-screws. Fitted with four machine guns and wireless carrying 600 km. Designed endurance: 15 hrs. at 2,500 m. at full speed.
12	(Building)						French Army airship.—*Tissandier*-class.

Le Berrier, Paris.—Builder of a pressure airship fitted with a ballonet which was the earliest forerunner of the modern airship. Propulsion by means of twenty oar-propellers worked by the crew. Enterprise financed by the Comte de Lennox.

Works No.	Name Trials	Length (m)	Beam (m)	Volume (mc)	Power (h.p.)	Speed (km)	Notes
1	L'Aigle (August 17, 1834)	42.2	11.4	2,800	?	?	On her trial the airship proved too heavy to lift her own weight and was destroyed by the infuriated spectators.

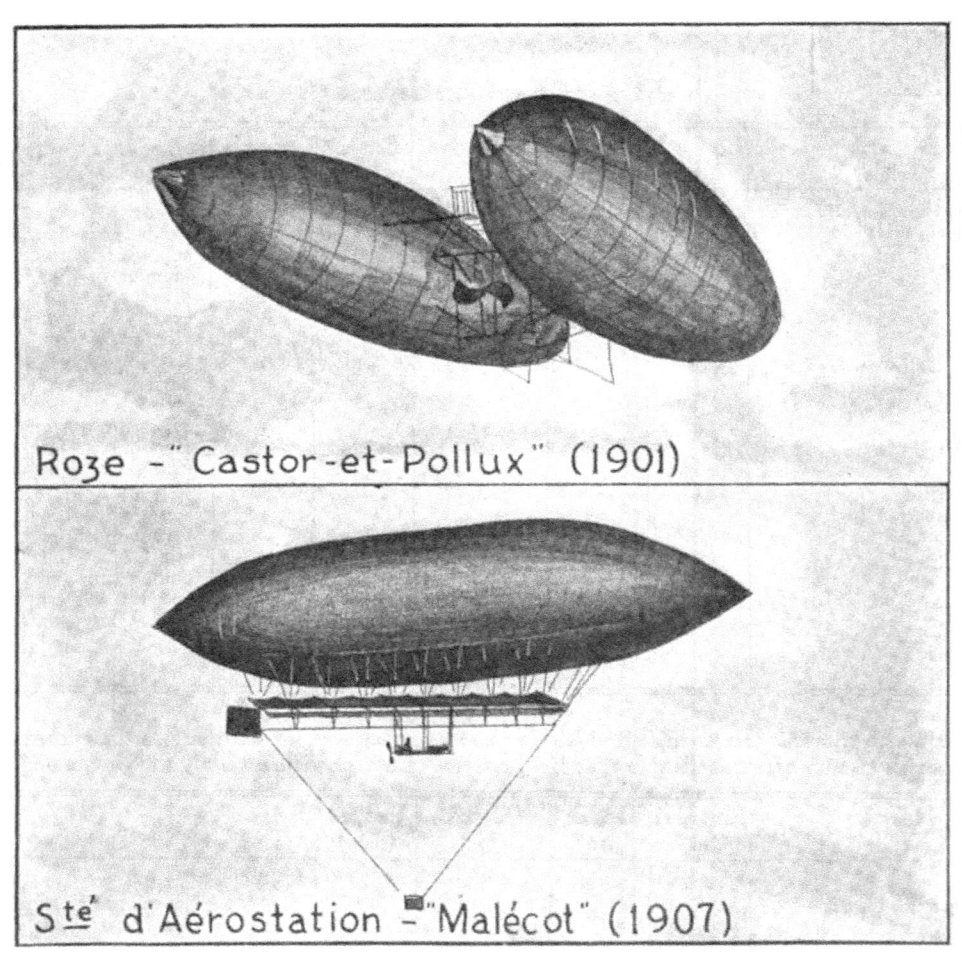

FRANCE—Continued

Le Compagnon (Armand), Paris.—Builder of a pressure airship of the keel-girder type. Propulsion through flapping wings.

Works No.	Name Trials	Length (m)	Beam (m)	Volume (mc)	Power (h.p.)	Speed (km)	Notes
1	Le Compagnon (1892)	20.4	3.5	156			Experimental airship.—No conclusive results were obtained.

Robert & Pillet, Paris.—Builders of a pressure airship of the keel-girder type. Trim controlled by lifting screws. Carton-Lachambre hull.

Works No.	Name Trials	Length (m)	Beam (m)	Volume (mc)	Power (h.p.)	Speed (km)	Notes
1	Robert-Pillet (1904)	38	9.5	2,100	35	?	Experimental airship.—One Aster engine; swivelling twin-screws and one pusher-screw. The trials were not satisfactory and the airship was eventually broken up.

Roze (Louis), Paris.—Builder of a structure airship characterized by twin-hulls rigidly connected side-by-side. Aluminum frame. Trim controlled by lifting screws. Fabric skin.

Works No.	Name Trials	Length (m)	Beam (m)	Volume (mc)	Power (h.p.)	Speed (km)	Notes
1	Castor-et-Pollux (September, 1901)	45	7.5	2,800	20	?	Experimental airship.—One Buchet engine; two co-axial screws for horizontal propulsion and two lifting screws. The trials remained inconclusive, being stopped for lack of funds after the second ascent, when the airship reached an altitude of 15 m.

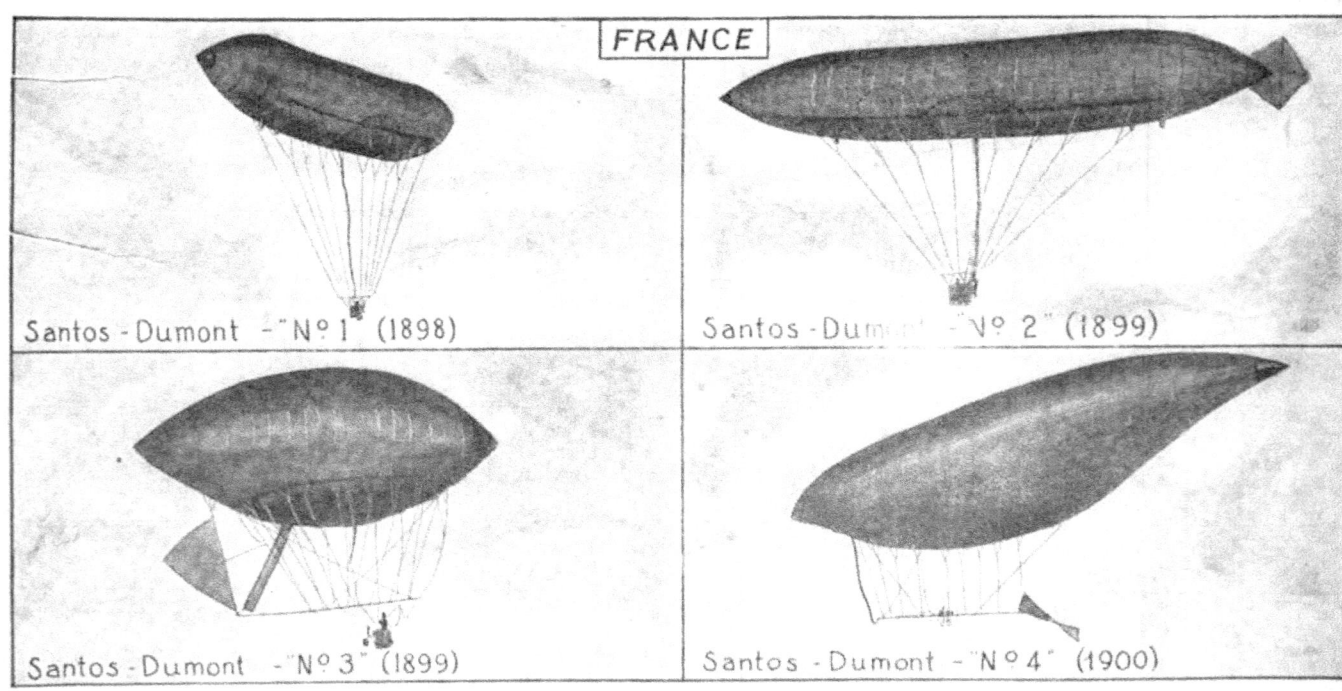

FRANCE—Continued

Santos-Dumont (Alberto), Paris.—Builder of small pressure airships for sporting purposes. Carton-Lachambre hulls. Trim controlled by ballast.

Works No.	Name Trials	Length (m)	Beam (m)	Volume (mc)	Power (h.p.)	Speed (km)	Notes
1	No. 1 (September, 1898)	25	3.5	180	3	?	No ballonet. One Dion-Bouton engine; one pusher-screw.—Was wrecked at her second ascent through a loss of shape of the hull. The pilot remained unhurt.
2	No. 2 (May, 1899)	25	3.8	200	3	?	No ballonet. Same power-plant as *No. 1*.—The only ascent caused the wrecking of the airship owing to a deformation of the hull. The pilot remained unhurt.
3	No. 3 (November, 1899)	20	7.5	500	5	20	No ballonet. Inflated with coal-gas. Made several short ascents, but was not very successful for want of longitudinal stability. One Buchet engine, one pusher-screw.
4	No. 4 (1900)	29	5.1	420	7	?	No ballonet. One Buchet engine; one pusher-screw. Trials were not successful.
5	No. 5 (July, 1901)	34	5	550	12	20	No ballonet. One Buchet engine; one pusher-screw. Made a few successful ascents; one of 33 km. over Paris during which a landing was made for repairs. Wrecked on August 8th, 1901, by stranding on the Trocadéro. Pilot unhurt.
6	No. 6 (1901)	33	6	620	16	29	Santos-Dumont's most successful airship. Ballonet: 60 mc. One Buchet engine; one pusher-screw. Won on Oct. 19th, 1901, the Deutsch de la Meurthe prize of 100,000 francs for a circuit from St. Cloud to the Eiffel tower in less than ½ hour. Wrecked on Feb'y 14th, 1902, off Monaco, by falling into the sea. The pilot remained unhurt.

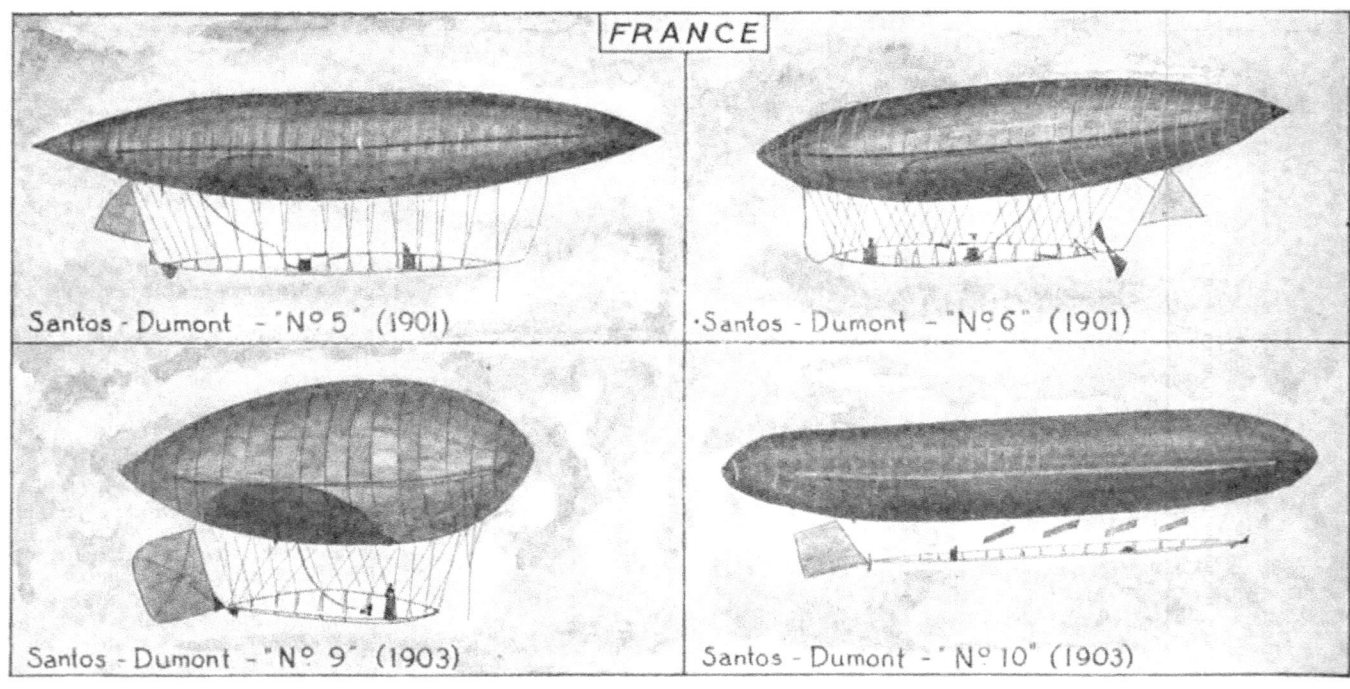

FRANCE—Continued

Works No.	Name Trials	Length (m)	Beam (m)	Volume (mc)	Power (h.p.)	Speed (km)	Notes
7	No. 7 (1901)	50	8	1,260	60	?	Built for the St. Louis airship race. One C.G.V. engine; one pusher-screw. Was accidentally put out of commission.
8	No. 8 (1902)	15.1	5	216	5	?	One Clément engine; one pusher screw. Made only one ascent, after which she was dismantled, having proved little satisfactory.
9	No. 9 (1903)	15.1	5.5	260	5	18	Same power plant as *No. 8*. Made numerous successful ascents over Paris; landed on June 23rd, 1903, on the Champs-Elysées. Named also "*La Balladeuse.*"
10	No. 10 (1903)	48	8.5	2,240	20	?	Passenger airship fitted with four cars; named also "*L'Omnibus.*" Failed to leave the ground.
11	No. 11 (1903)	34		1,200	16	?	Was not completed. One Buchet engine; one pusher-screw.
12	No. 12 (1903)						Was not completed.
13	No. 13 (December, 1904)	19	14.5	1,900			Built for experiments of statical climbing. Was not fitted with a power-plant.
14	No. 14 (August, 1905)	41	3.4	186	14	?	One Buchet engine; one pusher screw. Made but one ascent at Trouville; not successful.
15	No. 14-bis (1906)						Was not fitted with a power-plant, served as a buoy for aeroplane experiments.
16	No. 16 (June, 1907)	21	3	100	50	?	One Antoinette engine; one pusher screw. Stranded on a tree while landing after her first ascent.

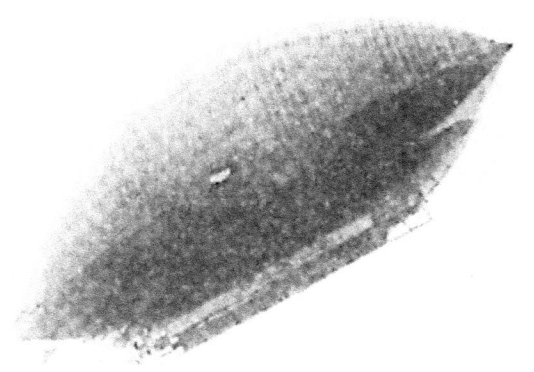

THE *PAX* (1902).

FRANCE—Continued

Severo (Maranhao), Paris.—Builder of keel-girder type pressure airships. Carton-Lachambre hulls. Trim controlled by lifting screws.

Works No.	Name Trials	Length (m)	Beam (m)	Volume (mc)	Power (h.p.)	Speed (km)	Notes
1	Bartholomeo-de-Gusmao (1894)	60	15				Built in Brazil. Was wrecked at the trials.
2	Pax (May 12th, 1902)	30	12.4	2,330	40	?	Built in Paris. Two Buchet engines, one of 24 h. p. driving one pusher-screw and one of 16 h. p. driving one tractor-screw, both mounted in the axis of the hull, on a bamboo frame. Two lifting screws. On her trials the *Pax* caught fire and exploded when 400 m. over Paris, killing Senhor Severo and his mechanician, M. Saché.

Société d'Aérostation, Paris.—Builders of a pressure airship of the keel-girder type to the designs of M. Malécot. Carton-Lachambre hull. Trim controlled by lifting planes.

Works No.	Name Trials	Length (m)	Beam (m)	Volume (mc)	Power (h.p.)	Speed (km)	Notes
1	Malécot (September, 1907)	34	7.4	1,050	30	32	Experimental airship.—One Buchet engine; one pusher-screw. Best endurance: 3 hrs. Was sold in 1908 to M. Jacques Faure, who rebuilt the airship in view of an oversea voyage from Monaco to Corsica.
1a	Faure (March, 1909)	33	7.5	1,035	30	30	On her trials at Monaco the airship proved unstable and was wrecked by the wind while attempting to land.

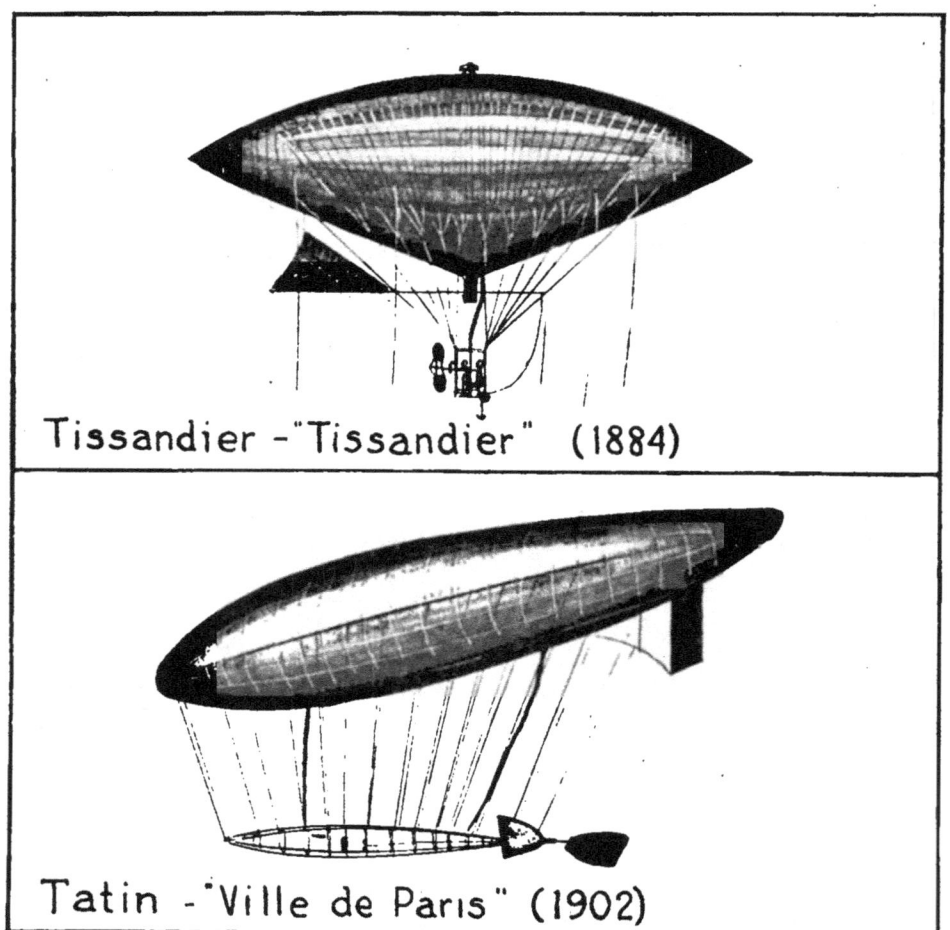

FRANCE—Continued

Tatin (Victor), Paris.—Builder of a pressure airship of the car-girder type. Trim controlled by ballast. Mallet hull.

Works No.	Name Trials	Length (m)	Beam (m)	Volume (mc)	Power (h.p.)	Speed (km)	Notes
1	Ville-de-Paris (1902)	58	8.2	2,000	60		Experimental airship, built for M. Henri Deutsch de la Meurthe. Ballonet: 200 mc. One Mors engine; one tractor screw. No free ascent was ever made, as the airship displayed considerable instability on her moorings.

Tissandier (Albert & Gaston), Paris.—Builders of a pressure airship of the keel-girder type. Trim controlled by ballast.

Works No.	Name Trials	Length (m)	Beam (m)	Volume (mc)	Power (h.p.)	Speed (km)	Notes
1	Tissandier (September, 1883)	28	9.2	1,060	2	15	Experimental airship.—No ballonet. One Siemens electric battery-motor; one pusher-screw. Several ascents were made with this airship, although only partial control was obtained. Best endurance: 25 km. in 2 hrs.

"Zodiac" (Anciens Etablissements Maurice Mallet), Puteaux (Seine).—Builders of pressure airships of the car-girder type to the designs of M. Maurice Mallet and of structure airships to the designs of M. Emile Spiess. Features of the Spiess type: hull-frame of hollow wood girders, cross-braced by wire stays and sub-divided into compartments for independent gas-cells. No ballonet. Fabric skin, re-inforced by a netting covering the entire hull-frame. Trim controlled by lifting planes (on both types of airships) and trimming tanks (on the Spiess type).

Works No.	Name Trials	Length (m)	Beam (m)	Volume (mc)	Power (h.p.)	Speed (km)	Notes
1	De la Vaulx (June, 1906)	32.5	6.4	730	14	25	Experimental airship of the keel-girder type, built to the designs of Count Henri de la Vaulx. One

TOP—THE *DUINDIGT* (1911) AND *LE TEMPS* (1911); BOTTOM—THE *CAPITAINE-FERBER* (1911) AND THE *COMMANDANT-COUTELLE* (1913).

FRANCE—Continued

Works No.	Name Trials	Length (m)	Beam (m)	Volume (mc)	Power (h.p.)	Speed (km)	Notes
							Ader engine; one tractor-screw, mounted on the keel-girder. Made numerous short ascents; was re-built to M. Mallet's designs in 1909 and re-named *Petit-Journal II*. (See below.)
2	Petit-Journal (April, 1909)	30	7	700	16	26	Publicity airship of the Parisian daily *Petit-Journal*.—One Clerget engine; one pusher-screw. Made numerous trips over Paris.
3	Petit-Journal II (1909)	32.3	7.2	900	45	30	Publicity airship of the *Petit-Journal*. One Ader engine; one pusher-screw.
4	Zodiac (October, 1909)	40.8	8.5	1,410	45	45	French Army airship.—Ballonet: 350 mc. One Ballot engine; one pusher-screw. Designed endurance: 4 hrs. Dismantled in 1914.
5	Davis (1910)	40.8	8.5	1,400	30	35	Excursion airship of Mr. Davis of New York. One Mercédès engine; one pusher-screw.
6	Zodiac (1910)	40.8	8.5	1,400	30	35	Belgian Army airship.—One Mercédès engine; one pusher-screw.
6a	(1913)	42.5	8.5	1,700	50	40	Was re-built by the Belgian Génie. One Ballot engine; one pusher-screw. Served at the outbreak of the Great War as a training airship.
7	Duindigt (May, 1911)	34.9	6.8	915	30	43	Dutch Army airship.—One Daimler engine; one pusher-screw. Ballonet: 125 mc. Presented to the Netherlands government by Mynheer Jochems. Was, however, little used as a training airship.

TOP—THE *SPIESS* (1913) AND ITS UNDERSTRUCTURE; *BOTTOM*—ONE OF THE ENGINES AND PROPELLERS OF THE *SPIESS*.

FRANCE—Continued

Works No.	Name / Trials	Length (m)	Beam (m)	Volume (mc)	Power (h.p.)	Speed (km)	Notes
8	Tchaïka (November, 1910)	48	10	2,140	60	40	Russian Army airships.—Ballonet: 550 mc. One Labor engine (*Korchoune*: one Dansette-Gillet engine); one pusher-screw. Best endurance: 4 hrs.
9	Korchoune (December, 1910)						
10	Le-Temps (March, 1911)	50.3	9	2,300	110	50	French Army airship.—Ballonets: 514 mc. One Dansette-Gillet engine; twin-screws. Best endurance: 5 hrs. Was presented to the government through a public subscription organized by the Paris daily, *Le Temps*. Trips in 1912 aggregated 700 km. and 23 hrs. 26 min.
11	Capitaine-Ferber (December, 1911)	76	12.4	6,000	220	56	French Army airship.—Two Dansette-Gillet engines; two pairs of twin-screws. Ballonets: 1,500 mc. Designed endurance: 15 hrs. Best endurance: 280 km. in 6 hrs. at 1,400 m. altitude. Trips in 1912 aggregated 5,900 km. and 152 hrs.
12	Commandant-Coutelle (May, 1913)	92	14	9,500	400	62	French Army airship.—Ballonets: 2,600. Two Dansette-Gillet engines; two pairs of twin-screws. Designed endurance: 24 hrs.; altitude: 2,000 m.
13	Spiess (April, 1913)	113	13.5	12,800	200	50	French Army airship.—Presented to the government by M. Spiess. Structure type. One Chenu engine in the bow-car; twin-screws. 14 compartments. After a short series of trials the airship was enlarged to contain 17 gas-cells and a second Chenu engine, mounted on the stern-car and driving twin-screws, was fitted. The trials were fairly satisfactory.
13a	(December, 1913)	140	13.5	16,400	400	70	

THE *SUCHARD* (1911–13).

FRANCE—Continued

Works No.	Name Trials	Length (m)	Beam (m)	Volume (mc)	Power (h.p.)	Speed (km)	Notes
14 15	} (Laid down 1913) {	130	15	23,000	1,000	80	French Army airships.—Car-girder, pressure type. Four Chenu engines; two pairs of twin-screws. Designed endurance: 15 hrs. at 2,500 m. altitude and full speed, 30 hrs. at ¾ speed. Wireless carrying 600 km. Four machine guns on the cars, one on the roof; flexible shaft leading to the platform on the roof.
16	(Laid down 1913)	130	15	23,000	1,000	80	Russian Army airship.—*Zodiac-14* type. Since the outbreak of t' Great War a certain number o -hips have been laid down r :ding which no information is ; sently available.

GERMANY

Baumgartner, Berlin.—Builder of a pressure airship, in association with Herr Woelfert. Trim controlled by ballast.

Works No.	Name Trials	Length (m)	Beam (m)	Volume (mc)	Power (h.p.)	Speed (km)	Notes
1	Baumgartner (March, 1882)	17.5	8				Experimental airship.—One pusher-screw, operated by hand. No appreciable results were obtained. Herr Baumgartner having given up the venture, Herr Woelfert continued the experiments alone (see *ibidem*).

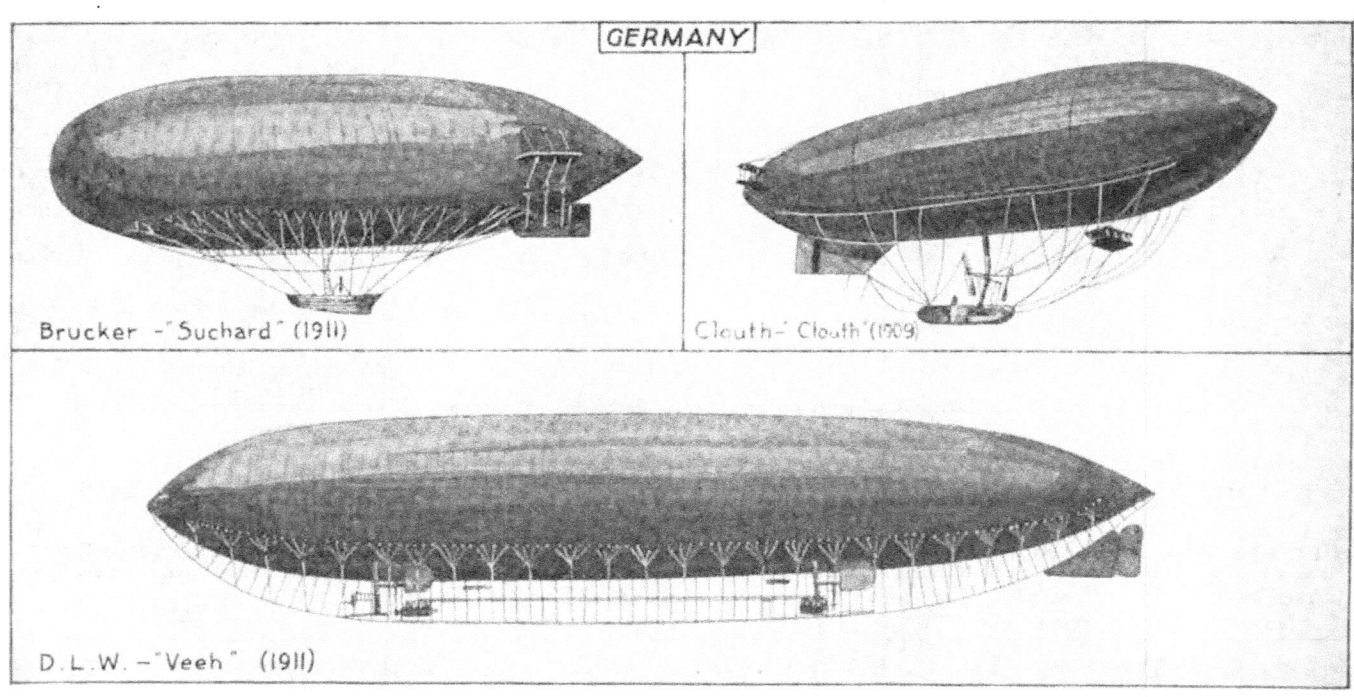

GERMANY—Continued

Brucker Transatlantic Flight Expedition, Berlin.—Builders of a girderless pressure airship. Riedinger hull; nacelle, built like a motor boat, by Lürssen. Trim controlled by lifting planes and a movable weight.

Works No.	Name Trials	Length (m)	Beam (m)	Volume (mc)	Power (h.p.)	Speed (km)	Notes
1	Suchard (1911)	60.5	17.2	9,730	220	44	Built for a transatlantic trip from the Canaries to the Lesser Antilles with the help of the trade-winds. Two N. A. G. engines; twin screws. Designed endurance 150 h. with a crew of six. One 6 h.p. N. S. U. auxiliary engine, actuating the ballonet blower, the dynamo for wireless telegraphy and the water-ballast winch. Ballonet: 3,600 mc. Was rebuilt after various trials and eventually the transatlantic trip was abandoned.
1a	(1913)	76	17.2	12,000	220	44	

Clouth (Luftschiffbau), Cologne-Nippes.—Builders of pressure airships of the keel-girder type. Girder consisting of articulated wooden struts; inserted in the bottom of the hull. Trim controlled by lifting planes.

Works No.	Name Trials	Length (m)	Beam (m)	Volume (mc)	Power (h.p.)	Speed (km)	Notes
1	Clouth (August, 1909)	42	8.3	1,720	40	35	Excursion airship.—Ballonet: 344 mc. One Buchet engine; twin-screws. After a few trial trips the airship was rebuilt and re-engined. One Adler engine; twin-screws. Best endurance: 150 km. in 4½ hrs. (Cologne to Brussels, June, 1910). Was dismantled in 1912, when the Clouth-Luftschiffbau merged with the Luft-Fahrzeug Gesellschaft of Berlin.
1a	(1910)	42	8.5	1,850	50	38	

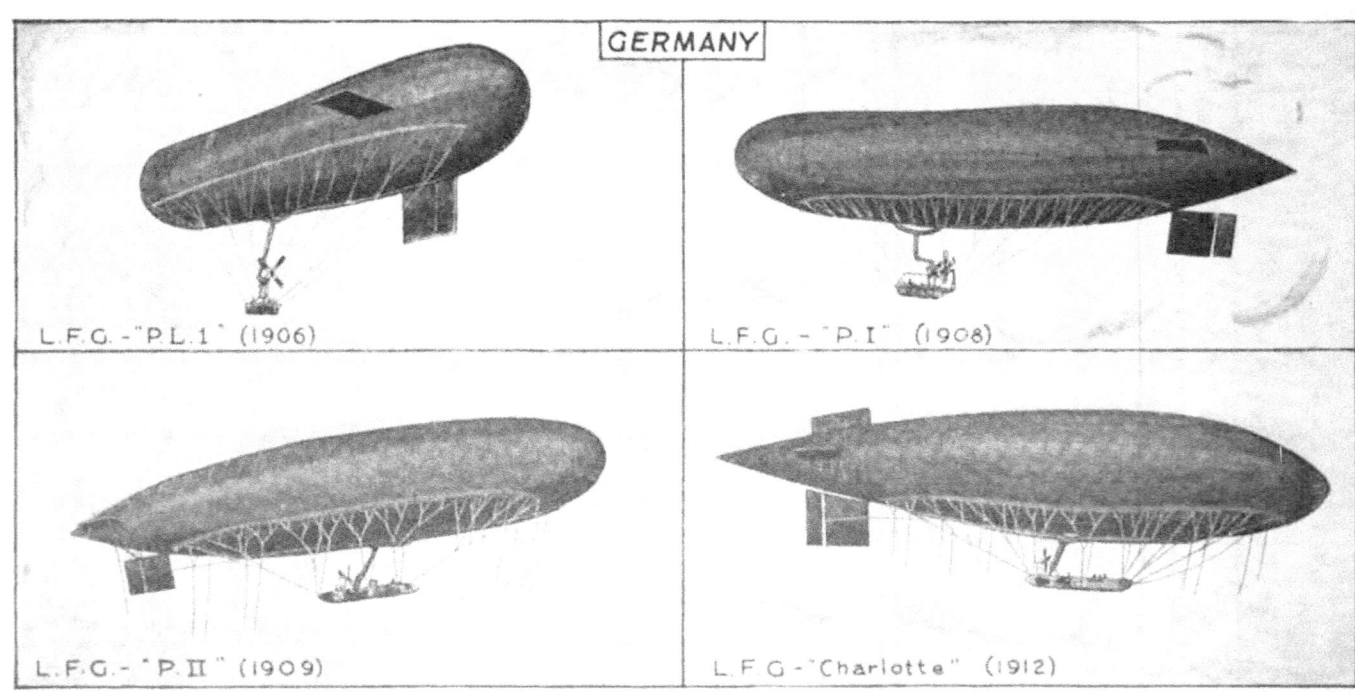

GERMANY—Continued

Deutsche Luftschiff-Werft, Munich (Bavaria).—Builders, to the designs of Herr Veeh, of a pressure airship of the keel-girder type. Keel of steel tubing, built into the hull and containing the navigation and engine rooms. Trim controlled by lifting planes and trimming tanks. The company was dissolved in 1914.

Works No.	Name Trials	Length (m)	Beam (m)	Volume (mc)	Power (h.p.)	Speed (km)	Notes
1	Veeh-I (1911)	70	12.4	6,780	360	60	Experimental airship.—Ballonet: 1,700 mc. Two Schneeweis engines; two pairs of twin-screws. Was tested with one-half the power plant, but did not prove satisfactory and was re-engined and enlarged in 1912.
1a	(July, 1913)	84.5	12.4	9,100	260	68	Two Mercédès engines; two pairs of twin-screws. Designed endurance: 20 hrs. Made numerous trial trips of short duration, but was broken up for lack of funds and sold at auction in 1914.

Dorhöfer, Cologne.—Builder of a pressure airship of the car-girder type. Trim controlled by lifting planes.

Works No	Name Trials	Length (m)	Beam (m)	Volume (mc)	Power (h.p.)	Speed (km)	Notes
1	Dorhöfer (1910)	28	7	1,000	60	.	Experimental airship.—One Mercédès engine; one tractor-screw. Failed on her trials.

Luft-Fahrzeug-Gesellschaft ("L. F. G."), Berlin.—Builders of girderless pressure airships to the patents of Major Von Parseval. Automatically shifting cars with self-blocking device for altering trim, combined with two compensating ballonets. Works at Bitterfeld (Saxony).

Works No.	Name Trials	Length (m)	Beam (m)	Volume (mc)	Power (h.p.)	Speed (km)	Notes
P. L. 1	P. L. 1 (May, 1906)	48.5	8.6	2,300	35	36	Experimental airship.—One Mercédès engine; twin-screws. Was re-built and re-fitted with one Mer-

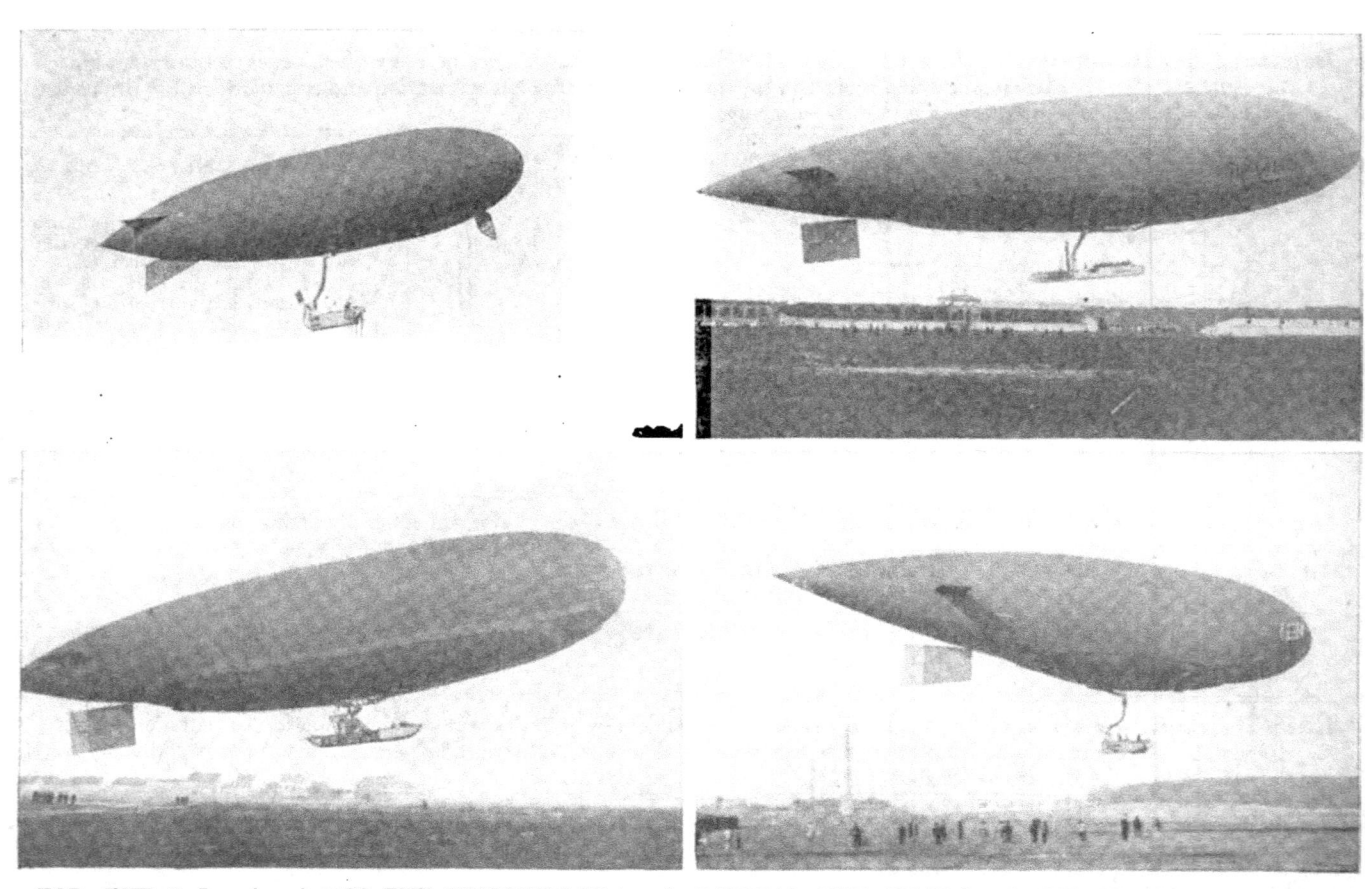

TOP—THE *P. L. 5* (1909) AND THE *STOLLWERCK* (1910); *BOTTOM*—THE *GRIFF* (1910) AND THE *P. L. 9* (1910-13).

GERMANY—Continued

Works No.	Name Trials	Length (m)	Beam (m)	Volume (mc)	Power (h.p.)	Speed (km)	Notes
1a	(1909)	60	9.4	3,200	85	40	cédès engine driving one pusher-screw. Ballonet: 600 mc. Purchased by the Imperial Aero Club of Berlin to serve for excursions. Dismantled 1911.
P. L. 2	P. I (August, 1908)	60	10.4	4,100	85	47	Prussian Army airship.—One Mercédès engine; twin-screws. Best endurance: 290 km. in 11½ hrs. Destroyed by the storm while landing near Grünewald, on Sept. 16th, 1908.
P. L. 3	P. II (February, 1909)	70	12.3	6,600	200	51	Prussian Army airship.—Two N. A. G. engines; twin-screws. Designed endurance: 14 hrs. Made numerous ascents at the Aeronautical Exhibition of Frankfort (1910). Destroyed by the storm on May 16th, 1911.
P. L. 4	M. I.						Austrian Army airship, built to L. F. G. designs by the Motor-Luftfahrzeug Gesellschaft of Vienna (See Austria).
P. L. 5	P. L. 5 (December, 1909)	40	8	1,450	25	36	Excursion airship of the L. V. G.—One Mercédès engine; one pusher-screw. Designed endurance: 5 hrs. Was destroyed by a fire on June 16th, 1911, at Münden.
P. L. 6	Stollwerck (June, 1910)	70	14	6,800	220	56	Excursion and advertisement airship of the L. V. G.—Two N. A. G. engines; twin-screws. Was rebuilt and refitted with a new envelope. Ballonet: 2,400 mc. Made 250 trips, covering 15,000 km. and carrying 2,300 passengers.
6a	(October, 1912)	75	15	8,000	220	59	

TOP—THE CAR OF THE *P. L. 5* AND OF THE *GRIFF*; *BOTTOM*—THE CAR OF THE *CITTÀ-DI-VENEZIA* AND A PARSEVAL AIRSHIP AS TRANSPORTED ON THE ROAD.

GERMANY—Continued

Works No.	Name Trials	Length (m)	Beam (m)	Volume (mc)	Power (h.p.)	Speed (km)	Notes
P. L. 7	Griff (October, 1910)	72	14	7,600	220	59	Russian Army airship.—Ballonet: 1,400 mc. Two N. A. G. engines; twin-screws. Best endurance: 7½ hrs.
P. L. 8	P. II. (February, 1913)	77	14	8,000	360	54	Prussian Army airship.—Two Maybach engines; twin-screws. Designed endurance: 20 hrs.
P. L. 9	P. L. 9 (October, 1910)	40	8	1,450	70	40	Excursion airship of the L. V. G.—Two Mercédès engines; twin-screws. Was refitted with one Körting engine when re-built to become a Turkish Army airship.
9a	(August, 1913)	50	10	2,200	50	42	
P. L. 10	P. L. 10 (1913)	45	8	1,700	50	45	Excursion airship.—One Körting engine; twin-screws. Was not completed until 1913, having remained four years on the yards.
P. L. 11	P. III. (December, 1911)	84	15.5	10,000	400	65	Prussian Army airship.—Ballonet: 3,000 mc. Two Körting engines; twin-screws. Best endurance: 16 hrs.
P. L. 12	Charlotte (May, 1912)	79	15.2	8,800	220	54	Excursion airship of the Rhenish-Westphalian Air Sport Co.—Two N. A. G. engines; twin-screws. Designed endurance: 20 hrs.; altitude: 2,800 m. Ballonet: 2,300 mc.
P. L. 13	Yuhi (April, 1912)	79	14.5	8,500	300	66	Japanese Army airship.—Two Maybach engines; twin-screws. Designed endurance: 20 hrs.; altitude: 2,000. Ballonet: 2,300 mc.
P. L. 14	(February, 1913)	86	15.5	9,600	360	67	Russian Army airship.—Two Maybach engines; twin-screws. Designed endurance: 20 hrs.; altitude: 2,500 m. Ballonet: 2,700 mc.
P. L. 15	(Building, 1914)	96	15.5	12,000	540	75	Italian Army airship.—Three Maybach engines; two pairs of twin-screws. Requisitioned by Germany

THE BRITISH NAVAL AIRSHIP *No. 2* (PARSEVAL).

GERMANY—Continued

Works No.	Name Trials	Length (m)	Beam (m)	Volume (mc)	Power (h.p.)	Speed (km)	Notes
P. L. 16	P. IV. (October, 1913)	86	15.5	10,000	360	71	at the outbreak of the war. (Photo wanted.) Prussian Army airship.—Ballonet: 3,000 mc. Two Maybach engines; twin-screws. *P.L.14* class.
P. L. 17	Città di-Venezia (September, 1912)	85	15.5	9,600	360	69	Italian Army airship.—Two Maybach engines; twin-screws. *P.L.14* type.
P. L. 18	No. 2 (April, 1913)	86	15.5	10,000	360	68	British naval airship.—Two Maybach engines; twin-screws. Designed endurance: 20 hrs.; altitude: 2,500 m.
P. L. 19 P. L. 20 P. L. 21							British naval airships, built to L. F. G. designs by Vickers, Sons & Maxim, Ltd. (See Great Britain.)
P. L. 22	P. V. (July, 1914)	96	15.5	12,000	540	75	Prussian Army airship.—*P.L.15* type. Three Maybach engines; two pairs of twin-screws. Was shot down by Russian motor-guns on Jan. 26th, 1915, while raiding Libava. The crew of seven were made prisoners. No definite information is available regarding the number of airships turned out during the war; it has been reported that the L. F. G. works of Bitterfeld have been turned into a repair station for Zeppelin airships and that the output of Parseval airships has consequently been greatly limited.

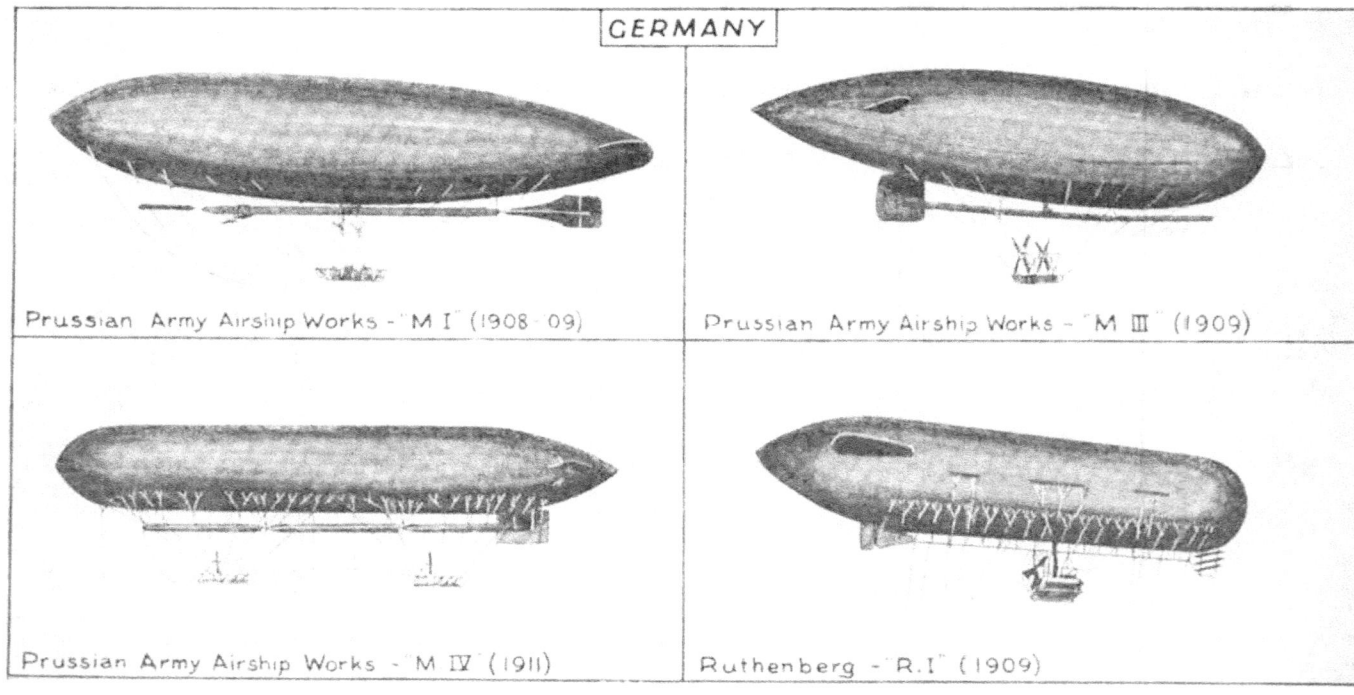

GERMANY—Continued

Luftschiff-Antriebs-Gesellschaft, Berlin.—Builders of airships fitted with a screwless propulsion system (Meyer's patents).

Works No.	Name Trials	Length (m)	Beam (m)	Volume (mc)	Power (h.p.)	Speed (km)	Notes
1	L. A. G. I (1912)	60	10.4	4,000	50		Experimental airship.—Hull of the condemned Prussian Army airship *P.I.* One Adler engine; orthopteric propellers. Trials were inconclusive.
2	L. A. G. II (Building, 1914)	98	15	18,000			Experimental airship built to the designs of Mr. Wischnewsky. (Data and photo wanted.)

Prussian Army Airship Works, Berlin-Tegel.—Builders of keel-girder pressure airships to the designs of Major Gross and Herr Basenach. Special feature: demountable metal keel hung from the hull. Trim controlled by compensating ballonets and trimming tanks, worked by compressed air.

Works No.	Name Trials	Length (m)	Beam (m)	Volume (mc)	Power (h.p.)	Speed (km)	Notes
1	M-a (July, 1907)	41	7	1,400	25	30	Experimental airship.—One Körting engine; twin-screws. Gave little satisfaction and was re-built. Best endurance: 200 km. in 8 hrs.
1a	(November, 1907)	42	9	1,800	30	32	
2	M. I (January, 1908)	71	12	5,000	150	42	Prussian Army airship.—Two Körting engines; twin-screws. Was twice entirely re-built and met with numerous accidents. Best endurance: 282 km. in 13 hrs.
2a	(August, 1909)	71	12.5	5,200	150	40	
2b	(June, 1911)	74	11	6,000	150	45	
3	M. II (April, 1909)	71	12.5	5,200	150	40	Prussian Army airship.—Two Körting engines; twin-screws. Best endurance: 460 km. in 16 hrs. Rebuilt to match the third type of M.L.; was destroyed on Sept. 13th, *1911* during the Army manœuvres by spontaneous combustion.
3a	(August, 1911)	74	11	6,000	150	50	

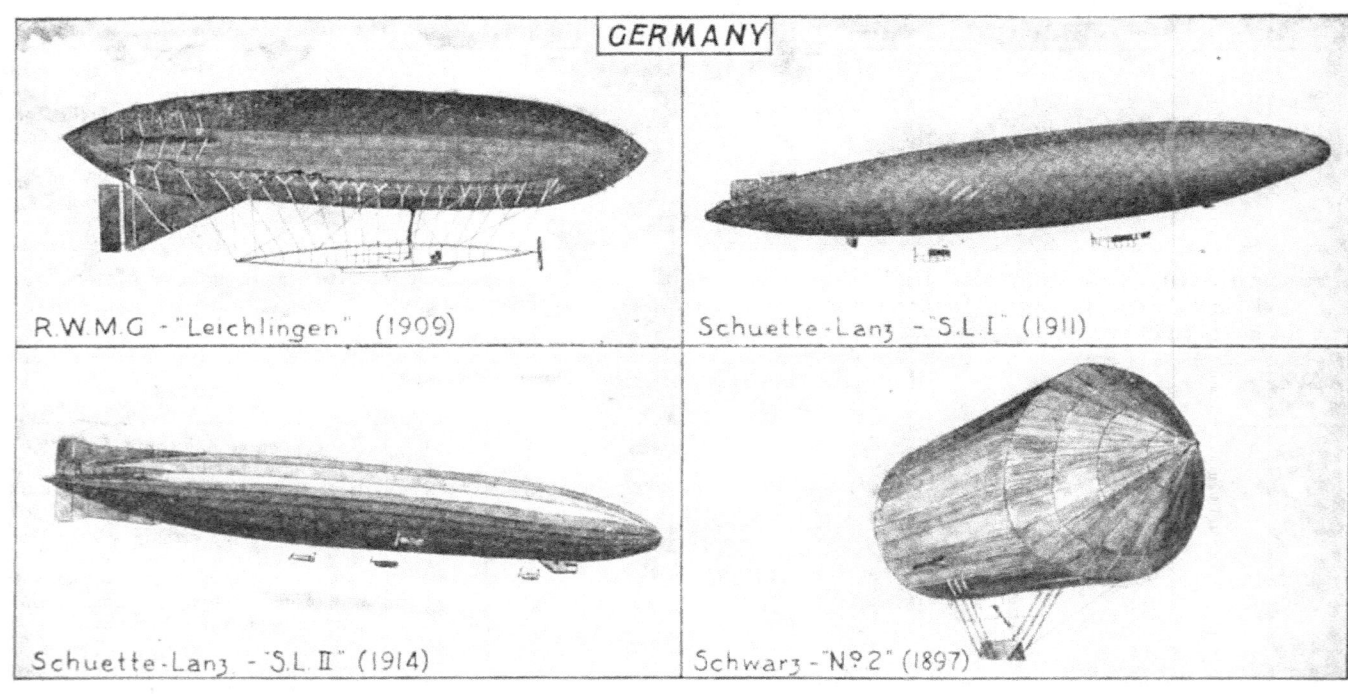

GERMANY—Continued

Works No.	Name Trials	Length (m)	Beam (m)	Volume (mc)	Power (h.p.)	Speed (km)	Notes
4	M. III (December, 1909)	84	12.4	6,700	200	52	Prussian Army airship.—Two Körting engines; twin-screws. Best endurance: 370 km. in 12½ hrs. Re-built and re-fitted with four 75 h.p. Körting engines; was destroyed in the shed of Tegel on Oct. 10th, 1911, by a fire.
4a	(January, 1911)	90	12.4	9,000	300	60	
5	M. IV (March, 1911)	96	12	10,000	400	68	Prussian Army airship.—Four Körting engines; two pairs of twin-screws. Best endurance: 400 km. (Gotha-Metz) in 8 h. 40 m. Re-built and re-fitted with three 150 h.p. Körting engines. (Photo wanted.)
5a	(1913)	102	13.5	12,000	450	75	

No definite information is available regarding the output of airships during the war; in view of the fact that the Prussian Army Airship Works served in time of peace chiefly as an experimental station, it does not seem, however, likely that large numbers of airships have been produced since.

Riedinger (A.), Ballonfabrik, Augsburg.—Builders of airship hulls and aerostatic matériel.

Rheinisch-Westfaelische Motorluftschiff Gesellschaft, Elberfeld.—Builders, to the designs of Herr Oscar Erbsloeh, of a car-girder pressure airship. Trim controlled by lifting planes and trimming tanks.

Works No.	Name Trials	Length (m)	Beam (m)	Volume (mc)	Power (h.p.)	Speed (km)	Notes
1	Leichlingen (October, 1909)	53.2	10	2,900	125	50	Excursion airship.—One Benz engine; one tractor screw. Ballonet: 450 mc. Designed endurance: 6 hrs. Was re-built and enlarged.

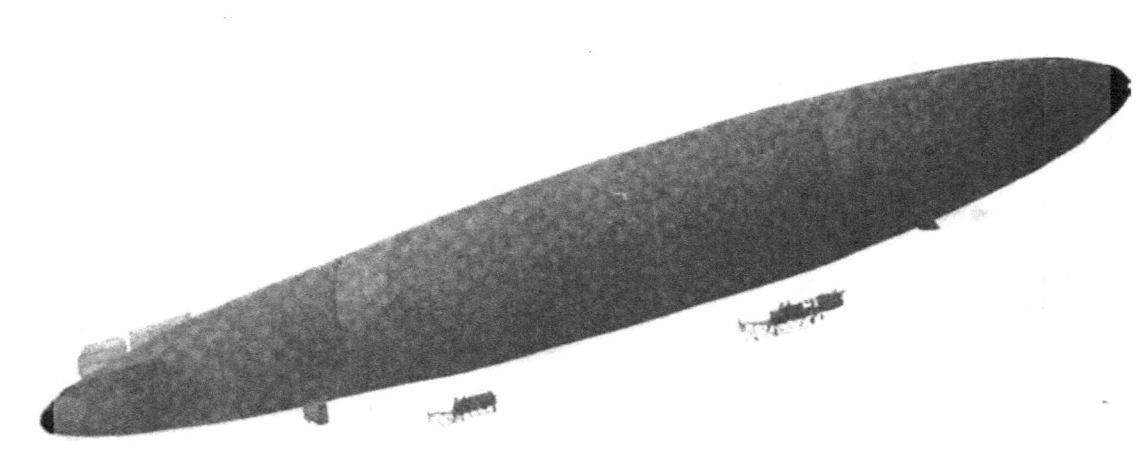

THE *S. L. I* (1911).

GERMANY—Continued

Works No.	Name Trials	Length (m)	Beam (m)	Volume (mc)	Power (h.p.)	Speed (km)	Notes
1a	(1910)			3,200	125	50	Ballonet: 580 mc. Exploded in mid-air on July 13th, 1910, killing the crew of five, including Herr Erbsloeh.

Ruthenberg (H.), Weissensee (Berlin).—Builder of pressure airships of the keel-girder type. Trim controlled by lifting planes. Girder of steel-tubing.

Works No.	Name Trials	Length (m)	Beam (m)	Volume (mc)	Power (h.p.)	Speed (km)	Notes
1	R. I (September, 1909)	40	6.5	1,150	24	36	Touring airship of Herr H. Haase of Hamburg. One Benz engine; one pusher-screw. Designed endurance: 5 hrs. with a crew of three. Ballonet: 230 mc.
2	R. II (1911)	46	7.4	1,700	75	45	Excursion airship.—One F. I. A. T. engine; one pusher-screw. No lifting planes; trim controlled by a movable weight. Ballonet: 300 mc. Was partly wrecked on landing near Crefeld on June 1st, 1911.
3	R. III (1913)	65	11	2,700	150	55	Excursion airship.—Two F. I. A. T. engines; twin-screws. Lifting planes. Ballonet: 450 mc.

Schütte-Lanz (Luftschiffbau), Rheinau, near Mannheim.—Builders of structure airships. Hull-frame of laminated wood girders, spirally wound and held under tension by wire-stays. Fabric skin. Suspended cars. Trim controlled by lifting planes. Gangway, connecting the cars, within the hull.

Works No.	Name Trials	Length (m)	Beam (m)	Volume (mc)	Power (h.p.)	Speed (km)	Notes
1	S. L. I (October, 1911)	131	18.4	19,500	540	71	Prussian Army airship.—11 compartments. Two Mercédès engines, mounted on two cars; each driving

ONE OF THE CARS OF THE *S. L. I.*

GERMANY—Continued

Works No.	Name Trials	Length (m)	Beam (m)	Volume (mc)	Power (h.p.)	Speed (km)	Notes
							one pusher-screw. Best endurance: 16½ hrs. Was destroyed by a storm while moored in the open near Schneidemuehl, on July 17th, 1913.
2	S. L. II (April, 1914)	144	18.4	23,000	800	87	Prussian Army airship.—Four Maybach engines, mounted on four crosswise hung cars, each driving one pusher-screw. One rigidly connected pilot-car near the bow. Best endurance: 1,400 km. in 20 hrs.; altitude: 2,100 m. Performed during the early part of the Great War on the Russian front until she was, in November, 1914, badly punished by Russian gunners and appears to have subsequently been dismantled.
3	L. 4 (1914)	165	18.4	30,000	1,080	90	German naval airship.—Four Mercédès engines driving four pusher-screws as on *S.L.II*. Was "ironcrossed" for her co-operation in the sinking of H. M. ships *Aboukir*, *Cressy* and *Hogue*, on Sept. 22nd, 1914, by the submarine *U.9*. Stranded in a storm, on Feb. 17th, 1915, near Esbjerg; all of the crew saved themselves but four, who perished when the airship was carried away by the storm.
?	S. L. III (January, 1915)	144	18.4	23,000	800	87	Prussian Army airship.—*S.L.II* type.
?	L. 7 (February, 1915)	165	18.4	30,000	1,080	90	German naval airship.—Same features as *L.4*. Was shot down on May 4th, 1916, off the Schleswig

THE *S. S. 1* (1911).

GERMANY—Continued

Works No.	Name Trials	Length (m)	Beam (m)	Volume (mc)	Power (h.p.)	Speed (km)	Notes
?	L. 21 (1915)	165	18.4	30,000	1,080	90	coast, by H. M. ships *Galatea* and *Phaëton;* seven of her crew were made prisoners. German naval airship.—Was set on fire and destroyed with all on board on Sept. 3rd, 1916, near Cuffley, by Lieut. William L. Robinson, V. C., R. F. C.

Schwarz (David), Berlin.—Builder of the first structure airships. Hull-frame of aluminum tubing; skin of 0.2 mm. aluminum sheeting. No compartments. Trim controlled by a lifting screw. No elevator, nor rudder. Upon the death of Herr Schwarz his patents were purchased by Count Zeppelin.

Works No.	Name Trials	Length (m)	Beam (m)	Volume (mc)	Power (h.p.)	Speed (km)	Notes
1	No. 1			5,000	12		Built in Petrograd. Burst during her inflation in 1893 through the breaking of the inner wire-stays. One Daimler engine; twin-screws.
2	No. 2 (November, 1897)	47.5	14	3,700	12	18	Built in Berlin. Hull of elliptical cross-section. One Daimler engine; twin-screws and one steering screw. On her trials the airship was unable to make any headway against a wind of 7.5 m./sec. and was damaged on landing. After having been emptied the airship was completely destroyed by the wind and the vandalism of the spectators.

THE CENTRAL CAR OF THE *S. S. 1.*

GERMANY—Continued

Siemens-Schuckert Works, Berlin.—Builders of a girderless pressure airship to the Krell-Dietzius patents, which were ultimately purchased by the Prussian Army Airship Works. Trim controlled by lifting planes, four ballonets, trimming tanks and one lifting screw.

Works No.	Name Trials	Length (m)	Beam (m)	Volume (mc)	Power (h.p.)	Speed (km)	Notes
1	S. S. 1 (January, 1911)	118	13.2	13,500	480	70	Experimental airship.—Four Daimler engines; two sets of triple-screws. Two 24 h.p. Benz auxiliary engines driving one lifting screw and the ballonet-blowers. Three cars, the one in the middle fitted for passengers, the front and rear cars serving as engine rooms. Designed endurance: 36 hrs. Best endurance: 500 km. in 7 hrs. Was rebuilt and eventually dismantled.
1a	(1912)	120	13.5	15,000	480	71	

Steffen (Franz), Kiel.—Builder of pressure airships of the keel-girder type. Trim controlled by lifting planes and two ballonets. Three compartments.

Works No.	Name Trials	Length (m)	Beam (m)	Volume (mc)	Power (h.p.)	Speed (km)	Notes
1	Kiel-I (March, 1910)	32	4.5	500	40	40	Excursion airship.—One Buchet engine; one pusher-screw. The trials were not very satisfactory and the airship was dismantled in 1912. (Photo wanted.)

Unger & Carter, Hannover.—Builders of a structure airship. Hull frame of steel tubing. Multi-cylindrical cross-section. Trim controlled by lifting planes.

Works No.	Name Trials	Length (m)	Beam (m)	Volume (mc)	Power (h.p.)	Speed (km)	Notes
1	Unger (Building, 1914)	150	22	20,000			Experimental airship, built to the designs of Herr E. Unger.

VIEWS OF THE *ZEPPELIN–I* (1900).

GERMANY—Continued

Woelfert, Berlin.—Builder of a pressure airship of the girderless type. Trim controlled by a lifting screw.

Works No.	Name Trials	Length (m)	Beam (m)	Volume (mc)	Power (h.p.)	Speed (km)	Notes
1	Deutschland (August, 1896)	27.5	8.5	875	8		Experimental airship.—One Daimler benzine engine; one tractor screw and one lifting screw. Ice-water cooling. No ballonet. Was originally fitted with a 3 h.p. Siemens electric battery-motor which was discarded on being found unsatisfactory. On her 8th ascent the airship was set on fire by the engine and fell from a height of 200 m., killing Herr Woelfert and his mechanic, Herr Knabe.

Zeppelin (Luftschiffbau), Friedrichshafen (Wurtemberg)—Builders of metal structure airships to the David Schwarz patents and the designs of Count Ferdinand Zeppelin. Hull-frame of aluminum-alloy lattice girders, cross-braced by wire-stays, and subdivided into compartments for independent gas-cells. No ballonets. Fabric skin. Trim controlled by lifting planes. Cars rigidly connected. Gangway affording passage between the cars.

Works No.	Name Trials	Length (m)	Beam (m)	Volume (mc)	Power (h.p.)	Speed (km)	Notes
LZ. 1	Zeppelin-I (July, 1900)	128	11.7	11,430	32	20	Experimental airship.—Two Mercédès engines; two pairs of twin-screws. Trim first controlled by a movable weight; later through lifting planes. Made only two short ascents after which the airship collapsed in her floating shed on Lake Constance and was dismantled in 1902.
LZ. 2	Zeppelin-II (November, 1905)	127	11.7	10,400	170	40	Experimental airship.—Two Mercédès engines; two pairs of twin-screws. Made a short ascent and

TOP—THE *ZEPPELIN-II* (1905) AND THE *ZEPPELIN-III* (1906); *BOTTOM*—THE STERN AND THE FORWARD CAR OF THE *ZEPPELIN-III*.

GERMANY—Continued

Works No.	Name Trials	Length (m)	Beam (m)	Volume (mc)	Power (h.p.)	Speed (km)	Notes
LZ. 3	Zeppelin-III (October, 1906)	128	11.7	11,430	170	40	landed near Kieslegg (Switzerland) where she was subsequently wrecked on her moorings by a storm. Experimental airship.—Two Mercédès engines; two pairs of twin-screws. Best endurance: 340 km. in 7 hrs. Was re-built and sold to the Prussian Army.
LZ. 3a	Z. I (1908)	136	11.7	12,200	220	46	Prussian Army airship.—Two Maybach engines; two pairs of twin-screws. (This power-plant and drive has become typical of all Zeppelin airships built prior to the Great War; therefore only increase in the number of engines mounted on the cars will henceforth be mentioned.) Best altitude: 1,720 m. Remained six years in commission.
LZ. 4	LZ. 4 (September, 1907)	136	13	15,200	220	47	Experimental airship.—Best endurance: 417 km. in 11 hrs. Destroyed through spontaneous combustion during an electrical storm, while moored at Echterdingen, on Aug. 8th, 1908.
LZ. 5	Z. II (June, 1908)	136	13	15,200	220	50	Prussian Army airship.—Best endurance: 970 km. in 37¾ hrs. Made a trip of 150 km. after her three bow compartments had been taken off upon the airship colliding with a tree. Was destroyed by a storm while moored near Weilburg, on April 24th, 1910.
LZ. 6	LZ. 6 (June, 1908)	136	13	15,200	220	51	Passenger airship.—Fitted with a cabin-car. Placed under charter of the Delag Line* after the loss of the

* Abbreviation for Deutsche Luftschiffahrt Aktien-Gesellschaft, Frankfort-on-the-Main.

THE *LZ. 4* (1907) AT FRIEDRICHSHAFEN.

GERMANY—Continued

Works No.	Name Trials	Length (m)	Beam (m)	Volume (mc)	Power (h.p.)	Speed (km)	Notes
LZ. 6a	(Winter, 1910)	144	13	16,500	330	53	*Deutschland.* Best endurance: 450 km. in 17 hrs. Was re-built and a third engine was mounted, first on the cabin-car (driving a third pair of twin-screws), then on the stern-car in a twin unit, each engine driving one of the stern twin-screws. Made 73 trips aggregating 9,145 km. Was destroyed by a fire, in her shed at Baden-Oos, on Sept. 14th, 1910.
LZ. 7	Deutschland (June, 1910)	148	14	19,300	330	55	Passenger airship of the Delag Line.—Cabin-car seating 20; crew of 8. Best endurance: 540 km. in 9 hrs. On her 7th trip the airship ran into a storm and stranded for lack of fuel in the Teutoburg Forest. None was injured.
LZ. 8	Deutschland-II (March, 1911)	148	14	19,300	360	56	Passenger airship of the Delag Line.—Three engines of a more powerful type. Made only 2 trips. Was wrecked on May 16th, 1911, by being blown against the airship shed of Düsseldorf.
LZ. 9	Z. II (October, 1911)	132	14	16,900	450	74	Prussian Army airship.—Best endurance (trials): 20 hrs. Was re-built in 1912. Turning circle: 680-700 m.
LZ. 9a	(1912)	140	14	17,800	450	74	
LZ. 10	Schwaben (June, 1911)	140	14	17,800	450	72	Passenger airship of the Delag Line.—Made 229 trips aggregating 27,570 km., on which 4,545 passengers were carried. Turning circle: 650 m. Was destroyed through

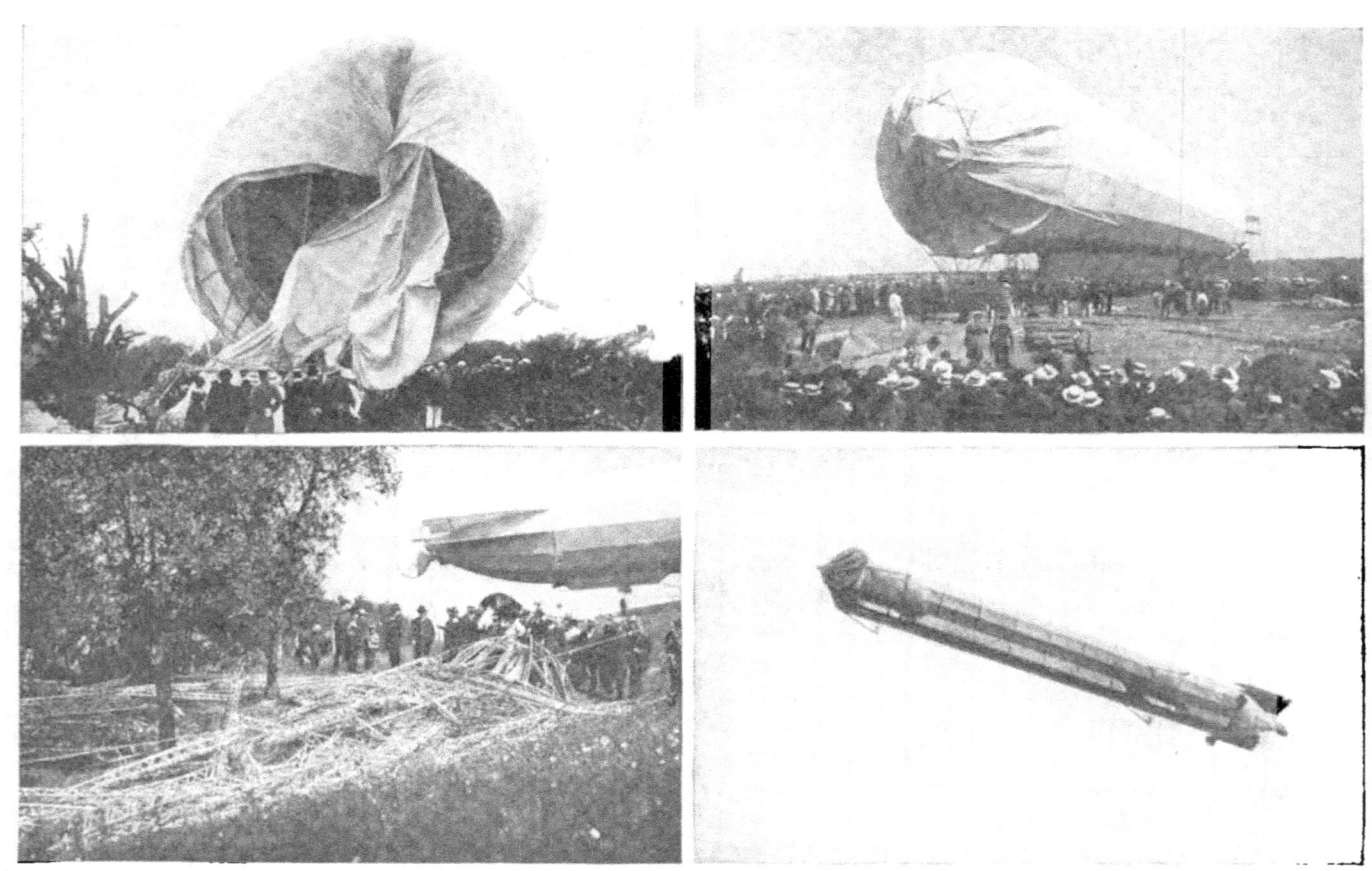

VARIOUS PHASES OF THE STRANDING AND REFLOATING OF THE *LZ. 5* (1909).

GERMANY—Continued

Works No.	Name Trials	Length (m)	Beam (m)	Volume (mc)	Power (h.p.)	Speed (km)	Notes
							spontaneous combustion after her hull had been damaged by the wind at the Düsseldorf airship shed, on June 28th, 1912.
LZ. 11	Viktoria-Luise (February, 1912)	148	14	18,700	450	75	Passenger airship of the Delag Line. Best endurance: 560 km. in 12 hrs. Made up to Oct. 31st, 1913, 384 trips, aggregating 46,284 km., on which 8,134 passengers were carried. Turning circle: 550 m. Was chartered in 1914 by the German Navy to serve as a training airship.
LZ. 12	Z. III (April, 1912)	140	14	17,500	450	78	Prussian Army airship.—Improved *LZ. 9* type.
LZ. 13	Hansa (July, 1912)	148	14	18,700	540	80	Passenger airship of the Delag Line.—Best endurance: 700 km. in 10½ hrs. Made up to Oct. 31st, 1913, 297 trips, aggregating 34,166 km., on which 6,217 passengers were carried. Was chartered in 1914 by the German Navy to serve as a training airship.
LZ. 14	L. 1 (October, 1912)	158	14.8	22,465	540	76	First German naval airship.—New type. Four Maxims on the cars, one on the roof near the bow. Wireless carrying 300 km. Best endurance: 1,900 km. in 31 hrs. with a crew of 21. Foundered in a storm on Sept. 9th, 1913, off Helgoland with 13 of the crew.
LZ. 15	Z. I (January, 1913)	141	14.8	19,500	540	77	Prussian Army airship.—Four Maxims on the cars. Best endurance: 16½ hrs. Was destroyed by a storm on her moorings near Karlsruhe on March 19th, 1913.

THE *LZ. 6* (1908-10). IN THE LOWER RIGHT-HAND CORNER THE THIRD ENGINE INSTALLED AMIDSHIPS.

GERMANY—Continued

Works No.	Name Trials	Length (m)	Beam (m)	Volume (mc)	Power (h.p.)	Speed (km)	Notes
LZ. 16	Z. IV (March, 1913)	141	14.8	19,500	540	77	Prussian Army airship.—*LZ. 15* type. Best endurance 18½ hrs.; altitude: 2,000 m.
LZ. 17	Sachsen (May, 1913)	141	14.8	19,500	540	76	Passenger airship of the Delag Line.—Made up to Oct. 31st, 1913, 206 trips, aggregating 21,683 km., on which 2,698 passengers were carried.
LZ. 17a	(March, 1914)	149	14.8	20,800	600	80	Was rebuilt and re-engined in 1914 when she was chartered by the German Navy to serve as a training airship.
LZ. 18	L. 2 (September, 1913)	158	16.6	27,000	720	80	German naval airship.—New type: gangway within the hull, pilot-car in front of the two engine-cars which contained two engines each. 19 compartments. Wireless carrying 500 km. Best endurance: 1,000 km. in 13 hrs. Was destroyed through spontaneous combustion on Oct. 17th, 1913, over Johannisthal. The crew of 17 and a testing commission of 11 were killed.
LZ. 19	Z. I (June, 1913)	141	14.8	19,500	540	77	Prussian Army airship.—*LZ. 15* type. Designed endurance: 20 hrs. Best endurance: 1,100 km. in 19 hrs. Was destroyed by a storm while moored at Thionville (Alsace) on June 13th, 1914.
LZ. 20	Z. V (July, 1913)	141	14.8	19,500	540	77	Prussian Army airship.—*LZ. 15* type. Best endurance: 20 hrs. Was re-built like the *Sachsen*.
	(July, 1914)	149	14.8	20,800	600	80	In the Great War the *Z. V* performed on the Russian front till Sept. 28th, 1914, when she was shot down near Warsaw and her crew made prisoners.

TOP—BOW AND STERN VIEW OF THE *Z.IV* (*LZ. 16*); *BOTTOM*—THE FORWARD CAR OF THE *Z.IV* AND OF THE *L. 1*.

GERMANY—Continued

Works No.	Name Trials	Length (m)	Beam (m)	Volume (mc)	Power (h.p.)	Speed (km)	Notes
LZ. 21	Z. VI (November, 1913) (1914)	141 149	14.8 14.8	19,500 20,800	540 600	77 80	Prussian Army airship.—*LZ. 15* type. Was being re-built at the outbreak of the war like the *Z.V*.
LZ. 22	Z. VII (January, 1914)	156	14.8	22,000	600	80	Prussian Army airship—Improved *LZ. 14* type.
LZ. 23	Z. VIII (February, 1914)	156	14.8	22,000	600	80	Prussian Army airship.—Improved *LZ. 14* type. Best altitude: 2,645 m. Was shot down by French gunners on August 22nd, 1914, near Badonviller (Lorraine). Part of the crew were killed.
LZ. 24	L. 3 (May, 1914)	158	16.6	27,000	800	80	German naval airship.—Improved *LZ. 18* type. No special pilot-car, nor masked gangway however. Best endurance: 35 hrs.; altitude: 2,700 m. Stranded in a storm on Feb. 17th, 1915, near Esbjerg (Denmark) and was scuttled by her commander, who was subsequently interned with the crew.
LZ. 25 LZ. 26 LZ. 27 LZ. 28 LZ. 29	Z. IX (July, 1914) Z. X (August, 1914) Z. XI (September, 1914) Z. XII (September, 1914) Z. XIII (October, 1914)	156	14.8	22,000	600	80	Prussian Army airships of the improved *LZ. 14* type. Built at Friedrichshafen. Vessels of this type have been built in large numbers until the summer of 1915, when the new type of Army airship was produced which follows.
	LZ. 77 type (1915-16)	156	16	25,000	840	85	Four Maybach engines of greater power; one, mounted on the bow-car, driving one pusher-screw and three, on the stern-car, driving triple-screws. Designed endurance: 25 hrs. Crew of 16. Altitude: 3,500 m. Four Maxims on the cars; 1½ tons of bombs. One airship of

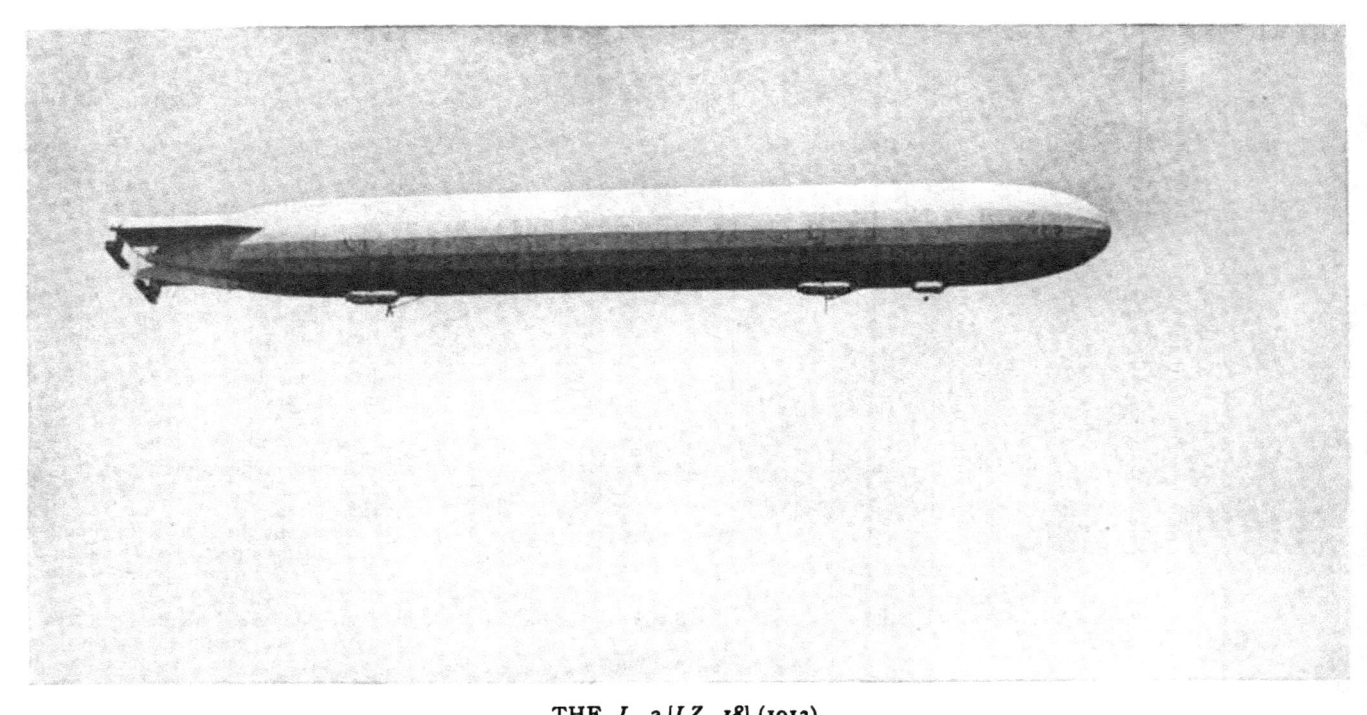

THE *L. 2* [*LZ. 18*] (1913).

GERMANY—Continued

Works No.	Name Trials	Length (m)	Beam (m)	Volume (mc)	Power (h.p.)	Speed (km)	Notes
							this type (Works No. *LZ. 77*) was shot down by French gunners on Feb. 2nd, 1916, near Révigny. Another Army airship of the same type (Works No. *LZ. 85*) was shot down by the Franco-British fleet on May 5th, 1916, near Salonica. In February, 1917, the Prussian Army decided to discontinue the use of Zeppelin airships.
	L. 5 (November, 1914) L. 6 (December, 1914) L. 8 (February, 1915) L. 9 (March, 1915) L. 10 (April, 1915)	158	16.6	27,000	840	80	German naval airships.*—*LZ. 24* type; fitted with more powerful engines. Endurance, fully loaded, 26 hrs. Crew of 16. Four Maxims on the cars; 1½ tons of bombs.
							The *L. 5* was destroyed on June 7th, 1915, in the airship shed of Evere (Belgium) by aeroplanes piloted by Flight Sub.-Lieuts. J. P. Wilson and J. S. Mills, R. N. A. S.—The *L. 6* was destroyed on the same day near Ghent (Gand) by an aeroplane piloted by Flight Sub.-Lieut. R. Warneford, V. C., R. N. A. S.—The *L. 8* broke up on landing by night, on March 5th, 1915, near Tirlemont.—The *L. 10*, while returning from a raid on England on Aug. 10th, 1915, was wrecked in the harbour of Ostende by the Dunkirk squadron of the R. N. A. S.

* According to an article by "Austerlitz" in *The Aeroplane*, London, Jan. 3rd, 1907.

THE END OF THE *L. 15* (1915).

GERMANY—Continued

Works No.	Name Trials	Length (m)	Beam (m)	Volume (mc)	Power (h.p.)	Speed (km)	Notes
	L. 11 (July, 1915) L. 12—L. 19 (August to November, 1915)	160	17.5	30,000	1,050	85	German naval airships.—Five engines; two on each car driving twin-screws, the fifth engine on the stern-car driving one pusher-screw. Designed endurance: 26 hrs.; altitude: 3,500 m. Crew of 16. Four Maxims on the cars and one on the roof, near the bow. 2 tons of bombs. The *L. 15* was damaged, while raiding England, by A.-A. guns and by Lieut. A. de B. Brandon, R. F. C., and came down on April 1st, 1916, in the mouth of the Thames, where the crew scuttled the airship and surrendered.—The *L. 18* caught fire and blew up on Nov. 17th, 1915, in the airship dock of Tondern.—The *L. 19* was damaged by A.-A. guns while raiding England and foundered on Feb. 2nd, 1916, in the North Sea with the entire crew.
	L. 20—L. 29* (November, 1915, to April, 1916)	170	20	35,000	1,260	95	German naval airships.—Six engines; triple-screws on both cars. Designed endurance: 30 hrs.; altitude: 3,500 m. Crew of 18. Masked gangway, like on *LZ. 18*, fitted as a bomb-chamber. One 12 mm. machine gun each on the roof near the bow and one on the bow-car; two Maxims each on the cars and the bomb-chamber, firing broadsides. 2½ tons of bombs.

* Minus L. 21, which was a Schütte-Lanz airship.

THE END OF THE *L. 20* (1916).

GERMANY—Continued

Works No.	Name Trials	Length (m)	Beam (m)	Volume (mc)	Power (h.p.)	Speed (km)	Notes
	L. 30—L. 40 (May, 1916, to January, 1917)	207	22	54,000	1,500	105	The *L. 20* stranded on May 3rd, 1916, near Stavanger (Norway), having run out of fuel and drifted with the wind while homeward bound from a raid on Scotland. The crew were interned and the airship was blown up by the Norwegian authorities as a measure of precaution.—The *L. 22* was shot down on May 14th, 1917, in the North Sea, by a British seaplane. German naval airships.—Six Maybach engines of a new model; one pusher-screw each on the bow-car and central twin-cars ("power-eggs") and triple-screws on the stern-car. Designed endurance: 30 hrs.; altitude: 4,000 m. Crew of 22. Two 12 mm. machine guns carried side-by-side on the roof, near the bow, on collapsible tripods; one such gun on the roof, near the stern. Six Maxims, viz., two each on the bow and stern cars and one each on the twin-cars. Sixty bombs, aggregating 3½ tons, carried amidships on racks. Electro-magnetic launching device. Masked gangway, connecting all stations. The *L. 31* was shot down on Oct. 2nd, 1916, while raiding London, by Sec. Lieut. W. J. Tempest, R. F. C., and fell near Potter's Bar. The crew were killed.—The *L. 32* was shot down on Sept. 24th, 1916, while

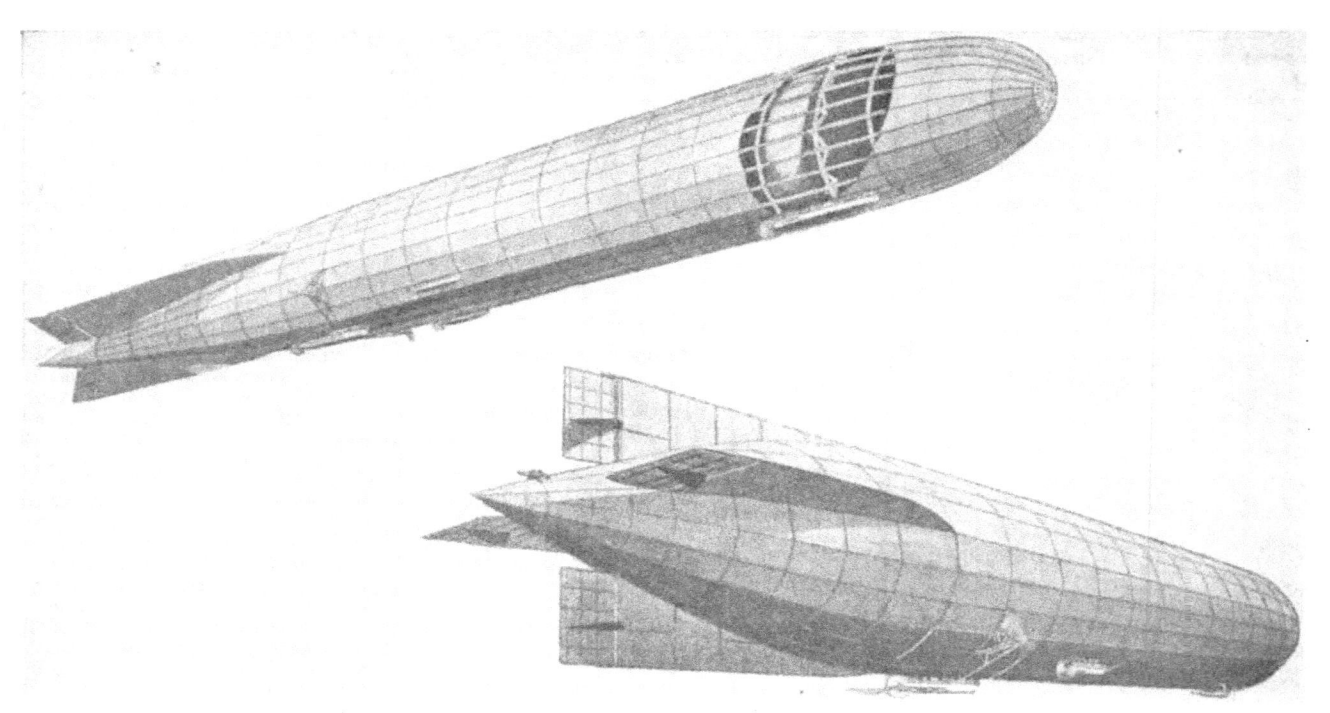

TWO SCHEMATIC VIEWS OF THE L. 33 [LZ. 76] (1916).

Courtesy of *The Aeroplane*.

GERMANY—Continued

Zorn, Berlin.—Builder of a structure airship. Wooden hull frame. Trim controlled by lifting planes and trimming tanks.

Works No.	Name Trials	Length (m)	Beam (m)	Volume (mc)	Power (h.p.)	Speed (km)	Notes
1	Zorn (1910)	120	13.8	13,600	210		Experimental airship.—Three Argus engines; three pairs of twin-screws. Three cars. On her trials the airship did not prove satisfactory and was eventually dismantled.

GREAT BRITAIN

"Airships", Ltd., Hendon, N. W.—Builders of pressure airships to the Astra and Astra-Torres patents.

Armstrong, Whitworth & Co., Ltd., Newcastle-on-Tyne.—Builders of pressure airships of the keel-girder type to Signor E. Forlanini's patents. Trim controlled by lifting planes.

Works No.	Name Trials	Length (m)	Beam (m)	Volume (mc)	Power (h.p.)	Speed (km)	Notes
AW-1	(Laid down, 1913)	90	18	15,000	320	80	British naval airship.—Four engines; twin-screws.
AW-2	(Laid down, 1913)	90	18	15,000	320	80	British naval airship.—As above.
AW-3	(Laid down, 1913)			25,000	1,000	100	British naval airship.

Barton (F. A.), London.—Builder of a pressure airship of the car-girder type. Trim controlled by lifting planes and trimming tanks. Suspension hems stiffened by bamboo strips.

Works No.	Name Trials	Length (m)	Beam (m)	Volume (mc)	Power (h.p.)	Speed (km)	Notes
1	Barton (July, 1905)	51.8	12.5	6,440	100	25	Experimental airship, built with the financial assistance of the War Office. Ballonet: 1,200 mc. Two Buchet engines, each driving one twin set of propellers consisting of three co-axial screws. Made on July 22, 1905, a partially controlled flight over London (40 km.), but drifted on landing into some trees and was wrecked.

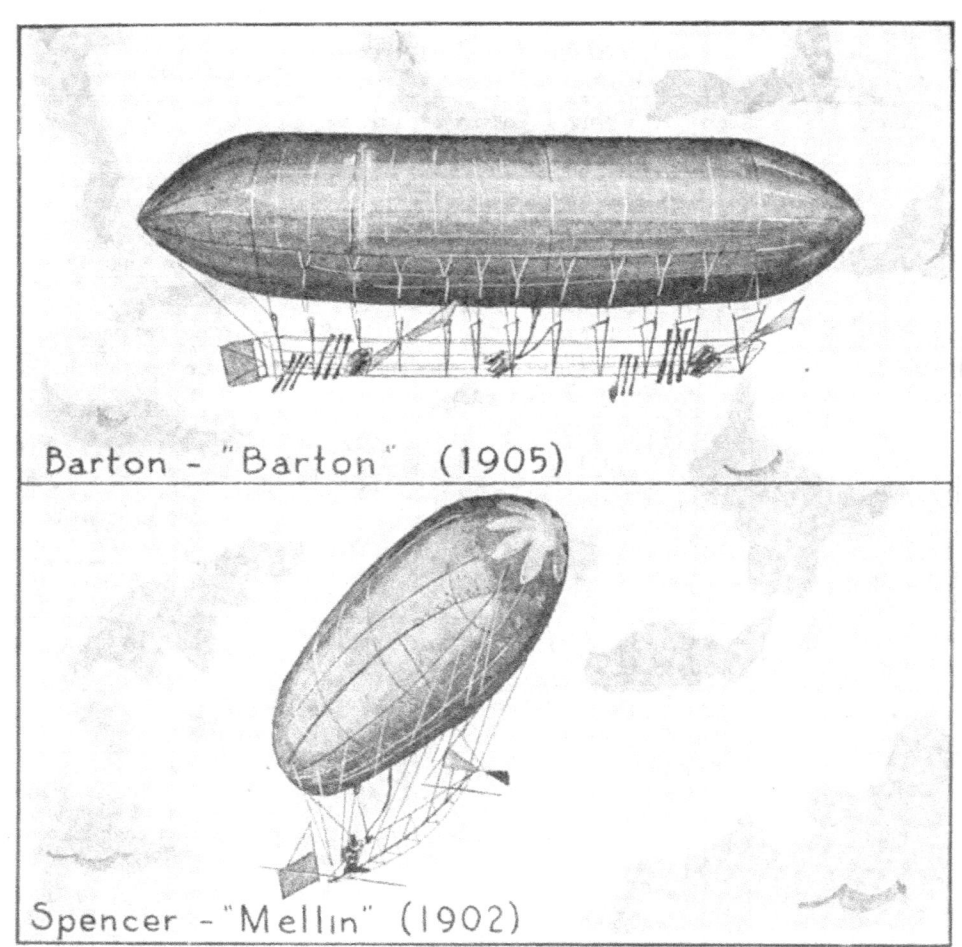

GREAT BRITAIN—Continued

Beedle (W.), London.—Builder of a structure airship.

Works No.	Name Trials	Length (m)	Beam (m)	Volume (mc)	Power (h.p.)	Speed (km)	Notes
1	Beedle (1901)	30.5	4.9	500	28		Experimental airship. One automobile engine; twin-screws. (Data and photo wanted.)

Bell (Hugh), London.—Builder of a pressure airship of the keel-girder type. Keel of steel tubing, running from end to end.

Works No.	Name Trials	Length (m)	Beam (m)	Volume (mc)	Power (h.p.)	Speed (km)	Notes
1	Bell (1848)	17	6.5				Propulsion by manually operated twin-screws. The trials, which took place at Vauxhall Gardens, did not furnish appreciable results.

Buchanan (F.), London.—Builder of a pressure airship.

Works No.	Name Trials	Length (m)	Beam (m)	Volume (mc)	Power (h.p.)	Speed (km)	Notes
1	Buchanan (1902)	30.5		1,260			The trials were not successful. (Photo, or sketch, and additional data wanted.)

Gaudron (Auguste), London.—Builder of a pressure airship of the girderless type. Trim controlled by ballast.

Works No.	Name Trials	Length (m)	Beam (m)	Volume (mc)	Power (h.p.)	Speed (km)	Notes
1	Gaudron (May, 1898)	18.3	8.5	600	2		Experimental airship.—One Siemens electric motor; one tractor screw. On her trials the airship made a partially controlled voyage over London, at the conclusion of which she was, however, unable to return against the wind to her starting place and was voluntarily stranded by the pilot.

THE *NULLI-SECUNDUS* (1907) AND THE *BABY* (1909).

GREAT BRITAIN—Continued

Royal Aircraft Factory (formerly Army Balloon Factory), Farnborough.—Builders of pressure airships to various designs. Trim controlled by lifting planes and (on later models) by swivelling screws.

Works No.	Name Trials	Length (m)	Beam (m)	Volume (mc)	Power (h.p.)	Speed (km)	Notes
1	Nulli-Secundus (September, 1907)	33.9	9.2	2,400	50	30	Experimental airship, built to the designs of Colonel Capper and S. F. Cody.—Keel-girder type; hull of goldbeater's skin. Ballonet: 400 mc. One Antoinette engine; twin-screws. Was badly damaged by a storm on Oct. 10th, 1907, near London, whither the airship had flown from Farnborough.
1a	Dirigible II (July, 1908)	36.6	9.2	2,700	100	32	Was re-built and fitted with a ballonet of 500 mc. and a second Antoinette engine, but proved unsatisfactory and was eventually broken up.
2	Baby (May, 1909)	25.6	7.6	600	16	29	British Army airship.—Car-girder type; inflated fins. Two Buchet engines; one pusher-screw above the car.
2a	Beta (June, 1910)	31.7	7.6	945	30	40	Was re-built and fitted with one Green engine driving twin-screws and with surface fins. Thus altered the *Beta* (ex-*Baby*) proved a very successful vessel for her size and made trips aggregating 5,000 km. till 1913, when she was dismantled.
3	No. 2A (February, 1910)	46	7.6	1,200	80		British Army airship.—One Green engine; twin-screws. Was little successful.

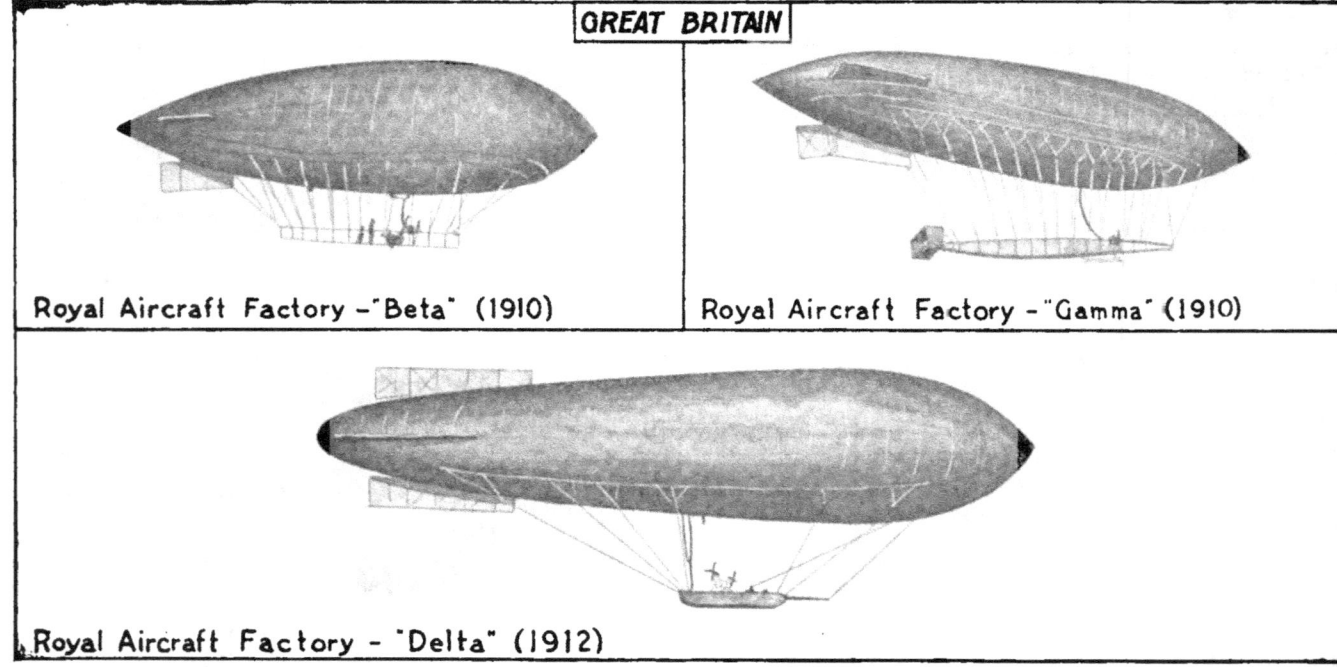

GREAT BRITAIN—Continued

Works No.	Name Trials	Length (m)	Beam (m)	Volume (mc)	Power (h.p.)	Speed (km)	Notes
4	Gamma (July, 1910)	46	9.1	2,265	100	45	British Army airship.*—One Green engine; swivelling twin-screws. Car-girder type.
5	Delta (1912)	60	13.4	4,530	200	60	British Army airship.*—Car-girder type. Two Wolseley engines; swivelling twin-screws.
6	Eta (1913)			6,000	300		British Army airship.*—Car-girder type. Two Salmson engines; swivelling twin-screws.

* In July, 1914, all the British Army airships were transferred to the (then) newly created Airship Section of the Royal Naval Air Service.

Short Brothers Battersea Park, London, S. W.—Builders of airships to various designs.

Spencer (C. G. & Sons), London.—Builders of airships to various designs. Trim controlled by ballast.

Works No.	Name Trials	Length (m)	Beam (m)	Volume (mc)	Power (h.p.)	Speed (km)	Notes
1	Mellin (June, 1902)	23	6.1	560	8	25	Experimental airship. Car-girder, pressure type. One Siemens electric motor; one tractor-screw. Made on Sept. 19th, 1902, a partially controlled flight from London to Harrow (32 km.), but lacked power to return, against a moderate wind, to her starting place.
2	Spencer II (No trials)	28.4	7.3	840	24		Experimental airship of the structure type. Aluminum hull; 8 compartments. Fabric skin. One Antoinette engine; one tractor screw. Laid down in 1903, was not completed.

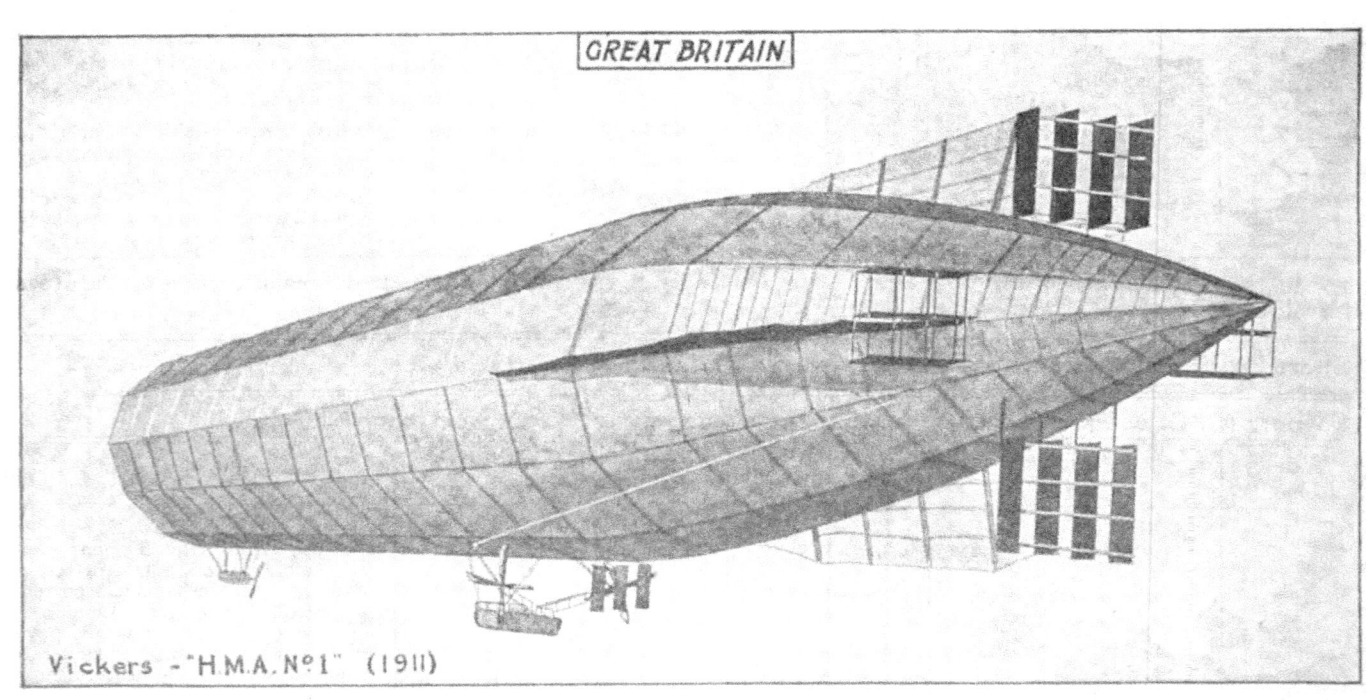

GREAT BRITAIN—Continued

Vickers, Sons and Maxim, Ltd., Barrow-in-Furness.—Builders of structure airships to their own designs and of girderless pressure airships to the Parseval patents. Trim controlled by lifting planes. (Vickers type.)

Works No.	Name Trials	Length (m)	Beam (m)	Volume (mc)	Power (h.p.)	Speed (km)	Notes
1	No. 1 (Laid down, 1910)	155	14.6	19,800	400		British naval airship.—Structure type; 19 gas-cells. Hull-frame of duralumin. Two Wolseley engines mounted in two cars, the front one driving twin-screws, the rear one driving one pusher-screw. On Sept. 24th, 1911, while being towed out of her shed, the airship was blown against the shed and broke in two. She was never repaired.
2	No. (Laid down, 1913)			23,000			British naval airship.—Structure type.
3	No. (Laid down, 1913)	84	15.5	12,000	400	75	British naval airship.—Parseval girderless pressure type.
4	No. (Laid down, 1913)	84	15.5	12,000	400	75	British naval airship.—As above.
5	No. (Laid down, 1913)	84	15.5	12,000	400	75	British naval airship.—As above.

Willows (E. T.), Cardiff.—Builder of pressure airships of the car-girder and keel-girder types. Trim controlled by swivelling screws.

Works No.	Name Trials	Length (m)	Beam (m)	Volume (mc)	Power (h.p.)	Speed (km)	Notes
1	No. 1 (1905)	22.6	5.5	340	7	30	Experimental airship.—Car-girder type. One Peugeot engine; one pusher-screw and one pair of twin-screws (the latter swivelling). No rudder, nor elevator. Notwithstanding her small power, this airship handled satisfactorily.

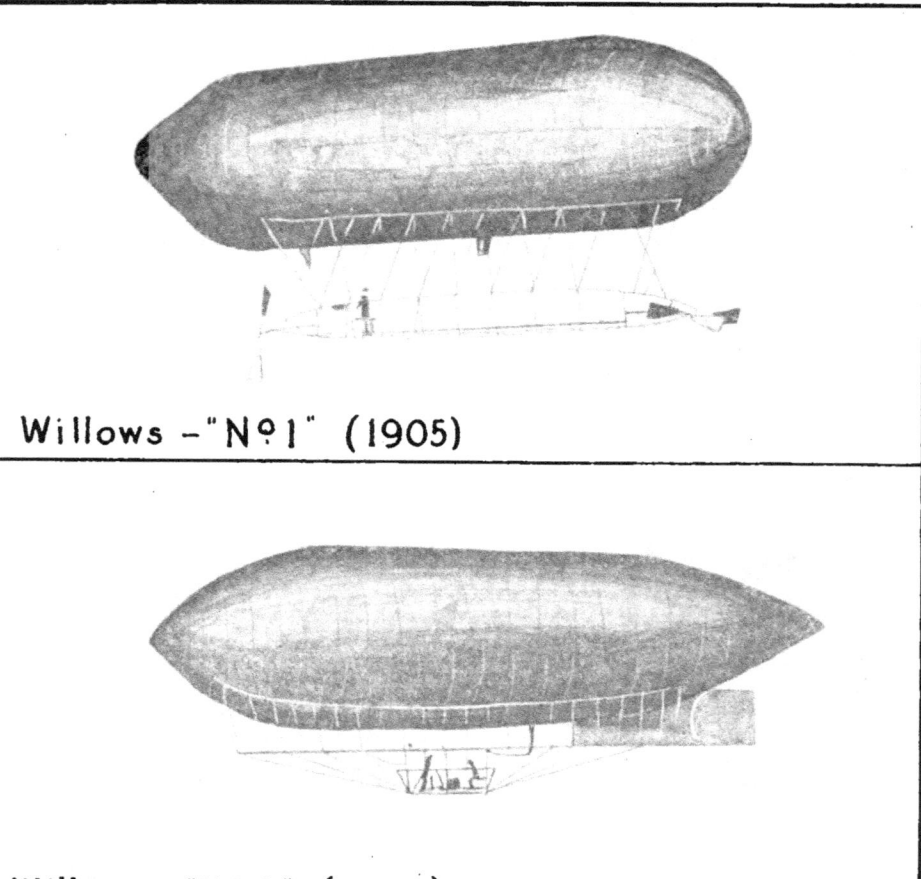

GREAT BRITAIN—Continued

Works No.	Name Trials	Length (m)	Beam (m)	Volume (mc)	Power (h.p.)	Speed (km)	Notes
2	No. 2 (November, 1909)	26.2	6.7	600	30	35	Excursion airship of Mr. Willows. Keel-girder type. One J. A. P. engine; one pair of swivelling twin-screws. Made many trips, including one from Cardiff to London (225 km. in 9 hrs.). Was re-built. Flew on Nov. 4th, 1910, with two on board from London, across the Channel to Douai (10½ hrs.).
2a	City-of-Cardiff (1910)	36.5	7	910	30	35	
3	No. 4 (October, 1912)	30.5	6.1	670	35	55	British naval airship.—Keel-girder type. One Anzani engine; swivelling twin-screws. Built to be carried on board ships.
4	No. 5 (1913)	39.6	7.9	1,400	70	60	Excursion airship of Mr. Willows.—Swivelling twin-screws.

ITALY

Army Airship Works, Vigna di Valle (Rome).—Builders of pressure airships of the keel-girder type to the designs of captains Crocco and Ricaldoni. Trim controlled by lifting planes. Gas-tight compartments. Articulated girder, consisting of a Gall's chain, inserted in the bottom of the hull.

Works No.	Name Trials	Length (m)	Beam (m)	Volume (mc)	Power (h.p.)	Speed (km)	Notes
1	No. 1 (October, 1908)	63	10	2,750	105	51	Experimental airship.—One Clément-Bayard engine; twin-screws. Ballonet: 500 mc. 7 compartments. Fitted with a rigid keel-girder, which was converted into an articulated one at the re-construction.
1a	No. 1-bis (August, 1909)	60	10.5	3,450	105	52	Ballonet: 650 mc. Best endurance: 300 km. in 7 hrs. Was again re-built.

THE WILLOWS *CITY OF CARDIFF* (1910) AND THE CAR OF THE *No. 4* (1912).

ITALY—Continued

Works No.	Name Trials	Length (m)	Beam (m)	Volume (mc)	Power (h.p.)	Speed (km)	Notes
1b	P. 1 (1910)	60	11.6	4,200	105	52	Ballonet: 800 mc. Best endurance: 470 km. in 14 hrs. Served as an Army training airship until 1914, when she was dismantled.
2 3	P. 2 (1910) P. 3 (1911)	63	11.6	4,400	120	52	Italian Army airships.—One Clément-Bayard engine; twin-screws. Designed endurance: 10 hrs. Altitude: 1,600 m. Ballonet: 900 mc. Both airships took a prominent part in Italy's Lybian campaign, being the first airships to see actual war service. The *P.2* was dismantled in 1914.
4 5	P. 4 (November, 1912) P. 5 (December, 1912)	63	12	4,700	160	65	Italian Army airships.—Ballonet: 1,200 mc. Two F. I. A. T. engines; twin-screws. Designed endurance: 12 hrs. at 2,000 m. altitude. Best endurance: 460 km. in 9 hrs. (for *P.5*). The *P.4* (called also the *Città di Iesi*) made during the Great War numerous raids on Dalmatia and Istria and was destroyed by Austrian seaplanes on Aug. 5th, 1915, while raiding Pola.—The *P.5* was destroyed by Austrian seaplanes on Aug. 12th, 1916, in the airship shed of Campalto.
6	M. 1 (1912)	83	17	12,000	500	70	Italian Army airship.—8 compartments. Armoured car. Two F. I. A. T. engines; twin-screws. Designed endurance: 24 hrs.
7	M. 2 (Summer, 1913)	83	17	12,100	500	70	Italian naval airship.—Improved *M.1* type. Four Wolseley engines. Best endurance: 1,000 km. in 21

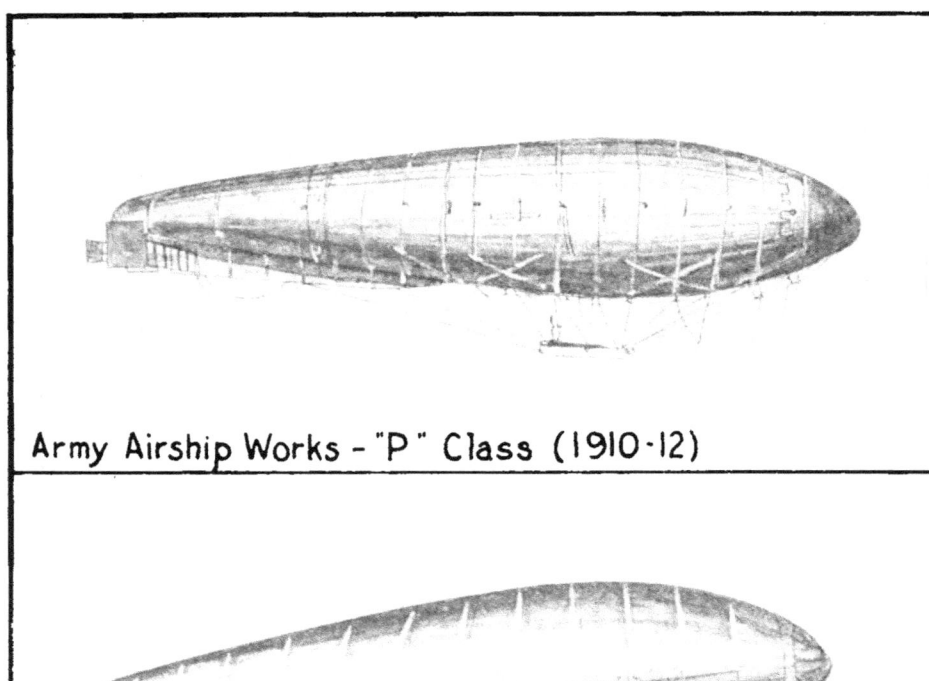

ITALY—Continued

Works No.	Name Trials	Length (m)	Beam (m)	Volume (mc)	Power (h.p.)	Speed (km)	Notes
							hrs. Called also the *Città di Ferrara*. Was shot down by Austrian seaplanes on June 8th, 1915, while homeward bound from a raid on Fiume.
8	M. 3 (October, 1913)	83	17	12,100	520	70	Italian Army airships.—*M.2* type. Four Clément-Bayard engines. The *M.3* was shot down by Austrian A.-A. guns on May 4th, 1916, near Gorizia, while homecoming from a raid on Lubiana.
9	M. 4 (January, 1914)						
10	V. 1 (February, 1915)	90	20	14,650	400	93	Italian naval airship.—New type, built to the designs of Capt. Verduzio. Rigid keel-girder of triangular trellis-work within the hull. Ballonet: 4,800 mc. 12 compartments. Two Maybach engines; twin-screws. Designed endurance: 15 hrs. at full speed and 2,000 m. altitude.
11	M. 5 (April, 1916)	83	17	12,100	520	70	Italian Army airship.—*M.2* type.
12-13	G. 1—G. 2 (Laid down 1914)			20,000	800	80	Italian naval airships.—Structure type.

Da Schio (Count A'merico), Vicenza (Venetia).—Builder of pressure airships of the car-girder type. Particular feature: hull fitted with an elastic underside, doing away with the ballonet. Trim controlled by lifting planes.

Works No.	Name Trials	Length (m)	Beam (m)	Volume (mc)	Power (h.p.)	Speed (km)	Notes
1	Italia (June, 1905)	39.2	6	1,200	12	30	Experimental airship, built with the financial assistance of the late King Humbert I.—One Buchet engine;

TOP—THE *LEONARDO DA VINCI* (1909); *BOTTOM*—THE *CITTÀ DI MILANO* (1913) AND HER CAR.

ITALY—Continued

Works No.	Name Trials	Length (m)	Beam (m)	Volume (mc)	Power (h.p.)	Speed (km)	Notes
							one tractor screw. Made only one ascent; was subsequently fitted with a new hull and made another ascent in 1909, at the conclusion of which she was partly wrecked by the wind.
2	Italia-II (1913)	50	10.5	2,600	50	40	Experimental airship.—One S. P. A. engine; twin-screws. (Information wanted regarding performances.)

Forlanini (Enrico), Baggio (Lombardy).—Builder of pressure airships of the keel-girder type to the designs of E. Forlanini and Capt. dal Fabbro. Features: metal keel, built into the envelope, containing the nacelle; ballonet heated by the engine-exhaust. No cable suspension. Trim controlled by lifting planes. Double envelope.

Works No.	Name Trials	Length (m)	Beam (m)	Volume (mc)	Power (h.p.)	Speed (km)	Notes
1	Leonardo da Vinci (November, 1909)	40	14	3,265*	40	50	Experimental airship.—Ballonet: 350 mc. One Antoinette engine; twin-screws. One 2 h.p. auxiliary engine for ballonet blowers. Laid down to be propelled by a 100 h.p. steam engine. Highly satisfactory trials in spite of small power plant. Best endurance: 3 hrs.
2	Città di Milano (August, 1913)	72	18	11,800*	170	63	Italian Army airship.—Purchased by a popular subscription of the citizens of Milan. Two Isotta-Fraschini engines; twin-screws. Best endurance: 150 km. in 2 hrs. (Milan-Turin). Was partly destroyed on Apr. 9th, 1914, near Cantù by an explosion while about to land.

* Gas capacity.

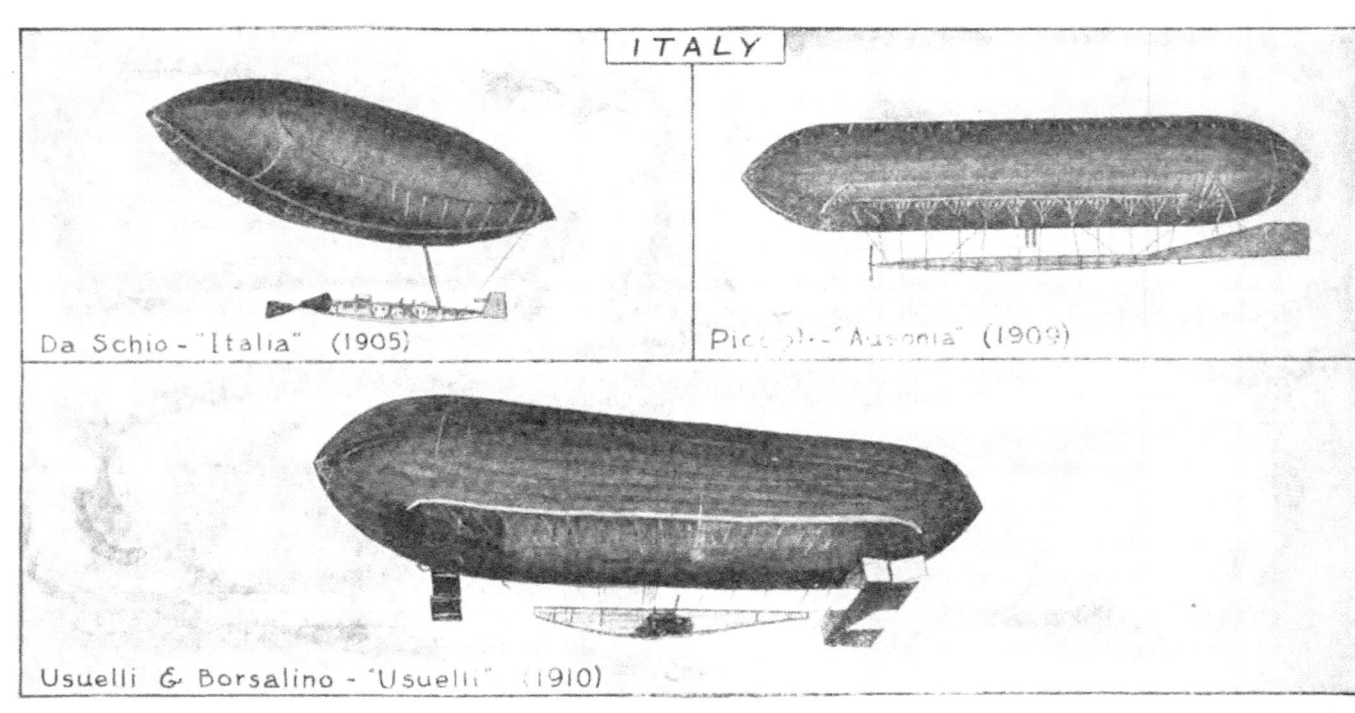

ITALY—Continued

Works No.	Name Trials	Length (m)	Beam (m)	Volume (mc)	Power (h.p.)	Speed (km)	Notes
3	F. 3 (1915)	90	18	13,800*	400	74	Italian naval airship.—Four F. I. A. T. engines; twin-screws. Designed endurance: 45 hrs. at 75 km. and 90 hrs. at 59 km.
4	No. (November, 1914)	90	18	13,900*	320	73	British naval airship.—Two engines; twin-screws. Endurance as above.
5	F. 5 (Building)	90	20	17,800*	480	70	Italian Army airship.—Two engines; twin-screws.
6	F. 6 (Building)	90	20	17,800*	760	75	Italian Navy airship.—Four engines; twin-screws.

Piccoli (Nico), Magré (Venetia).—Builder of pressure airships of the car-girder type. Trim controlled by lifting planes.

Works No.	Name Trials	Length (m)	Beam (m)	Volume (mc)	Power (h.p.)	Speed (km)	Notes
1	Ausonia (1909)	42	8.3	1,800	40	40	Excursion airship belonging to her builder. One S. P. A. engine; one tractor screw. Designed endurance: 8 hrs. Was partly wrecked by the storm when landing on June 10th, 1910, at Mantua. Was re-built and re-fitted with a larger S. P. A. engine, but was again wrecked by the storm.
1a	Ausonia-bis (1910)	37	7.8	1,500	55	40	

Usuelli & Borsalino, Turin.—Builders of pressure airships of the car-girder type. Trim controlled by lifting planes.

Works No.	Name Trials	Length (m)	Beam (m)	Volume (mc)	Power (h.p.)	Speed (km)	Notes
1	Usuelli (August, 1910)	51	9.8	3,870	100	50	Excursion airship belonging to her builders. Car-girder type. One S. P. A. engine; twin-screws. Best endurance: 150 km. (Turin to Milan). Was partly wrecked by the storm when landing, on May 13th, 1913, near Musocco.

*Gas Capacity.

THE YAMADA *No. 2* (1910).

JAPAN

Army Airship Works, Tokorozawa.—Builders of airships to various designs.

Works No.	Name Trials	Length (m)	Beam (m)	Volume (mc)	Power (h.p.)	Speed (km)	Notes
1	(Building)	130		20,000	1,200	72	Army airship, structure type. Four engines. Designed endurance: 30 hrs. Crew: 20.

Yamada (Isaburo), Tokyo.—Builder of pressure airships to various designs.

Works No.	Name Trials	Length (m)	Beam (m)	Volume (mc)	Power (h.p.)	Speed (km)	Notes
1	No. 1 (1904)						Experimental airship of the kite-balloon type. Was not successful and was converted into a kite-balloon during the Russo-Japanese war. (Data wanted.)
2	No. 2 (1910)	35	7.5	1,400	50	22	Experimental airship of the car-girder type. One ballonet. One Maximotor engine; one pusher-screw. Was wrecked by the wind in March, 1911.
3	I (1911)	58	9.4	3,000	72		Japanese Army airship.—Car-girder type. Two Koerting engines; twin-screws. (Information regarding performances wanted.)
4	II (1912)	58	9.4	3,000	75		Japanese Army airship.—As above, excepting the power plant, which is one Koerting engine.

THE VASTREE (1910)

RUSSIA

Army Airship Works, Petrograd.—Builders of airships to various designs.

Works No.	Name Trials	Length (m)	Beam (m)	Volume (mc)	Power (h.p.)	Speed (km)	Notes
1	Outchebny (September, 1908)			1,800	50	35	Experimental airship, built to the designs of Captain A. Chabsky. Girderless pressure type. One Vivinus engine; one pusher-screw. Served for years as a training airship for the Russian Army.
2	Kretchet (1911)	70	14	5,680	200	50	Russian Army airship.—Built to Messrs. Lebaudy Frères' designs. Keel-girder, pressure type. Two Panhard-Levassor engines; twin-screws.
3	(Building)						Russian Army airship.—(Data and photo wanted.)

Danilewsky, Kharkoff.—Builder of two small pressure airships propelled by flapping wings which were operated by the pilot through a bicycle transmission. Various ascents were made in 1897 and 1898, but no practical results were achieved.

"Doux" Aircraft Works, Moskow.—Builders of airships to various designs.

Works No.	Name Trials	Length (m)	Beam (m)	Volume (mc)	Power (h.p.)	Speed (km)	Notes
1	Yastreb (1910)	50	13	2,500	70	47	Russian Army airship.—One Dansette-Gillet engine; one pusher-screw. (Photo wanted.)

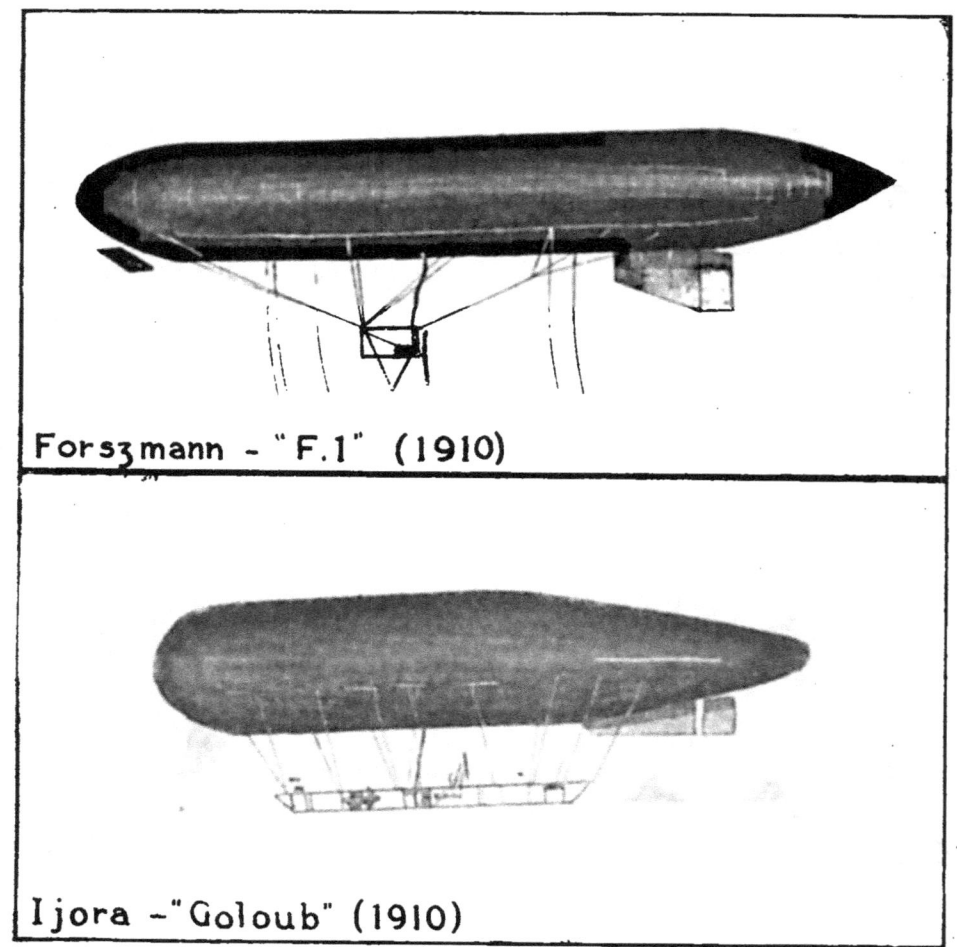

RUSSIA—Continued

Duflou & Constantinovitch, Petrograd.—Builders of pressure airships of the car-girder type. Trim controlled by lifting planes.

Works No.	Name Trials	Length (m)	Beam (m)	Volume (mc)	Power (h.p.)	Speed (km)	Notes
1	Kobtchik (1912)	48	9.5	2,150	90	50	Russian Army airship.—Two engines; two pairs of twin-screws. Built to modified designs of the Zodiac Co. (Photo wanted.)

Forszmann (v.), Petrograd.—Builder of pressure airships of the girderless type. Trim controlled by lifting planes. Riedinger hulls

Works No.	Name Trials	Length (m)	Beam (m)	Volume (mc)	Power (h.p.)	Speed (km)	Notes
1	F. 1 (1910)	37	6	800	40	37	Russian Army airship.—One Koerting engine; one pusher-screw.
2	F. 2 (1911)	35	6	600	25	35	Russian Army airship.—One Koerting engine; one pusher-screw.

Kostévitch, Petrograd.—Builder of a pressure airship of the keel-girder type, which was tested in November, 1908. (Photo and data wanted.)

"Ijora" Aircraft Works, Petrograd.—Builders of pressure airships of the car-girder type. Trim controlled by lifting planes.

Works No.	Name Trials	Length (m)	Beam (m)	Volume (mc)	Power (h.p.)	Speed (km)	Notes
1	Golub (1910)	46	9.5	2,270	75	50	Russian Army airship.—One Koerting engine; twin-screws.
2	Sokol (1911)	50	10	2,500	80	54	Russian Army airship.—One De Dion-Bouton engine; twin-screws.
3	Albatros (1914)			8,000	300	61	Russian Army airship.—Two Koerting engines; twin-screws. (Data and photo wanted.)

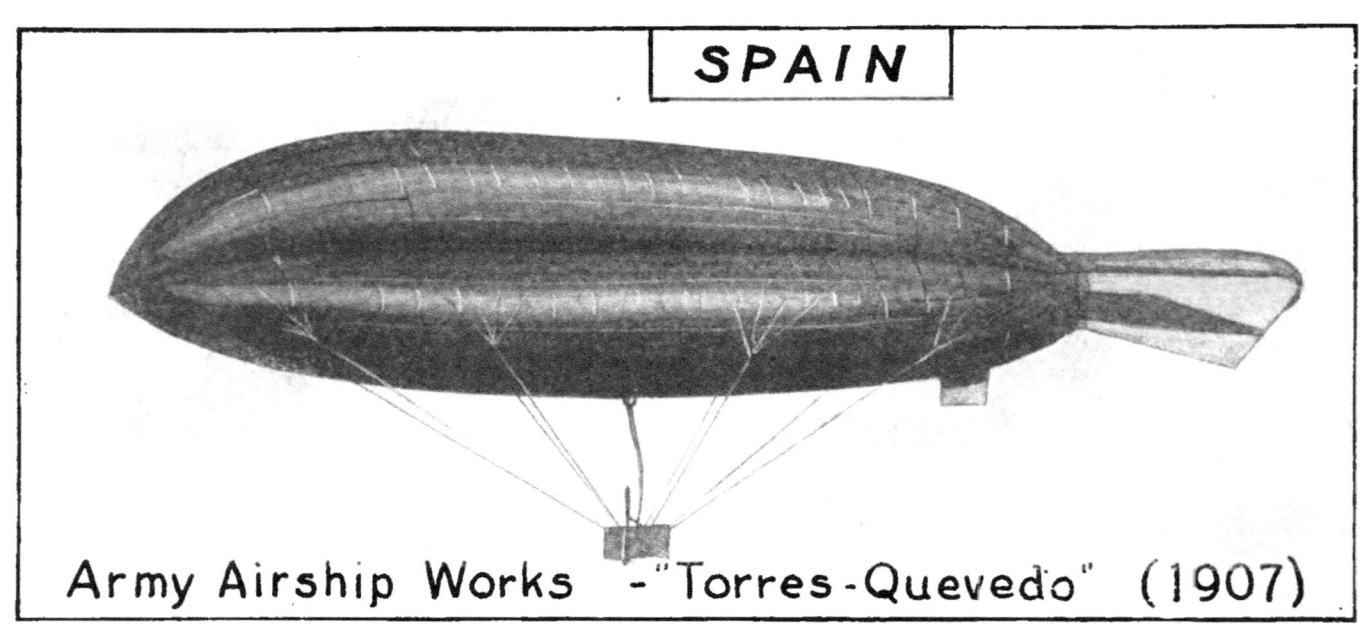

RUSSIA—Continued

Russo-Baltic Aircraft Works, Riga.—Builders of airships to various designs.

Works No.	Name Trials	Length (m)	Beam (m)	Volume (mc)	Power (h.p.)	Speed (km)	Notes
1	(Building)	80		13,000	320		Experimental airship of the Russian Army.—Structure type, built to the designs of General Kovanko. Two engines; two pairs of twin-screws.

SPAIN

Army Airship Works, Guadalajara.—Builders of airships to various designs.

Works No.	Name Trials	Length (m)	Beam (m)	Volume (mc)	Power (h.p.)	Speed (km)	Notes
1	Torrès-Quevedo (August, 1907)	36	6	960	48		Experimental airship, built to the designs of Sr. L. Torrès-Quevedo and Capt. A. Kindelàn for the Centro de Ensayos Aeronàuticos (Aeronautical Experiment Centre), created by the Spanish Chambers.—Tension-truss pressure type; two Antoinette engines; twin-screws. Trim controlled by ballonets and self-shifting car. The trials were sufficiently satisfactory to warrant the purchase of Sr. Torrès-Quevedo's patents by the Astra Co.
2	Alfonso XIII (1915)						Spanish Army airship.—Torrès-Quevedo type. Blew up on Aug. 10th, 1915, in the airship harbour of Guadalajara. (Data and photo wanted.)

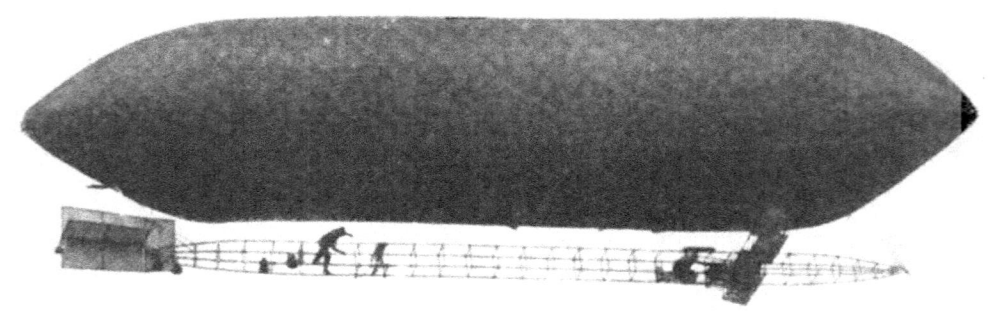

THE U. S. ARMY TRAINING AIRSHIP *No. 1* (1908).

UNITED STATES

Baldwin (Thomas Scott), New York.—Builder of pressure airships of the car-girder type. Trim controlled by lifting planes.

Works No.	Name Trials	Length (m)	Beam (m)	Volume (mc)	Power (h.p.)	Speed (km)	Notes
6	Baldwin-6 (1908)	29.1	5.8	580	20	25	Exhibition airship. Owner: Thos. S. Baldwin.—One Curtiss engine; one tractor-screw.
7	H. 1 (1908)	29.1	5.8	580	20	28	Touring airship of Capt. Hildebrandt, Berlin.—*Baldwin-6* type.
8	No. 1 (1908)	36	6	800	20	31	Training airship of the U. S. Army Signal Corps.—One Curtiss engine; one tractor-screw. Made only a limited number of ascents and was dismantled in 1910. Cost: $10,000.
9	Baldwin-9 (1909)	26.2	6.1	530	20	35	Exhibition airship. Owner: Thos. S. Baldwin.—One Curtiss engine; one tractor-screw.
10	Tomlinson (1909)	26.2	5.5	500	20	36	Exhibition airship. Owner: C. Tomlinson.—*Baldwin-9* type. The *Tomlinson* and the *Baldwin-9* participated in the Hudson-Fulton Celebration of Summer 1909.

Curtiss Aeroplane Company, Buffalo, N. Y.—Builders of airships to various designs.

Works No.	Name Trials	Length (m)	Beam (m)	Volume (mc)	Power (h.p.)	Speed (km)	Notes
1 2 3	DN-4 DN-5 (Building) DN-6	48.8	9.6	2,180	100	72	Coast patrol airships, U. S. Navy.—Girderless pressure type. Trim controlled by trimming tanks, lifting planes and ballonets (545 mc.). One Curtiss engine; one tractor-screw. Designed endurance: 10 hrs. at full speed; altitude: 2,300 m. Cost: $40,750 each.

THE U. S. NAVY TRAINING AIRSHIP *DN. 1* (1917).

UNITED STATES—Continued

Connecticut Aircraft Company, Bridgeport, Conn. (U. S. A.).—Builders of pressure airships to various designs.

Works No.	Name Trials	Length (m)	Beam (m)	Volume (mc)	Power (h.p.)	Speed (km)	Notes
1	DN-1 (April, 1917)	53.4	10.7	3,315	140	40	Training airship, U. S. Navy.—Cargirder type. Ballonet: 425 mc. One Sturtevant engine; twin-screws. Trim controlled by ballonets and lifting planes.—Authorized in 1915. Cost: $46,000.
2 3	DN-2 (Building) DN-3 (Building)	48.8	9.6	2,180	100	72	Coast patrol airships, U. S. Navy.—Girderless pressure type. Trim controlled by trimming tanks, lifting planes and ballonets (545 mc.). One Curtiss engine; one tractor-screw. Designed endurance: 10 hrs. at full speed; altitude: 2,300 m. Cost: $42,000 each.

Goodyear Tyre and Rubber Company, Akron (Ohio, U. S. A.).—Builders of airships to various designs.

Works No	Name Trials	Length (m)	Beam (m)	Volume (mc)	Power (h.p.)	Speed (km)	Notes
1	Akron (May, 1912)	88	15	9,800	280	50	Transatlantic airship, built to the designs of Mr. Melvin Vaniman. Keel-girder type pressure airship. Trim controlled by lifting planes, compensating ballonets and swivelling screws. "Hydrolevitor" for taking on water ballast. Two 100 h.p. and one 80 h.p. engines each driving one pair of twin-screws, the middle and rear pairs being

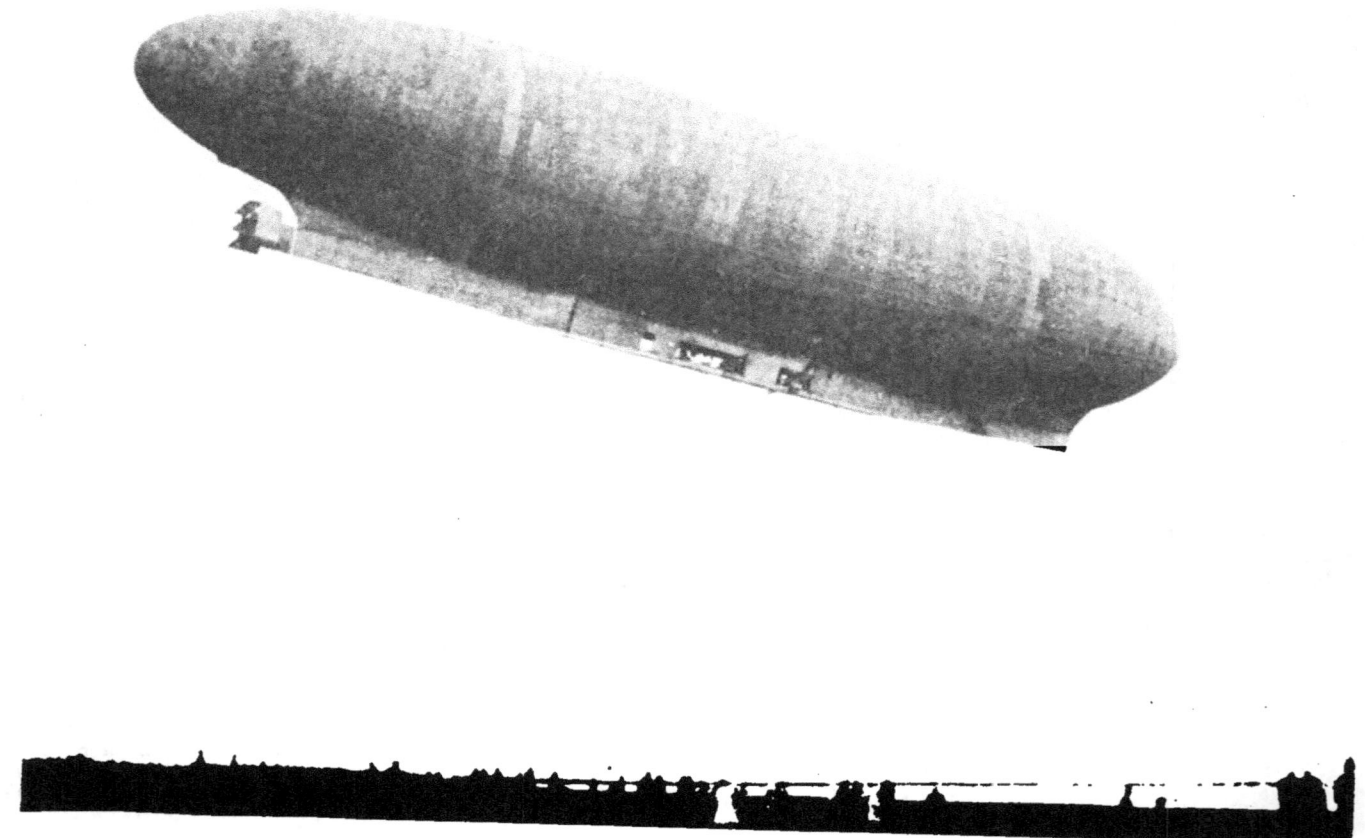

THE *AKRON* (1912).

UNITED STATES—Continued

Works No.	Name Trials	Length (m)	Beam (m)	Volume (mc)	Power (h.p.)	Speed (km)	Notes
							mounted to swivel. One 17 h.p. auxiliary engine driving the ballonet blowers and a dynamo working the wireless plant. Fitted with the lifeboat of W. Wellman's *America*. Blew up on July 2nd, 1912, over Atlantic City, owing probably to the insufficient capacity of the balloon valves. The crew of five, including Mr. Vaniman, were killed in the fall.
2—10	DN-7—DN-15 (Building)	48.8	9.6	2,180	100	72	Coast patrol airships, U. S. Navy.—Girderless pressure type. Trim controlled by lifting planes, trimming tanks and ballonets (545 mc.). One Curtiss engine; one tractor screw. Designed endurance: 10 hrs. at full speed; altitude: 2,300 m. Cost: $40,000 each. Best endurance for *DN-7* (May, 1917): 640 km. in 16 hrs.

Goodrich (B. F.) Company, Akron, Ohio.—Builders of airships to various designs.

Works No.	Name Trials	Length (m)	Beam (m)	Volume (mc)	Power (h.p.)	Speed (km)	Notes
1	DN-16 (Building)	48.8	9.6	2,180	100	72	Coast patrol airships, U. S. Navy.—Girderless pressure type. Trim controlled by lifting planes, trimming tanks and ballonets (545 mc.). One Curtiss engine; one tractor-screw. Designed endurance: 10 hrs. at full speed, altitude: 2,300 m. Cost: $41,500 each.
2	DN-17 (Building)						

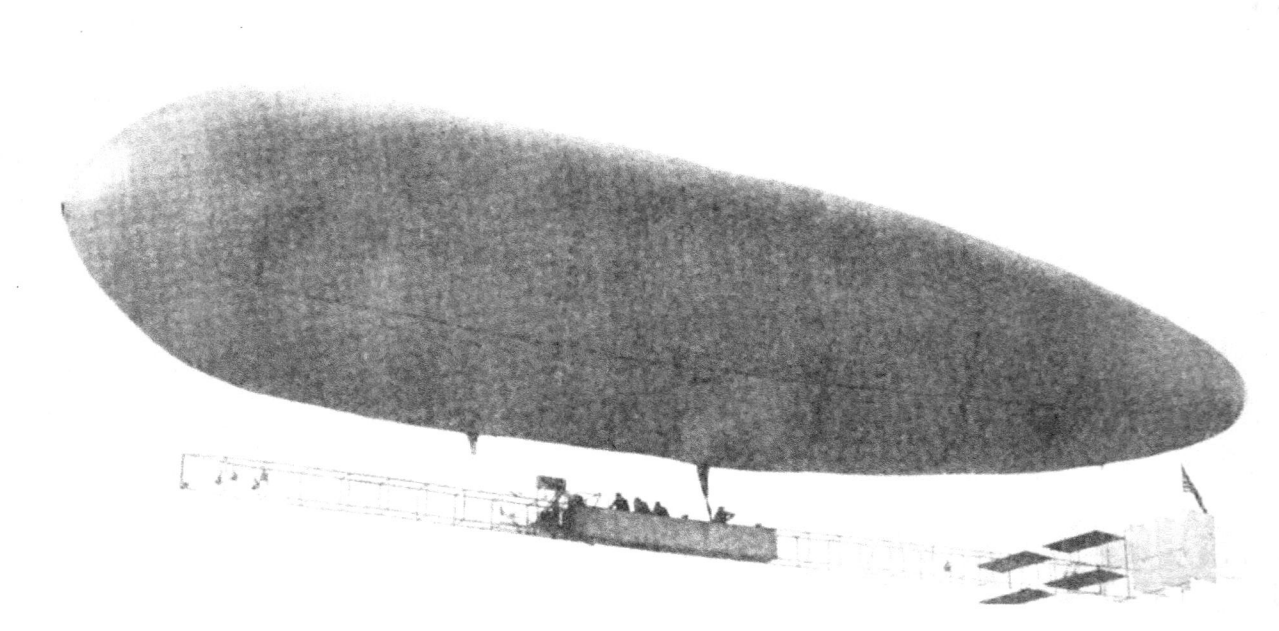

THE *PASADENA* (1913).

UNITED STATES—Continued

Knabenshue (Roy), Pasadena, Cal.—Builder of numerous airships of the car-girder, pressure type, all of which served exhibition purposes but one which is listed herewith.

Works No.	Name Trials	Length (m)	Beam (m)	Volume (mc)	Power (h.p.)	Speed (km)	Notes
	Pasadena (1913)	45.8	9.2	2,130	30	50	Excursion airship.—Designer: Mr. Charles F. Willard. One Hansen engine; twin-screws. Trim controlled by lifting planes. The *Pasadena* made in 1913 and 1914 numerous trips with passengers in California and near Chicago.

Knabenshue Aircraft Corporation, New York.—Builders of pressure airships.

National Airship Company, Berkeley, Cal.—Builders, to the designs of Mr. Morrell, of a girderless pressure airship.

Works No.	Name Trials	Length (m)	Beam (m)	Volume (mc)	Power (h.p.)	Speed (km)	Notes
1	Morrell (May, 1908)	157.5	10	12,580	180	?	Six Hansen engines; six pairs of twin-screws. No ballonet. Six cars. Disastrous trials: the airship lost her shape in mid-air and stranded on a row of houses, killing three and injuring six of the crew. Cost: $40,000.

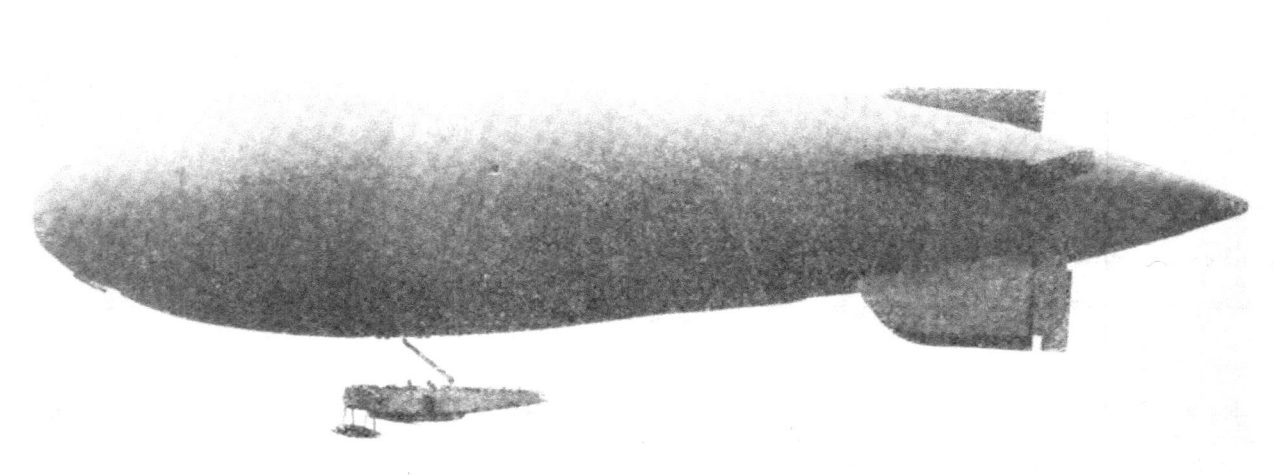

A U. S. NAVY SCOUT AIRSHIP (1917).

UNITED STATES—Continued

Rekar Airship Construction Company, Portland, Ore.—Builders of a structure airship.

Works No.	Name Trials	Length (m)	Beam (m)	Volume (mc)	Power (h.p.)	Speed (km)	Notes
1	Preble-Rekar	76.3	7.6	4,000			Was not completed.

Riggs & Rice, New York.—Builders of a pressure airship of the car-girder type. Designer, A. Leo Stevens.

Works No.	Name Trials	Length (m)	Beam (m)	Volume (mc)	Power (h.p.)	Speed (km)	Notes
1	American Eagle (November, 1909)	30.5	7.6	980	35		Experimental airship.—One Hansen engine; twin-screws and one tractor-screw. Was not successful, although short ascents were made.

Toliver Aerial Navigation Company, San Diego, Cal.—Builders of a pressure airship of the keel-girder type. Trim controlled by lifting planes.

Works No.	Name Trials	Length (m)	Beam (m)	Volume (mc)	Power (h.p.)	Speed (km)	Notes
1	Toliver (Laid down 1911)	76.3	12.2				Was not completed.

U. S. Army & Navy Joint Board, Washington, D. C.—The construction of an experimental structure airship, called the *DR-1*, has been decided upon in 1917.

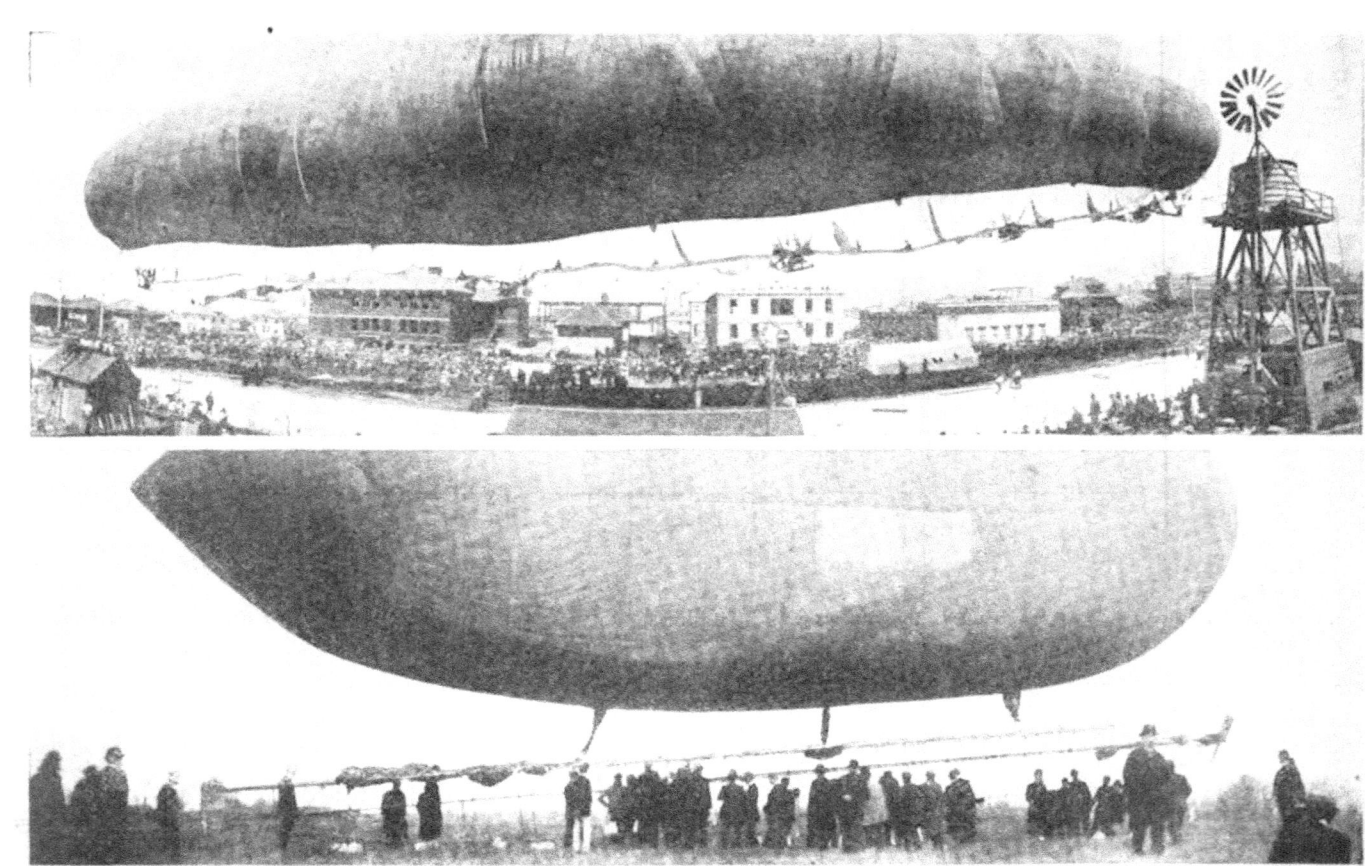

TOP—THE MORRELL (1908); BOTTOM—THE AMERICAN EAGLE (1909).

II. THE WORLD'S AIRSHIP PRODUCTION

II. THE WORLD'S AIRSHIP PRODUCTION
(VOLUME IN CUBIC METERS)

Country	1901	1902	1903	1904	1905
Austria	....	....	....	....	....
Belgium	....	....	....	....	....
Brazil	....	....	3,900	....	....
France	5,230	7,464	3,440	2,100	3,400
Germany	....	....	....	....	10,400
Great Britain	500	1,820	840	....	6,440
Italy	....	....	....	....	1,200
Japan	....	....	....	....	....
Russia	....	....	....	....	....
Spain	....	....	....	....	....
United States	....	....	....	....	....
Total	5,730	9,284	8,180	2,100	21,440

II. THE WORLD'S AIRSHIP PRODUCTION—Continued
(VOLUME IN CUBIC METERS)

Country	1906	1907	1908	1909	1910
Austria	....	....	....	3,150	4,800
Belgium	....	....	....	2,700	....
Brazil	....	....	....	....	....
France	3,930	10,700	7,540	21,950	43,155
Germany	13,730	16,600	39,500	25,720	50,350
Great Britain	....	2,400	....	1,200	5,140
Italy	....	....	2,750	5,065	8,780
Japan	....	....	....	....	1,400
Russia	....	....	1,800	....	5,570
Spain	....	960	....	....	....
United States	....	....	14,540	6,010	....
Total	17,660	30,660	66,130	65,795	118,195

II. THE WORLD'S AIRSHIP PRODUCTION—Continued
(VOLUME IN CUBIC METERS)

Country	1911	1912	1913	1914	1915
Austria	11,750	2,750	....	*	*
Belgium	....	....	....	....	*
Brazil	....	....	....	....	*
France	37,005	24,850	41,400	*	*
Germany	125,210	104,265	230,000	594,000**	1,031,000**
Great Britain	....	25,530	1,400	*	*
Italy	4,400	21,400	38,800	*	*
Japan	3,000	3,000	....	*	*
Russia	8,780	2,150	....	....	*
Spain	....	....	....	....	*
United States	....	9,800	2,130	....	....
Total	190,145	193,745	313,730	....	....

* No reliable information available.
** Approximate estimate, based on the productive capacity of the Schütte-Lanz and Zeppelin factories only.

II. THE WORLD'S AIRSHIP PRODUCTION—Continued
(VOLUME IN CUBIC METERS)

Country	1916	1917	1918	1919	1920
Austria	*				
Belgium	*				
Brazil	*				
France	*				
Germany	1,329,000**				
Great Britain	*				
Italy	*				
Japan	*				
Russia	*				
Spain	*				
United States					

* No reliable information available.
** Approximate estimate, based on the productive capacity of the Schütte-Lanz and Zeppelin factories only.

III. THE MILITARY AIRSHIP FLEETS

III. THE MILITARY AIRSHIP FLEETS *
On August 1st, 1914

BELGIUM
2 SCHOOL AIRSHIPS

La Belgique (1909-14), 5 tons; 120 h.p.; 52 km.—Vivinus.
Zodiac (1910-14), 2 tons; 50 h.p.; 40 km.—Zodiac.

FRANCE
7 FIRST CLASS AIRSHIPS

Tissandier (bldg.), 31 tons; 1,300 h.p.; 80 km.—Lebaudy.
Pilâtre-de-Rozier (bldg.) } 27 tons; 1,000 h.p.; 97 km.—Astra.
III (bldg.) .... }
IV (bldg.) } 23 tons; 1,400 h.p.; 85 km.—Clement-Bayard.
V (bldg.) }
VI (bldg.) } 25 tons; 1,000 h.p.; 80 km.—Zodiac.
VII (bldg.) }

6 SECOND CLASS AIRSHIPS

VIII (bldg.), 19 tons; 1,200 h.p.; 80 km.—Army Works.
Spiess (1913), 18 tons; 400 h.p.; 70 km.—Zodiac.
Commandant-Coutelle (1913), 11 tons; 400 h.p.; 62 km.—Zodiac.
Dupuy-de-Lôme (1912), 10 tons; 260 h.p.; 55 km.—Clément-Bayard.
Adjudant-Vincenot (1911-13), 10 tons; 260 h.p.; 56 km.—Clément-Bayard.
Lieut. Selle-de-Beauchamp (1910), 11 tons; 200 h.p.; 45 km.—Lebaudy.

---

* The airships herewith listed are divided into vessels of *first class*, corresponding to the French *cruiser* class and to the Italian *grande* (large) class; *second class*, corresponding to the French *éclaireur* (scout) class and to the Italian *medium* class; and *third class*, corresponding to the French *vedette* class and to the Italian *piccolo* (small) class.

III. THE MILITARY AIRSHIP FLEETS—Continued

4 THIRD CLASS AIRSHIPS

E. Montgolfier (1913), 7 tons; 160 h.p.; 69 km.—Clément-Bayard.
Fleurus (1912), 8 tons; 160 h.p.; 60 km.—Army Works.
Capitaine-Ferber (1911), 7 tons; 220 h.p.; 56 km.—Zodiac.
Capitaine-Marchal (1910), 8 tons; 160 h.p; 45 km.—Lebaudy.

GERMANY
15 FIRST CLASS AIRSHIPS

L. 4, L. 7 (bldg.), 33 tons; 1,080 h.p.; 80 km.—Schutte-Lanz.
L. 3 (1914), L. 5, L. 6 (bldg.); 30 tons; 800 h.p.; 85 km.—Zeppelin.
S. L. II (1914), 25 tons; 720 h.p.; 87 km.—Schütte-Lanz.
Z. VII (1913), Z. VIII, Z. IX, Z. X (bldg.); 24 tons; 600 h.p.; 80 km.—Zeppelin.
Z. IV, Z. V, Z. VI (1913), 22 tons; 540 h.p.; 77 km.—Zeppelin.
Z. III (1912), Z. II (1910–11), 20 tons; 450 h.p.; 76 km.—Zeppelin.

4 SECOND CLASS AIRSHIPS

P. V (1914), 13 tons; 400 h.p.; 75 km.—Parseval.
M. IV (1913), 14 tons; 450 h.p.; 75 km.—Army Works.
P. IV (1913), 11 tons; 360 h.p.; 71 km.—Parseval.
P. III (1911), 11 tons; 400 h.p.; 65 km.—Parseval.

2 THIRD CLASS AIRSHIPS

P. II (1910), 9 tons; 360 h.p.; 51 km.—Parseval.
M. I (1912), 7 tons; 150 h.p.; 45 km.—Army Works.

III. THE MILITARY AIRSHIP FLEETS—Continued

GREAT BRITAIN
2 FIRST CLASS AIRSHIPS

No. 15 (bldg.), 27 tons.—Armstrong.
No. ? (bldg.), 25 tons; 1,500 h.p.—Vickers & Maxim.

9 SECOND CLASS AIRSHIPS

Three of 13 tons; 200 h.p.; 72 km.; building.—Armstrong-Forlanini.
Three of 13 tons; 360 h.p.; 75–80 km; building.—Vickers-Parseval.
No. 3 (1913) and one building; 10 tons; 400 h.p.; 82 km.—Astra.
No. 2 (1913), 11 tons, 360 h.p.; 68 km.—Parseval.

4 SCHOOL AIRSHIPS

Delta (1912), Eta (1913); 5 tons; 200 h.p.; 45 km.—R. Aircraft Factory.
Gamma (1910); 2 tons; 100 h.p.; 45 km.—R. Aircraft Factory.
Willows (1912); 1 ton; 35 h.p.; 45 km.—Willows.

ITALY
3 FIRST CLASS AIRSHIPS

G. 1–G. 2 (bldg.), 22 tons; 800 h.p.; 80 km.—Army Works.
One, unnamed, building, 27 tons; 1,000 h. p.; 100 km.—Forlanini.

6 SECOND CLASS AIRSHIPS

V. 1 (bldg.), 16 tons; 400 h.p.; 90 km.—Army Works.
M. 5, M. 4 (bldg.), M. 3, M. 2 (1913), M. 1 (1912); 13 tons, 500 h.p.; 70 km.—Army Works.

III. THE MILITARY AIRSHIP FLEETS—Continued

2 THIRD CLASS AIRSHIPS
P. 4 (1912), **P. 5** (1913), 5 tons; 160 h.p.; 62–65 km.—Army Works.

JAPAN
1 SECOND CLASS AIRSHIP
Yuhi (1912); 10 tons; 300 h.p.; 66 km.—Parseval.

RUSSIA
3 FIRST CLASS AIRSHIPS
Three 25 ton, 1,000 h.p. airships building at Astra, Clément-Bayard and Zodiac respectively.

6 SECOND CLASS AIRSHIPS
Albatros (1914), 10 tons; 300 h.p.; 61 km.—Ijora.
"B" (1913), 11 tons; 400 h.p.; 63 km.—Astra.
"C" (1913), 11 tons; 360 h.p.; 67 km.—Parseval.
"D" (1913), 10 tons; 360 h.p.; 55 km.—Clément-Bayard.
Two building, at Ijora and Russo-Baltic, respectiv ly.

2 THIRD CLASS AIRSHIPS
Kretchet (1911), 6 tons, 200 h. p.; 50 km.—Army Works.
Griff (1910), 8 tons, 220 h.p.; 59 km.—Parseval.

6 SCHOOL AIRSHIPS
Bercout, Korchoune, Kobtchik, Sokol, Tchaïka, Yastreb (1909–12), 2–4 tons, 60–105 h.p.; 47–54 km.

TURKEY
1 SCHOOL AIRSHIP
No. 1 (1910–13), 2 tons; 50 h.p.; 40 km.—Parseval.

**SCALE-DRAWN SILHOUETTES
OF THE PRINCIPAL GERMAN AIRSHIP TYPES**

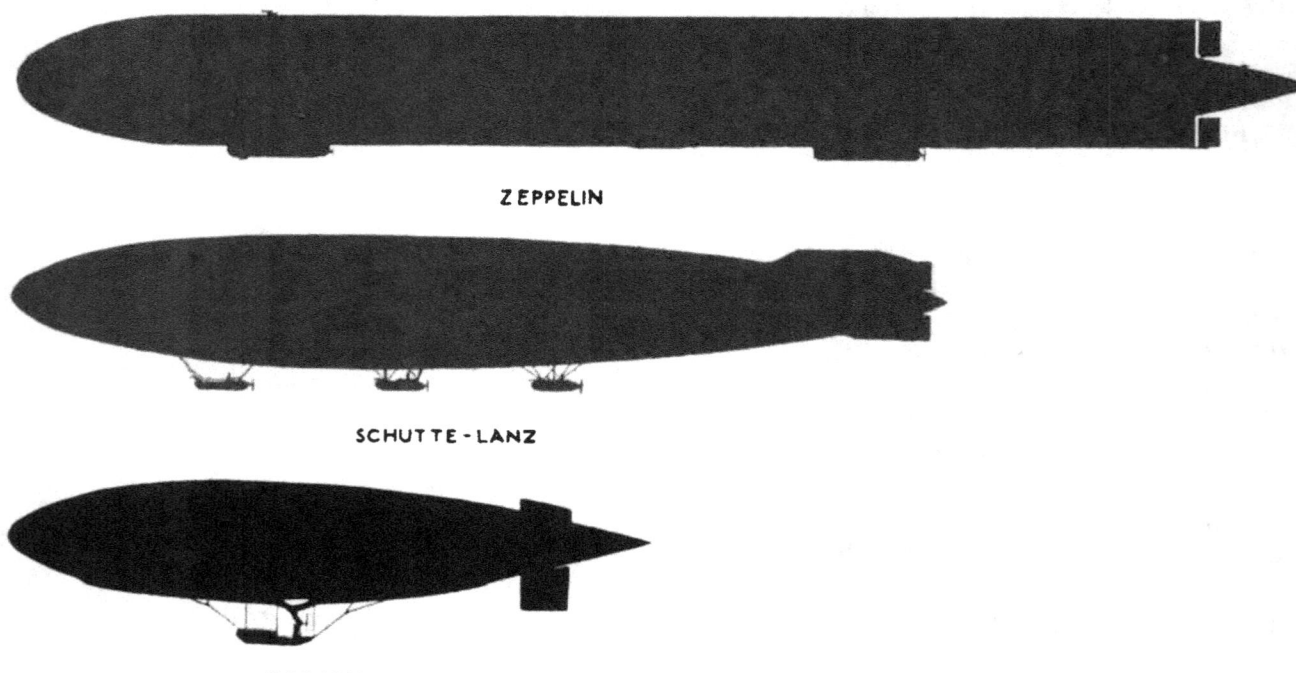

IV. COMPARATIVE STRENGTH OF THE MILITARY AIRSHIP FLEETS

IV. COMPARATIVE STRENGTH OF THE MILITARY AIRSHIP FLEETS
On August 1st, 1914

Germany	13 airships of 237 tons, commissioned. 8 airships of 211 tons, building.
France	9 airships of 90 tons, commissioned. 8 airships of 200 tons, building.
Russia	12 airships of 74 tons, commissioned. 5 airships of 95 tons, building.
Italy	5 airships of 49 tons, commissioned. 6 airships of 113 tons, building.
Great Britain	6 airships of 34 tons, commissioned. 9 airships of 140 tons, building.
Japan	1 airship of 10 tons, commissioned. No airship building.
United States	No airship commissioned No airship building.

V. AIRSHIP LOSSES OF THE ALLIES

V. AIRSHIP LOSSES OF THE ALLIES
August 1st, 1914—June 1st, 1917
(Compiled from Official Data)

FRANCE

No.	Name	Date	Place	Cause of Loss
1	D...	Sept., '14	France	Accident.
2	Alsace	10-3-'15	Rethel, France	Shot down by German guns.
3	T...	5-13-'16	Porto Torres, Italy	Caught fire and blew up, killing the crew of six.
4		2-25-'17	Sarreguemines, Lorraine	Shot down by German guns.

GREAT BRITAIN

No.	Name	Date	Place	Cause of Loss
1		7-28-'15	Wormwood Scrubs, England	Blew up in shed during inflation.
2		4-21-'17	Strait of Dover	Shot down by German seaplane.

ITALY

No.	Name	Date	Place	Cause of Loss
1	M. 2	6-8-'15	Fiume, Hungary	Shot down by Austrian seaplane.
2	P. 4	8-5-'15	Pola, Austria	Shot down by Austrian seaplane.
3	M. 3	5-4-'16	Gorizia, Italy	Caught fire and blew up, killing the crew of four.
4	P. 5	8-12-'16	Campalto, Italy	Destroyed in shed by Austrian seaplanes.

RUSSIA

No.	Name	Date	Place	Cause of Loss
1		Apr. 27, '17	Stanislawow, Galicia	Shot down by Austrian guns; fell in Russian lines. Crew saved.

VI. GERMANY'S AIRSHIP LOSSES

VI. GERMANY'S AIRSHIP LOSSES

(August 1st, 1914—July 1st, 1917)

OFFICIAL LIST

The following list includes only airships: (1) officially claimed by the Allies as having been captured or destroyed by their forces and (2) officially acknowledged by Germany as having been lost.

No.	Name	Date	Place	Cause of Loss
1	Z. VIII	Aug. 22, 1914	Badonviller, France	Shot down by French artillery; 4 of crew taken prisoner.
2	?	Sept. 6, 1914	Seradz, Russia	Captured on her moorings by a troop of Cossacks. Crew taken prisoner.
3	Z. V	Sept. 28, 1914	Warsaw, Russia	Shot down by Russian artillery. Crew of 10 taken prisoner.
4	P. V	Jan. 1, 1915	Libava, Russia	Shot down by Russian artillery. Crew of 7 taken prisoner.
5	L. 3	Feb. 17, 1915	Fanö Island, Denmark	Stranded and broke up. Crew of 16 were interned.
6	L. 4	Feb. 17, 1915	Esbjerg, Denmark	Foundered off the coast. Four of the crew were lost, 12 were interned.
7	L. 8	March 5, 1915	Tirlemont, Belgium	Broke up on landing by night.
8	LZ. 37	June 9, 1915	Ghent, Belgium	Destroyed in mid-air by British aeroplane. Crew killed in fall.
9	L. ?	Aug. 10, 1915	Ostende, Belgium	Destroyed by British seaplanes while berthing.
10	Z. ?	Aug. 24, 1915	Vilna, Russia	Shot down by Russian artillery. Crew of 10 taken prisoner.
11	Z. ?	Dec. 5, 1915	Kalkun, Russia	Shot down by Russian artillery. Crew killed in fall.
12	L. 19	Feb. 2, 1916	North Sea	Damaged by artillery, while raiding England. Foundered with crew of 16.
13	LZ. 77	Feb. 21, 1916	Révigny, France	Shot down by French artillery. Crew of 15 killed in fall.
14	L. 15	Apr. 1, 1916	Kentish Knock, England	Shot down by British aeroplane. Seventeen of crew taken prisoner; 1 killed in fall.
15	L. 20	May 3, 1916	Stavanger, Norway	Stranded and broke up. Sixteen of crew interned; 3 killed in fall.

VI. GERMANY'S AIRSHIP LOSSES—Continued

No.	Name	Date	Place	Cause of Loss
16	L. 7	May 4, 1916	Schleswig Coast, Germany	Shot down by British warships. Seven of crew taken prisoner.
17.	LZ. 85	May 5, 1916	Salonica, Greece	Shot down by Allied warships. Crew of 14 taken prisoner.
18	L. 21	Sept. 3, 1916	Cuffley, England	Shot down by British aeroplane. Crew of 18 killed in fall.
19	L. 32	Sept. 24, 1916	Essex County, England	Shot down by British aeroplane. Crew of 22 killed in fall.
20	L. 33	Sept. 24, 1916	Essex County, England	Shot down by British aeroplane. Crew of 22 taken prisoner.
21	L. 31	Oct. 1, 1916	Potter's Bar, England	Shot down by British aeroplane. Crew of 19 killed in fall.
22	L. ?	Nov. 27, 1916	Off Durham Coast, England	Shot down by British aeroplanes. Crew killed in fall.
23	L. ?	Nov. 28, 1916	Norfolk Coast, England	Shot down by British aeroplanes. Crew killed in fall.
24	L. 39	M'ch 17, 1917	Compiègne, France	Shot down by French artillery. Crew of 19 killed in fall.
25	L. 22	May 14, 1917	North Sea	Shot down by British seaplane. Crew killed in fall.
26	L. 43	June 14, 1917	North Sea	Shot down by British warships. Crew killed in fall.
27	Z. 48	June 17, 1917	East Coast of England	Shot down by British aeroplane. Five of the crew were taken prisoner; the remainder were killed in the fall.

SUPPLEMENTARY LIST

The following list includes airships semi-officially or privately reported to have been destroyed by Allied forces or to have been otherwise lost. No official confirmation of these losses is presently available, but the sources of information appear on the main as fairly reliable.

No.	Name	Date	Place	Cause of Loss
1	Z. ?	Aug. 6, 1914	Metz, Germany	Bombed in shed by French aeroplane.
2	Z. ?	Oct. 10, 1914	Düsseldorf, Germany	Bombed in shed by British aeroplanes.
3	LZ. 31	Nov. 21, 1914	Friedrichshafen, Germany	Bombed in shed by British aeroplanes.
4	P. ?	Dec. 24, 1914	Brussels, Belgium	Bombed in shed by British aeroplane.
5	P. ?	Dec. 25, 1914	Cuxhaven, Germany	Bombed in shed by British seaplanes.
6	?	Jan. 23, 1915	North Sea	Foundered during a storm.
7	?	Feb. 26, 1915	Pola, Austria	Foundered during a storm.

VI. GERMANY'S AIRSHIP LOSSES—Continued

No.	Name	Date	Place	Cause of Loss
8	?	M'ch 5, 1915	Cologne, Germany	Broke up on landing in a storm.
9	?	M'ch 5, 1915	Off Calais, France	Lost with all on board.
10	Z. ?	Apr. 12, 1915	Thielt, Belgium	Broke up on landing. Eleven of crew killed.
11	?	Apr. 26, 1915	Gontrode, Belgium	Bombed in shed by French aeroplanes.
12	?	May 13, 1915	Gierlesche, Belgium	Broke up on stranding in a wood.
13	?	May 21, 1915	Königsberg, Prussia	Broke away, unmanned. Foundered off Heligoland.
14	LZ.	June 7, 1915	Evere, Belgium	Bombed in shed by British aeroplanes.
15	P. ?	June 16, 1915	Adamello, Austria	Broke up on stranding against a mountain. Crew killed.
16	?	Aug. 17, 1915	North Sea	Foundered on returning from a raid on England.
17	?	Sept. 8, 1915	Brussels, Belgium	Broke up on berthing during a storm. Four of crew killed.
18	?	Oct. 13, 1915	Saint-Hubert, Belgium	Blew up in mid-air. Crew killed in fall.
19	L. 18	Nov. 17, 1915	Töndern, Germany	Blew up in shed, having accidentally been set on fire.
20	?	Nov., 1915	Grodno, Russia	Damaged by Russian artillery; broke up on landing.
21	Z. 28	Nov., 1915	Hamburg, Germany	Foundered during a storm.
22	P. ?	Nov., 1915	Bitterfeld, Germany	Broke up on landing.
23	?	Jan. 30, 1916	Mainvault, Belgium	Damaged by French aeroplane over Paris; broke up on landing.
24	?	Apr. 26, 1916	Bruges, Belgium	Bombed in mid-air by French aeroplane.
25	?	May 10, 1916	Veles, Serbia	Broke up on landing during a storm.
26	?	July 20, 1916	Tukkum, Russia	Damaged by Russian artillery, over Riga; broke up on landing.
27	?	Sept. 3, 1916	Off Sylt, Germany	Damaged by British artillery while raiding London; foundered.
28	?	Sept. 22, 1916	Rheinau, Germany	Bombed in shed by French aeroplanes.
29	?	Nov. 21, 1916	Mayence, Germany	Wrecked by a storm. Twenty-seven of the crew were killed, 1 was saved.
30	?	Dec. 28, 1916	Töndern, Germany	Collided, while berthing.
31	?	Dec. 28, 1916	Töndern, Germany	
32	?	Apr. 1, 1917	Odobesci, Roumania	Bombed by Russian aeroplanes.
33	?	Apr. 21, 1917	Duisburg, Germany	Wrecked by a storm. Entire crew killed.

VII. THE GERMAN AIRSHIP RAIDS ON GREAT BRITAIN

VII. THE GERMAN AIRSHIP RAIDS ON GREAT BRITAIN
(List closed on July 1st, 1917)

1915

Date	Raid On	Killed	Injured
Jan. 19	Yarmouth and District	4	9
Apr. 14	Tyneside	—	2
Apr. 15	Lowestoft and East Coast	—	—
Apr. 29	Ipswich and Bury St. Edmunds	—	—
May 10	Southend	1	1
May 16	Ramsgate	2	8
May 27	Southend	3	2
May 31	Outer London	6	3
June 4	East and Southeast Coasts	24	40
June 6	East Coast.—Zeppelin LZ. 38 destroyed on return trip near Ghent	5	40
June 15	North-East Coast	16	40
Aug. 9	East Coast.—Zeppelin L. 10 destroyed on return trip off Ostende	15	14
Aug. 12	East Coast	6	23
Aug. 17	Eastern Counties	10	36
Sept. 7	Eastern Counties	17	43
Sept. 8	Eastern Counties and London District	20	86
Sept. 11	East Coast	—	—
Sept. 12	East Coast	—	—
Sept. 13	East Coast	—	—
Oct. 13	London Area and Eastern Counties	56*	114†
	*15 soldiers. †13 soldiers.		
	Total	1~5	459

1916

Date	Raid On	Killed	Injured
Jan. 31	Norfolk, Suffolk, Lincolnshire, Leicestershire, Staffordshire and Derbyshire.—Zeppelin L. 19, damaged by defense, foundered on return trip in the North Sea	67	101
M'ch 5	Yorkshire, Lincolnshire, Rutland, Huntingdon, Cambridgeshire, Norfolk, Essex, and Kent	18	52
M'ch 31	Eastern Counties and North-East Coast	43	66

VII. THE GERMAN AIRSHIP RAIDS ON GREAT BRITAIN—Continued

1916

Date	Raid On	Killed	Injured
Apr. 1	North-East Coast—Zeppelin L. 15 brought down in Thames.	16	100
Apr. 2	South-Eastern Counties of Scotland.	10	11
Apr. 4	East Coast.	—	—
Apr. 5	North-East Coast	1	8
Apr. 24	Norfolk and Suffolk.	—	1
Apr. 25	Essex and Kent.	—	—
Apr. 26	East Kent Coast.	—	—
May 2	North-East Coast of England and South-East Coast of Scotland.	9	27
July 29	Lincolnshire and Norfolk.	—	—
July 31	Southeastern and Eastern Counties.	—	—
Aug. 3	Eastern and Southeastern Counties.	—	—
Aug. 9	East and North-East Coast.	8	17
Aug. 24	Northeastern Coast.	—	—
Aug. 25	Southeastern Coast and London Area.	8	36
Sept. 2–3	Eastern Counties and London by large number of airships.—Schütte-Lanz L. 21 brought down at Cuffley.	2	11
Sept. 23–24	Lincolnshire, Eastern Counties and London by 14 or 15 airships.—Zeppelin L. 32 destroyed, L. 33 captured in Essex.	38	125
Sept. 25–26	East and North Coasts.	36	37
Oct. 1–2	East Coast and London District by 10 airships.—Zeppelin L. 31 brought down at Potters Bar.	1	1
Nov. 27–28	Northeastern and Norfolk Coast.—One Zeppelin destroyed a mile off Durham coast, and another nine miles off Norfolk coast.	4	37
		241	620
	Total for 1915 and 1916.	426	1,079

1917

Date	Raid On	Killed	Injured
M'ch. 16–17	S. E. Coast and London Area.—Zeppelin L. 39 brought down on return trip, near Compiègne, by French gunners.	—	—
May 23–24	Eastern counties by 5 airships	1	—
June 16–17	Kent and East Anglia by 2 airships.—Zeppelin Z. 48 destroyed on the East Coast.	2	16

THE END OF A RAIDER.

VIII. THE COMMERCIAL AIRSHIP FLEETS OF 1914

THE *SCHWABEN* OF THE DELAG LINE, AND HER ACCOMMODATIONS.

VIII. THE COMMERCIAL AIRSHIP FLEETS OF 1914

FRANCE

Compagnie Générale Transaérienne, Paris.—Established in March, 1909, for the commercial exploitation of Astra airships. Fleet: *Ville-de-Nancy* (1909), 4 tons, and *Ville-de-Pau* (1910), 5 tons. Both dismantled. One 10 ton airship ordered in 1913.

No balance sheet available.

GERMANY

"Delag" Line (Deutsche Luftschiffahrt Aktien-Gesellschaft), Frankfort-on-the-Main.—Established in November, 1909, for the commercial exploitation of Zeppelin airships. Fleet: *Deutschland* (1910), 21 tons; *LZ. 6* (1908), 18 tons; *Deutschland-II* (1911), 21 tons; *Schwaben* (1911), 20 tons; all lost. *Viktoria-Luise* (1912), *Hansa* (1912), *Sachsen* (1913), all of 21 tons. The three latter were chartered in 1914 by the German Navy and placed in commission as training airships.

BALANCE SHEET, 1910-13

Year	1910	1911	1912	1913
Number of airships commissioned	2([1])	2([2])	3([3])	3([4])
Gross tonnage (total lift)	39	41	62	63
Total horse-power	690	810	1,080	1,530
Number of days commissioned	35	136	302	353
Number of voyages	41	158	392	737
Distance travelled (in km.)	4,167	20,330	52,924	63,365
Time travelled	93 h. 41 m.	360 h. 38 m.	932 h. 9 m.	1,169 h. 42 m.
Number of passengers and crews carried	868	3,263	8,299	14,010
Number of airships lost	2([1])	1([5])	1([6])	—
Passengers killed	—	—	—	—
Passengers injured	—	—	—	—

([1]) *Deutschland* and *LZ. 6*.
([2]) *Deutschland II* and *Schwaben*.
([3]) *Schwaben, Viktoria-Luise* and *Hansa*.
([4]) *Viktoria-Luise, Hansa* and *Sachsen*.
([5]) *Deutschland II*.
([6]) *Schwaben*.

IX. THE WORLD'S AIRSHIP SHEDS

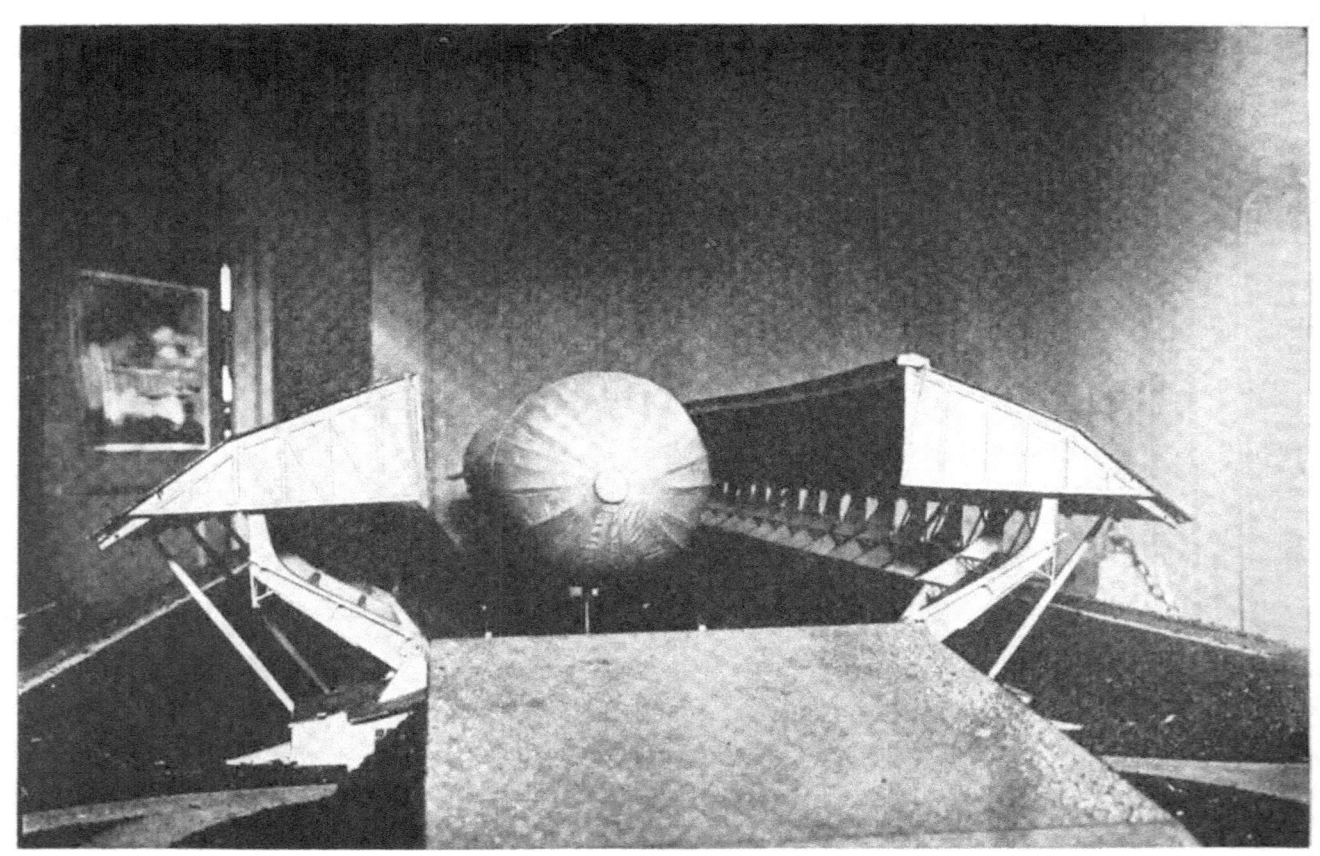

MODEL OF A GERMAN AIRSHIP SHED WITH DISAPPEARING ROOF.

IX. THE WORLD'S AIRSHIP SHEDS

Dimensions are given in metres (m).
In the column "Type": Dem. = demountable; Sta. = stationary; Rev. = revolving; Flo. = floating.

AUSTRIA

Place	Owner	Length (m)	Width (m)	Height (m)	Type	Year
Budapest	Army	70	20	18	Sta.	1911
Fischamend (Vienna)	"	70	20	18	"	1909
"	"	70	20	18	"	1911
"	"	120	25	20	"	1913
Innsbruck	"					1914
Lemberg (or Lwoff)	"					1914
Prague (or Praha)	"					1914
Sarayevo	"					1914
Trieste	"	100			"	1913

BELGIUM

Place	Owner	Length (m)	Width (m)	Height (m)	Type	Year
Wilryck (Antwerp)	Army	90	18	20	Sta.	1911
"	"	70	20	20	"	1912

(Note.—During the German occupation of Belgium a large number of airship sheds have been erected, particularly at Brussels, Evere, Ghent, Liège, Namur, Ostende and Wavre, most of which are over 150 m. long and of permanent character. The sheds of Wilryck have, furthermore, been lengthened.)

AIRSHIP SHED AT LA MOTTE-BREUIL (FRANCE).

IX. THE WORLD'S AIRSHIP SHEDS—Continued

FRANCE

Place	Owner	Length (m)	Width (m)	Height (m)	Type	Year
Beauval (Meaux)	Army	70			Sta.	1909
Belfort	"	100				1911
"	"	100				1911
"	"	100				1912
"	"	100				1912
Chalais-Meudon	"	130			Sta.	1906–13
"	"	140			"	1906–13
Châlons-sur-Marne	"	70			"	1909
"	"	100			"	1909
"	"	70			Dem.	1909
"	"	70			"	1909
"	"	70			"	1909
Epinal	"	100			Sta.	1912
Issy-les-Moulineaux	Astra	90	20	20	"	1908
"	Clément-Bayard	70	20	18	"	1909
La Motte-Breuil	" "	80	20	18	"	1909
"	" "					1914
Maubeuge	Army	80			"	1912
Moisson	Lebaudy	70			"	1900
"	"	60			"	1905
"	Army	130	38	30	"	1911
Nancy	"	70			"	1908
Pau	Astra	80			"	1910
Reims	Army	100			Sta.	1911
"	"	100			"	1911
"	"	130	30	20	Rev.	1914
Sartrouville	Astra	90	20	20	Sta.	1906
Saint-Cyr	Zodiac	60			"	1911
"	"	160	25	24	"	1913
Toul	Army	100			"	1912
Verdun	"	100			"	1911
"	"	100			"	1911

AIRSHIP SHED AT MANNHEIM (GERMANY).

IX. THE WORLD'S AIRSHIP SHEDS—Continued
GERMANY

Place	Owner	Length (m)	Width (m)	Height (m)	Type	Year
Aix-la-Chapelle (Aachen)	Army	150			Rev.	1914
Allenstein	"	150				1914
Baden-Oos	Delag Line	158	25	25	Sta.	1910
Berlin-Biesdorf	Siemens-Schuckert	135	25	25	Rev.	1909
Berlin-Jungfernheide	Army	150	50	30	Sta.	1913
Berlin-Johannistal	City	82	25	25	"	1908
"	"	163	45	28.5	"	1911
Berlin-Tegel	Army	50	18	20	"	1905
"	"	70	22		"	1907
"	"	101	25	25	"	1910
Bitterfeld	L. F. G.	75	25	25	"	1908
"	"	100	33	25	"	1909
Braunschweig	City	180	35	28	"	1914
Bremen	Delag Line	140	40	25	"	1913
Breslau	Army	150	40	25	"	1913
Cannstadt	Delag Line	150	40	25	"	1914
Carlsruhe		150	40	25	"	project
Cologne (Köln)-Bickendorf	Army	150	50	27.5	"	1909
Cologne-Nippes	Clouth	40	16	12.5	"	1909
Cuxhaven	Navy	180	75	30	Rev.	1913
Darmstadt	Army	150	50	30	"	1914
Dresden	City	191.6	58	33	Sta.	1914
Düsseldorf	"	152	25	24	"	1910
Emden	Navy	150	25	25	Rev.	1914
Frankfort-on-the-Main	Delag Line	160	30	24	Sta.	1911
Friedrichshafen	Zeppelin Co.	180	46	20	"	1908
"	"	250				1915
Gotha	City	176	26	26	"	1910
Graudenz	Army	150			Rev.	1914
Hannover	City	150	25	25	"	1914
Hamburg-Fuhlsbüttel	Private	80	35	25	Sta.	1911
"	City	165	51	32	"	1911
Helgoland	Navy	180	60	30	Rev.	1914
"	"				"	1915
Kiel	Private	170	30	25	Sta.	1910
Königsberg	Army	170	42	38	"	1911
Lahr	"	150	40	25	Rev.	1914
Leichlingen	Private	80	23	24	Sta.	1909

AIRSHIP SHED AT FRANKFORT-ON-THE-MAIN (GERMANY)

IX. THE WORLD'S AIRSHIP SHEDS—Continued

Place	Owner	Length (m)	Width (m)	Height (m)	Type	Year
Leipzig-Lindental	Private	120	25	20	Sta.	1911
Leipzig-Mockau	City	194	69	32.5	"	1914
Liegnitz	Army	150	50	30	"	1914
Mannheim-Rheinau	Schütte-Lanz	150	28	25	"	1910
"	Army				Rev.	1914
Mayence (Mainz)	City					project
Metz	Army	150	28	25	Sta.	1910
"	"	150	28	25	"	1911
Munich	Private	80	25	25	"	1912
"	Army				Rev.	1914
Posen	"	150				1914
Potsdam	Zeppelin Co.	175	50	35	"	1911
"	"				"	1914
Putzig	Navy				"	1914
Schneidemühl	Army	150			"	1914
Strasbourg	"	150	28	25	Sta.	1910
Stuttgart	City	150				1914
Thorn	Army	150	40	25		1913
Töndern	Navy	180	60		Rev.	1914
"	"	180	60		"	1915
"					"	1915
Treves (Trier)	Army	176	40	35	Sta.	1914
Wanne	Private	100	32	28	"	1912
Wilhelmshaven	Navy	180			Rev.	1915

GREAT BRITAIN

Place	Owner	Length (m)	Width (m)	Height (m)	Type	Year
Barrow-in-Furness	Vickers	164	45	33	Sta.	1911
Brighton	Army	60			"	1911
Farnborough	"	60			"	1909
"	"	90			"	1910
"	"	115			"	1911
Hoo-on-Medway	Navy	164	45	33	"	1914
Kingsnorth	"	164	45	33	"	1914
Wormwood Scrubbs	Private	100			"	1911
"	"	60			"	1910

REVOLVING SHED AT BERLIN-BIESDORF (GERMANY).

IX. THE WORLD'S AIRSHIP SHEDS—Continued

HOLLAND

Place	Owner	Length (m)	Width (m)	Height (m)	Type	Year
Soesterberg (Utrecht)	Army	60			Sta.	1911

ITALY

Place	Owner	Length (m)	Width (m)	Height (m)	Type	Year
Alessandria	Army	68	30	23.6	Sta.	1913
Baggio (Milan)	"	92	36	27	"	1911
Bosco Mantico (Verona)	"	91	30	24	"	1910
Bovisa (Milan)	Usuelli	90			"	1911
Campalto (Venice)	Army	84	18	21	"	1909
"	Navy	110	24	32	"	1911
Ferrara	Army	110	24	32	"	1911
Iesi	Navy	110	24	32	"	1913
Magré (Vicenza)	Piccoli				"	1913
Mirafiori (Turin)	Army	103	41	35	"	1909
Schio	Da Schio				"	1909
Tripoli (Lybia)	Army	100	25	25	"	1911
Vigna di Valle (Rome)	"	71	14	20.6	"	1907
"	"	71	14	20.6	"	1908
"	"	90	22	25.6	"	1911

JAPAN

Place	Owner	Length (m)	Width (m)	Height (m)	Type	Year
Makano	Army	80	25	20	Sta.	1910
Tokyo–Osaki	Yamada	80	20	18	"	1910
Tokorozawa	Army	100	25	22	"	1911
"	"	130	30	25	"	1912

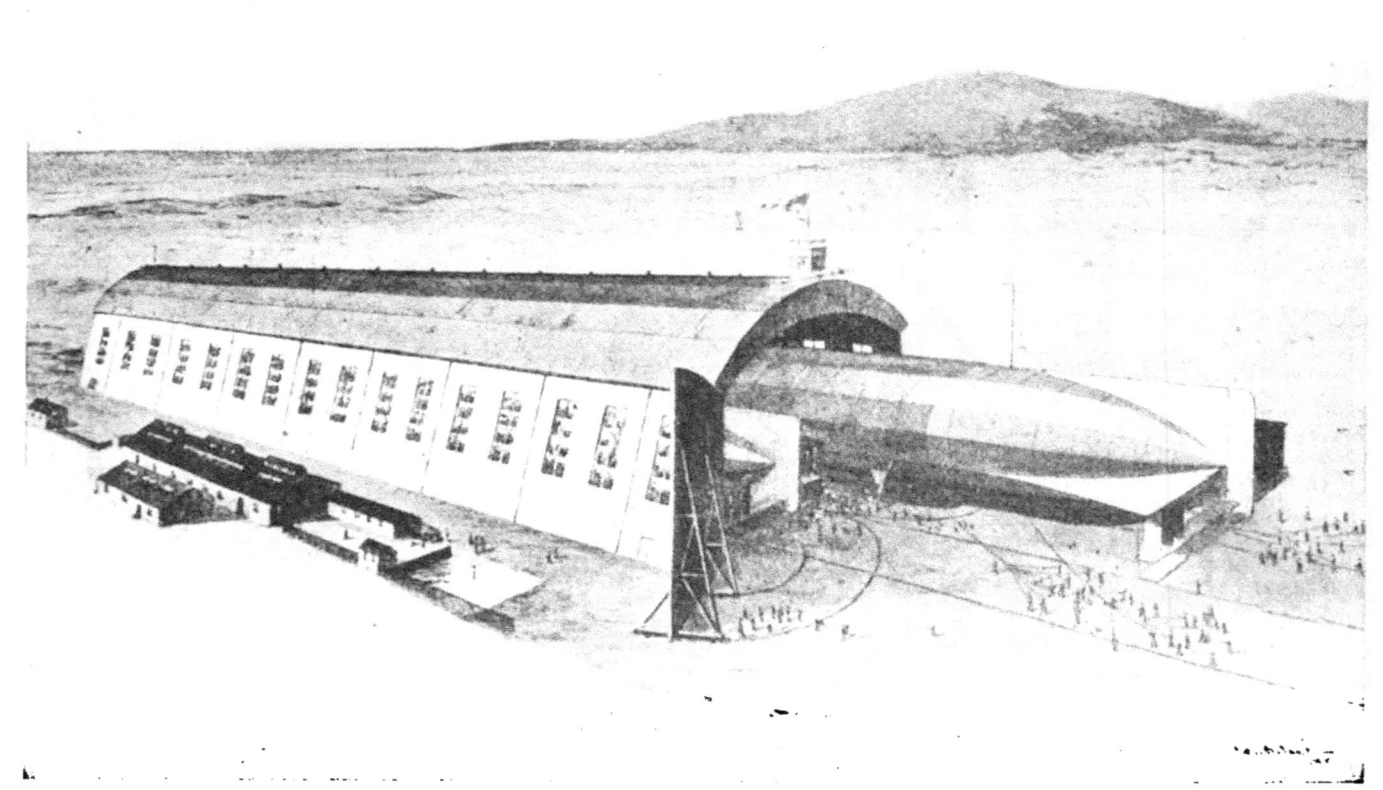

AIRSHIP SHED AT BARROW-IN-FURNESS (GREAT BRITAIN).

IX. THE WORLD'S AIRSHIP SHEDS—Continued

RUSSIA

Place	Owner	Length (m)	Width (m)	Height (m)	Type	Year
Berditcheff	Army	70	20		Sta.	1911
"	"	166	48		"	1914
Brest-Litovsk	"	80			"	1908
"	"	80			"	1908
"	"	166	48		"	1914
Dvinsk	"	166	48		"	1914
Homel	"				"	
Kieff	"	70	20		"	1911
Kovno	"				"	
Libava	"	70	20		"	1911
Lutsk	"	100	25	25	"	1912
Minsk	"				"	
Moscow	"	80			"	
"	"	80			"	
Petrograd	"	80			"	
"	"	80			"	
"	"	50			"	
"	"	166	48		"	1914
Reval	"				"	
Riga	"				"	
"	"				"	
Salisi-Gatchina	"				"	1909
"	"				"	1911
Sebastopol	"	70			"	
Sveaborg	"	80			"	
Vitebsk	"				"	
Vladivostok	"				"	
Warsaw	"	70			"	

THE SHED OF THE *PASADENA* AT PASADENA, CAL.

IX. THE WORLD'S AIRSHIP SHEDS—Continued

SPAIN

Place	Owner	Length (m)	Width (m)	Height (m)	Type	Year
Guadalajara	Army	80	15	20	Sta.	1908
"	"				"	1914

SWITZERLAND

Place	Owner	Length (m)	Width (m)	Height (m)	Type	Year
Lucerne	Astra Co.	90			Sta.	1910

TURKEY

Place	Owner	Length (m)	Width (m)	Height (m)	Type	Year
San Stefano	Army	52	15	18	Sta.	1913
"	"	150			"	1915

UNITED STATES

Place	Owner	Length (m)	Width (m)	Height (m)	Type	Year
Fort Omaha, Neb.	Army	60			Sta.	1908
Pensacola, Fla.	Navy				Flo.	1915

THE U. S. NAVY FLOATING SHED AT PENSACOLA, FLA.

INDEX OF THE WORLD'S AIRSHIPS

NOTE.—The letter, or group of letters, bracketed after each airship's name indicates the latter's registry, regardless of the builder's nationality or of the country in which the airship was built. "The registry of an aircraft is determined by the nationality of its owner." (Code of the Air, Article III.)

ABBREVIATIONS.—B, Belgium; BR, Brazil; D, Germany; DM, Denmark; E, Spain; F, France; GB, Great Britain; I, Italy; J, Japan; NL, Netherlands; OE, Austria; R, Russia; T, Turkey; US, United States

A

Adjudant-Réau (F), 21, 66, 67, 68.
Adjudant-Vincenot (F), 72, 73, 74.
Akron (US), 177, 178.
Albatros (R), 171.
Alfonso XIII (E), 173.
Alsace (F), 200.
America (US), 79, 80.
American Eagle (US), 183, 184.
Astra-Torrès I (F), 27, 64, 65, 66, 68.
Ausonia (I), 164, 165.
Austria (OE), 54, 57.

B

Baby (GB), 150, 151.
Baldwin-6, -9 (US), 175.
Bartholomeo-de-Gusmao (BR), 95.
Barton (GB), 147, 148.
Baumgartner (D), 103.
Beedle (GB), 149.
Bell (GB), 149.
Berkout (R), 63.
Beta (GB), 151, 152.
Boemches (OE), 53.
Bradsky (D), 71, 76.
Buchanan (GB), 149.

C

Capitaine-Ferber (F), 98, 101.
Capitaine-Marchal (F), 82, 84, 86, 87.
Castor-et-Pollux (F), 88, 89.
Charlotte (D), 106, 111.
Città di Ferrara (I), 159.
Città di Iesi (I), 159.
Città di Milano (I), 162, 163.
Città di Venezia (I), 110, 113.
City-of-Cardiff (GB), 157, 158.
Clément-Bayard I (F), 63, 71.
Clément-Bayard II (GB), 71, 72.
Clouth (D), 104, 105.
Colonel-Renard (F), 63, 68.
Commandant-Coutelle (F), 98, 101.
Conté (F), 66, 67.

D

Davis (US), 99.
Debayeux (F), 75.
Delta (GB), 152, 153.
De Marçay (F), 75.
Deutschland (D), 127, 131.
Deutschland II (D), 131.
Dirigible II (GB), 151.
DN-1 (US), 176, 177.
DN-2, DN-3 (US), 38, 177.
DN-4—DN-6 (US), 175.
DN-7—DN-15 (US), 179, 182.
DN-16, DN-17 (US), 179.
Dorhöfer (D), 107.
DR-1 (US), 183.
Duindigt (NL), 98, 99.
Dupuy-de-Lôme (F), 24, 72, 73, 76, 77.

E

E. Montgolfier (F), 72, 73.
España (E), 65.
Estaric (OE), 55.
Eta (GB), 153.
Eubriot (F), 77.

F

F. 1, F. 2 (R), 170, 171.
F. 3, F. 5, F. 6 (I), 165.
Faure (F), 95.
Fionia (DM), 59.
Fleurus (F), 58, 60, 61.

G

G. 1, G. 2 (I), 161.
Gamma (GB), 152, 153.
Gaudron (GB), 149.
Général-Meusnier (F), 61.
Giffard No. 1, No. 2 (F), 78, 79.
Goloub (R), 170, 171.
Griff (R), 29, 108, 110, 111.

H

H. 1 (D), 175.
Haenlein (D), 52, 53.
Hansa (D), 133.

I

Italia I, II (I), 161, 163, 164.

K

Kiel I (D), 125.
Kobtchik (R), 171.
Korchoune (R), 101.
Kretchet (R), 85, 169.

L

L. 1 (D), 133, 136.
L. 2 (D), 135, 138.
L. 3 (D), 137.
L. 4 (D), 121.
L. 5 (D), 139.
L. 6 (D), 139.
L. 7 (D), 121.
L. 8—L. 10 (D), 139.
L. 11—L. 19 (D), 140, 141.
L. 20 (D), 141, 142, 143.
L. 21 (D), 121.
L. 22—L. 29 (D), 141.
L. 30—L. 40 (D), 143.
L. 43 (D), 203.
La Belgique (B), 56, 57.
La France (F), 58, 59.
L. A. G. I, II (D), 115.
L'Aigle (F), 87.
Lebaudy-I, -II, -III, -IV (F), 81, 82, 83.
Lebedj (R), 85.
Le Compagnon, (F), 89.
Leichlingen (D), 116, 117.
Leonardo da Vinci (I), 162, 163.
Le Temps (F), 98, 101.
Liberté (F), 82, 85.
Lieutenant-Chauré (F), 65.
Lieutenant-Selle-de-Beauchamp (F), 87.
LZ. 4 (D), 129, 130.
LZ. 5 (D), 129, 132.
LZ. 6 (D), 129, 134.
LZ. 77 (D), 137.
LZ. 85 (D), 139.

M

M. I (D), 114, 115.
M. II (D), 115.
M. III (D), 114, 117.
M. IV (D), 114, 117.
M. I, M. II (OE), 55.
M. III (OE), 31, 52, 53.
M. 1 (I), 159, 160.
M. 2 (I), 159, 160.
M. 3 (I), 160, 161.
M. 4 (I), 160, 161.
M. 5 (I), 160, 161.
M-a (D), 115.
Malécot (F), 88, 95.

Mayfly (GB), 45, 154, 155.
Méditerranéen-II (F), 75.
Mellin (GB), 148, 153.
Morrell (US), 181, 184.
Morning-Post (GB), 85.

N

No. 1 (GB), 45, 154, 155.
No. 2 (GB), 112, 113.
No. 2A (GB), 151.
No. 3 (GB), 32, 67.
No. 4 (GB), 157, 158.
No. 1, 1-bis (I), 157.
No. 1 (US), 174, 175.
Nulli-Secundus (GB), 150, 151.

O

Outchebny (R), 169.

P

P. I (D), 106, 109.
P. II (D), 106, 109.
P. III (D), 111.
P. IV (D), 113.
P. V (D), 113.
P. 1—P. 5 (I), 159, 160.
Pasadena (US), 180, 181.
Patrie (F), 82, 83.
Pax (BR), 94, 95.
Petit-Journal I, II (F), 99.
Pilâtre-de-Rozier (F), 69.
PL. 1 (D), 106, 107.
PL. 5 (D), 108, 109.
PL. 9 (D), 108, 111.
PL. 10 (D), 111.
Preble-Rekar (US), 183.

R

R. I-III (D), 119.
République (F), 83.
Robert-Pillet (F), 89.
Russie (R), 85.

S

Sachsen (D), 135.
Santa Cruz (BR), 59.
Santos-Dumont No. 1-16 (BR), 90-93.
Schwaben (D), 5, 131, 210.
Schwarz No. 1 (OE), 123.
Schwarz No. 2 (OE), 116, 123.
SL. I (D), 43, 118, 119, 120.
SL. II (D), 116, 121.
SL. III (D), 121.
Sokol (R), 171.
Spencer II (GB), 153.
Spiess (F), 100, 101.
SS. I (D), 31, 122, 124, 125.
S. S. type (GB), 69, 70.
Stollwerck (D), 108, 109.
Suchard (D), 102, 104, 105.

T

Tchaika (R), 101.
Tissandier (F), 87, 96, 97.
Toliver (US), 183.
Tomlinson (US), 175.
Torrès-Quevedo (E), 172, 173.

U

Unger (D), 125.
Usuelli (I), 164, 165.

V

V. 1 (I), 161.
Veeh I (D), 104, 107.
Viktoria-Luise (D), 133.
Ville-de-Bordeaux (F), 63.
Ville-de-Bruxelles (B), 65, 66.
Ville-de-Lucerne (F), 65.
Ville-de-Nancy (F), 63.
Ville-de-Paris (F), 61, 62, 96, 97.
Ville-de-Pau (F), 62, 65.
Ville-de-Saint-Mandé (F), 77.

W

Willows No. 1–No. 5 (GB), 155–158.

Y

Yamada No. 1, 2 (J), 166, 167.
Yastreb (R), 168, 169.
Yuhi (J), 111.

Z

Z. I (D), 129, 133, 135.
Z. II (D), 129, 131, 132.
Z. III (D), 133.
Z. IV (D), 135, 136.
Z. V (D), 135.
Z. VI–XIII (D), 137.
Z. 48 (D), 203.
Zeppelin I (D), 126 127.
Zeppelin II (D), 127, 128.
Zeppelin III (D), 128, 129.
Zodiac (B), 99.
Zodiac (F), 99.
Zorn (D), 147.

Introduction to D'Orcy's Essays

By Vladimir Verano

How will history remember you?

It's a question that runs through every person's mind at least once in their lives. In this modern, interconnected, social-media-saturated era there's a strong chance **none** of us will be forgotten by history—all our glories, mistakes, our most banal moments recorded forever. Back before the internet, before computers even, the printed word was the way to be remembered by history. Sure, there was also artwork, photography and, in the case of the early 20th century, film, but print was the medium of empires and historians. How is it then, that a man as prolific a writer & multi-faceted as Ladislas d'Orcy has fallen into the folds and margins of history?

D'Orcy's Airship Manual began its modern life as part of a book digitization initiative in the early 1990s called Project Gutenberg. Hundreds of volunteers painstakingly typed, scanned, and collated as many works in the public domain as they could. By the time Google stepped in with its vast resources and man-power, Gutenberg had an archive of over 1.5 million titles (now part of the wonderful *www.archive.org*). It was through Google, that this book came across my desk. We had just started Third Place Press (now VertVolta Press) in late 2009, and were testing our Espresso Book Machine ('Ginger') with public domain titles of varying sizes and page-lengths, and one of our earliest customers ordered the Google edition of this book. The odd-shaped book bounced out of our machine and into my hands and I was spell-bound with the information inside: this exhaustive compilation of all manner of airships in existence in 1917, with commentary on their construction and materials, with dozens of schematics and photographs. A few months, and a few more printed copies later, I decided to create our own version of *D'Orcy's Airship Manual* for our Rediscovery Editions. It was not simply a matter of simply printing the PDF of the book; there was much work to be done on the sizing, and all manner of marginalia and markings. I also discovered that the edition we were printing was missing pages. After some careful work I managed to 'stitch' together a complete edition of the book, but still there was one thing missing: a biography or even a mention of Ladislas d'Orcy.

And this is where the story truly began. It started with a book and became about a man. A man with no Wikipedia entry, and no biography to speak of. So I proceeded to do what any modern lay-researcher would do: I began scouring the internet via Google. Over time, and many sessions searching I managed to dig up a wisp of biography, and like the book itself, I've managed to stitch together something coherent, albeit brief.

Baron Ladislas Emile D'Orcy was born in Gratz, Austria in 1887 and raised in Paris. His barony is part of the Austro-Hungarian aristocratic families. With such privilege comes a fine education, and Ladislas was educated in Hungary and Italy, after which he traveled extensively as a young man throughout Europe, the Balkans, India and the Far East.

Sometime during this period, it seems he became fascinated with the nascent aviation field. Pre-World War I was, by all accounts, a vibrant and exciting (not to mention dangerous) time to be involved in the business of flight. D'Orcy himself was involved in many ventures, including the Henry Farman Company in the United States. In doing so, D'Orcy and his colleagues stimulated aeronautical innovation and competition in a nation woefully behind its European counterparts.

D'Orcy helped found many Aviation clubs around the world, including the most secretive & prestigious of them all, The Society of Quiet Birdmen. Aviators were a daring and small community—aviation was still looked-upon as more of a hobby by the public at large—and it seems that they thrived in their outsider nature. D'Orcy was in the middle of all this revelry and camaraderie, soaking up life to the fullest.

As a writer, D'Orcy was precise, detail-oriented, and broadly knowledgeable. He was considered an authority on lighter-than-air craft (Zeppelins, dirigibles, etc.), and wrote articles for *Scientific American*, *Flight*, *L'Aero* and *Hydro*. He was also editor of several aviation journals, including *Aviation* and *Aircraft Journal*.

The essays included in this book allow the reader to step into the mind of D'Orcy and experience his bright intellect. SUPER-ZEPPELINS is remarkable in that it is an article written in 1916, at the height of World War I, based on scant information on two downed German Zeppelins; one sunk beneath the Thames and the other destroyed off the English coast. With only eye-witness accounts, some photographs and analysis of wreckage, D'Orcy reverse-engineers these Zeppelins with astounding detail: length, payload and fuel capacity, munitions, crew-capacity and more. Here is a man moving across disciplines easily—physics, engineering, chemistry, aeronautics—to deduce, correctly the true shape of these war machines. In MASTERY OF THE AIR VS. THE CONTROL OF THE SEA (also written in 1916) we see D'Orcy's capacity for military analysis, already foreseeing that a military with a strong air presence will dominate in 20th century conflicts. Moreso, he uses science and mathematics to back up his reasoning. In ON THE THRESHOLD OF THE FLYING AGE, and IS TRANSport by *Air a Success?* (both written in 1921), we see D'Orcy the pragmatist and businessman, discussing the evolution of the aviation industry in the United States and Europe. D'Orcy is equally optimistic and tough, demanding such visionary things as government subsidies, sound-proofed passenger cabins, and parachutes, which may sound ludicrous but at the dawn of the flying age it was a free-for-all of safety standards and regulations.

Sadly, in my research I discovered that D'Orcy died on February 12th, 1928. It is a rather curt single sentence mentioned in *Aircraft Year Book, 1928*. Just the date, and that he was an editor of an aviation journal. That's all.

But I know that it's ***not*** all. There is more to uncover in this clever man's life, and so for me it's a journey that has only started. D'Orcy died in 1928. He missed out on seeing many of his hopes and fears for aviation realized during the horrors and necessity of World War II; he missed out on the advent of the Space Race and the moon landing. It would have been a treat to read his analysis of all of this, his inquisitive mind bringing insight to us all.

For now though, we have this book and his essays, and perhaps in the future there will be more to know about Baron Ladislas D'Orcy and the dawn of the flying age.

X. Essays.

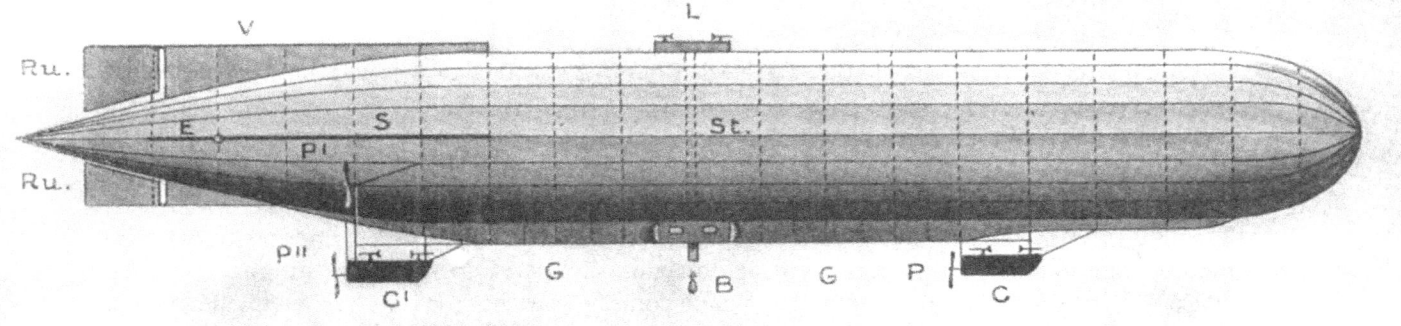

Outline (side-view) of a 30-ton super-Zeppelin. Drawn to data obtained from the wrecks of LZ-77 and L-15

(C C') engine cars (the one in front containing the pilot house); (P. P.' P") propellers; (G) gangway connecting the cars and containing water-ballast and fuel tanks; (St) starway leading from bomb-room (B) to armed lookout (L); stabilizing fin; (E) elevator; (V) vertical fin; (Ru) rudders.

Super Zeppelins.**

By Baron Ladislas d'Orcy,
Member, American Institute of Aeronautical Engineers

**(originally published in Scientific American, May 13th, 1916)*

It is common knowledge, that for some time past a new type of Zeppelin, far more powerful than any of its predecessors, has been commissioned with the Air Service of the German Navy. The recent destruction, by the agency of the Allies' anti-aircraft artillery, of two of these vessels has now afforded the long-sought opportunity for getting a closer view of this type of aircraft—which for the sake of convenience we shall term Super-Zeppelin.

A layman might hardly discern any change in the outward appearance of a super-Zeppelin, when compared with previous types; it appears, however, upon examination of what remained of the vessels destroyed at Revigny (the LZ-77) and in the mouth of the Thames (the L-15), that the hull, steering organs and propelling apparatus have been redesigned to a great extent on the latest types.

· Essays ·

It is a matter of discussion whether there exists but one new type or whether the Zeppelin Works still turn out a large long-range type for naval raids and one, smaller but faster, for military reconnaissances. The fact remains, however, that the Germans possess at preset a large type of Zeppelin whose features, as far as they are known, shall be discussed herewith.

THE HULL—The hull of the *ante-bellum* Zeppelins was in the shape of a cylinder with two symmetrical ogival ends—a very poor form, aerodynamically speaking; and it was still made worse by an exaggerated aspect ratio of ten to one, which comes to say that the hull was ten diameters long.

On the super-Zeppelin this defect had been remedied to some extent. The bow is slightly blunter than before, while the stern is nearly conical; furthermore the aspect ratio has been somewhat decreased, so that now the hull is only about eight or nine diameters long. Although this ratio is still some way off the one disclosed by aerodynamic research work to effect the smoothest airflow (6:1), it must materially assist the super-Zeppelin in attaining greater speed without the expenditure of additional power.

Regarding the size of super-Zeppelins, an examination of the wreck of the LZ-77 reveals that this vessel (which undoubtedly belonged to a recent type, as is disclosed by her factory number) was about 540 feet long with a displacement of over 1,100,000 cubic feet which would furnish a lift of about 33 tons.

Table Showing Probable Zeppelin Losses from August 1st, 1914 to May 3rd, 1916

No.	Name.	Place.	Date.	Cause of Loss.
1	Z-8*	Badonvillers, France	22- 8-1914	Destroyed by French gunners. Part of crew lost.
2	Z-5*	Mlava, Russia	29- 8-1914	Destroyed by Russian gunners. Crew lost.
3	?*	Seradz, Russia	6- 9-1914	Captured, while at anchor, by a cavalry patrol. Crew of 30, prisoners.
4	?	Düsseldorf, Germany	9-10-1914	Destroyed in shed by British aviators.
5	LZ-31*	Friedrichshafen, Germany	21-11-1914	Destroyed in shed by British aviators.
6	?	North Sea	23- 1-1915	Foundered during a storm.
7	L-3*	Esbjerg, Denmark	17- 2-1915	Stranded, having run out of fuel, and broke up. Crew of 16 interned.
8	L-9*	Boulogne, France	5- 3-1915	Foundered during a storm, after having raided Calais. Crew lost.
9	L-8*	Tirlemont, Belgium	4- 3-1915	Damaged by British aviator; wrecked on landing. 21 of crew killed.
10	?	Thielt, Belgium	12- 4-1915	Damaged, over Béthune, by French gunners; wrecked on landing.
11	?*	North Sea	26- 5-1915	Broke away without crew; foundered off Heligoland.
12	LZ-37*	Evere, Belgium	7- 6-1915	Destroyed in shed by British aviators.
13	LZ-38*	Ghent, Belgium	7- 6-1915	Destroyed in mid-air by British aviator; crew lost.
14	L-?*	Ostende, Belgium	10- 8-1915	Raided London. Destroyed, upon her return, by British aviators.
15	?*	Vilna, Russia	24- 8-1915	Shot down by Russian gunners; crew of 10 made prisoners.
16	?*	Saint-Hubert, Belgium	13-10-1915	Destroyed by exploding in mid-air.
17	?	Maubeuge, France	16-10-1915	Stranded on a chimney and broke up.
18	?	Grodno, Russia	5-11-1915	Destroyed by the storm on landing.
19	L-18*	Tondern, Germany	17-11-1915	Wrecked in shed through an accidental (?) explosion.
20	Z-28	Hamburg, Germany	17-11-1915	Wrecked by the storm.
21	L-22*	Tondern, Germany	1-12-1916	Destroyed in shed through accidental explosion of a bomb.
22	?*	Kalkun, Russia	5-12-1916	Shot down by Russian gunners. Crew lost.
23	?*	Mainvault, Belgium	30- 1-1916	Raided Paris. Damaged by French aviator; wrecked on landing.
24	L-19*	North Sea	21- 2-1916	Raided England. Probably ran out of fuel; foundered. Crew lost.
25	LZ-77*	Révigny, France	21- 2-1916	Shot down by French motor guns; destroyed in fall. Crew of 15 killed.
26	L-15*	Kentish Knock, England	1- 4-1916	Shot down by British gunners; crew of 18 surrendered. Vessel sank.
27	L-20*	Stavanger, Norway	3- 5-1916	Raided Scotland. Stranded, having run out of fuel and drifted with the wind. Blown up by crew: 3 killed, 16 interned.

* Destruction authenticated.

· Essays ·

THE STEERING ORGANS—The Steering organs have been greatly simplified on the super-Zeppelin.

A picture of the L-15 (which was photographed before she broke up and sank) shows clearly, that in place of a large number of small and parallel rudders and elevators, there is now a compact *empennage*, very similar to that of a tractor aeroplane. Both rudder and elevator now consist of simple "flaps" which are hinged to the vertical and horizontal fins, respectively.

Their surface area is naturally increased, as the conical stern takes up les space than when it was blunt; as a consequence and, owing to a smoother air-flow, the efficiency of the steering organs should have materially increased.

THE PROPELLING APPARATUS—The distribution of power has been very radically re-designed on the super-Zeppelin, the new system being one that follow marine practice closer than was customary hitherto.

While the 1914-15 type of naval Zeppelin was propelled by two sets of two 200-horse-power engines, each set driving two air-screws mounted on outriggers on either side of the hull, the super-Zeppelin carries but one engine in the front car and three engines in the rear car. Two of the stern engines drive side propellers in the old fashion; but the third one, as well as the front engine each drive a directly couple propeller at the rear of the cars.

The advantages derived from mounting the propellers astern are manifold. Firstly, as there is nothing to interfere with the air thrown back by the propellers, the efficiency of the latter should be somewhat increased; secondly, the danger of sparks from the exhaust, which might ignite hydrogen, is rendered very remote; and thirdly, the mounting of the engines in the stern car should afford more room in the front car for the navigating personnel.

One might therefore assume that ultimately the stern car will become the sole engine room, while the bow car will be the navigating room and nothing else. If this has not been done yet, it should rather be attributed to a lack of higher powered engines, than to some obscure reason for keeping one propeller ahead.

ARMAMENT—The armament of these vessels has hardly changed. The bomb-room has remained in the middle of the gangway; but the crude way of dropping bombs by hand has been superseded by a scientific appliance, whereby the bombs are released electrically.

In addition to the two machine guns mounted on each car, two more have been provided for arming the lookout post, atop of the hull, which is connected with the bomb-room by means of a stairway encased in a chimney.

· *Essays* ·

Thus far the apparent changes affecting super-Zeppelins.

Modifications relative to the ratio of dead weight to useful load, are more or less a matter of speculation. On the *ante-bellum* Zeppelins the useful load amounted to about one fourth of the total lift. According to a statement emanating from Count Zeppelin's secretary, the climbing power of the new type is two fifths better than on previous types and the load of ammunition amounts to two tons; it might therefore be assumed that the useful load is also at least two fifths better than heretofore, in which case its ratio would be 35 per cent of the total lift.

Such an improvement is entirely within the present-day possibilities, if one bears in mind that the ratio of dead weight to useful load *decreases* with the Zeppelin's size and that the super-Zeppelins displace about ten tons more than the vessels of the previous type. Some weight may also have been saved through an improved system of construction, as well as by the new 200-horse-power engines which weigh only 880 pounds, instead of 985 pounds. On the basis of the above ratio a 33-ton super-Zeppelin carries a useful load of about 11 ½ tons—more than double the load the previous type was capable of lifting. If such is the case, allowance for two tons of ammunition leaves nine and one half tons available for crew, ballast and fuel.

THE CREW—Of the two super-Zeppelins destroyed lately, the LZ-77 carried 15 men and the L-15, whose crew was captures, two officers and 16 men. Supposing the latter figure represents the war compliment of the largest super-Zeppelin, it remains to be computed how these 18 men are detailed for navigating and fighting.

The three-engined passenger Zeppelins required a navigating personnel of nine men, distributed as follows: the commander, two helmsmen and two mechanics in the front car (housing one engine); and a chief engineer and three mechanics in the rear car (housing two engines).

Although a super-Zeppelin mounts a third astern, it might be assumed that the engine crew has not been increased, five mechanics and one engineer being quite sufficient for looking after four engines. But in view of the super-Zeppelins' long cruising radius a third helmsman might have been added to the crew; this would leave eight men, including the lieutenant, for manning the bomb tube and the machine guns. Six men are required for manning the latter; the remaining two would constitute the bomb-crew with the lieutenant as gunnery officer, and possibly, second in charge of navigation.

A compliment of 18 officers and men represents a load of about one and one half tons; there would then remain eight tons for ballast and fuel.

· Essays ·

THE BALLAST—There are very good reasons for believing that the water-ballast has been considerably increased on the 33-ton airships. Vessels of the previous (23-ton) type, which carried 1½ tons of ballast, used to navigate at an altitude of 5,000 feet and hardly ever reached the 9,000 feet mark, excepting trials; super-Zeppelins, however, often reach an altitude of 10,000 feet and are currently seen navigating at 7,000 feet.

Whereas the buoyancy of a Zeppelin is just sufficient to keep the vessel floating at a low level, great heights can be reached only through a combination of dynamic lift (expenditure of engine power) and of static lift, the latter being attained both through jettisoning ballast and burning fuel, and in extreme cases, by a forced dropping of bombs.

The question of ballast is one closely allied with that of compensating losses of buoyancy at great heights. Lack of space unfortunately forbids a detailed discussion of this subject; suffice it to say, that losses of buoyancy cannot be made up entirely by jettisoning ballast and one might assume that some artifice, possibly a system compensating balloonets for each of the 20 or more gasbags, has been devised for remedying this defect on super-Zeppelins.

Such a course should not be astonishing at all in view of the several airships the German navy lost in the North Sea, for the sole reason that when they came down from a great height, the gas, after having expanded, contracted through the greater atmospheric pressure and proved insufficient for insuring the necessary buoyancy. It was this phenomenon which caused the loss of L-3 and L-4, not to speak of others.

Anyhow, one can safely assume that the ballast of a 33-ton vessel is at least double that of the *ante-bellum* Zeppelin, say three tons, but more probably four tons, leaving for tons for fuel.

CRUISING RADIUS—As the fuel consumption of the four-engine unit amounts to about 450 pounds per hour, four tons of fuel would keep the engines running for about 18 hours at full speed (55 knots) and thus insure a cruising radius of 990 nautical miles. The latter figure will possibly necessitate a reduction of, say 10 per cent, if allowance be made for the fuel burnt while climbing.

If it were feasible to run the vessel on the homeward journey (after she has been lightened up through the expenditure of fuel, ballast and bombs), with two engines only, the radius of action might be somewhat increased. By using the formula:

$$\text{Speed at x power} = \sqrt{\frac{\text{Full Speed}}{\frac{\text{Full Power}}{\text{x Speed}}}}$$

One finds that by running with two engines the airship would develop a speed of 38.8 knots, which means a saving of 225 pounds of fuel per hour and consequently an additional cruising radius of about 200 nautical miles (9 hours at 55 knots = 495 nautical miles + 18 hours at 38.3 knots = 698 nautical miles, total: 1,193 nautical miles).

The accuracy of these figures, based on more or less plausible assumptions, cannot obviously be vouchsafed to a mile; still they seem to bear out pretty well in the light of the latest Zeppelin incursions, when some of the raiders went as far as Liverpool and Edinburgh.

Here it should be noted that the raiders which attacked these places, or at least their environs, were all reported as coming from the East, i.e. from across the North Sea and not from the South, i.e. from Belgium, which means that they belonged to some of the numerous "airship-harbors" which dot the German coast from Tondern (in Schleswig-Holstein) to Emden, on the Dutch frontier. The distances between Tondern and Edinburgh (440 nautical miles) and between Emden and Liverpool (400 nautical miles) would seem to bear out the assumed cruising radius of the super-Zeppelin.

As th the reason, why these vessels should choose a long and perilous journey across the North Sea rather than proceed from Belgium, one might argue that the latter course, while comparably shorter, has been now rendered exceedingly unpleasant to the Zeppelins through the vigilant activity of the Allies' airmen and anti-aircraft guns. This the casualty list of the Zeppelins proves to the best satisfaction.

Mastery of the Air vs. the Control of the Sea.**

By Baron Ladislas d'Orcy,
Member, American Institute of Aeronautical Engineers

**(originally published in Scientific American, June 17th, 1916)*

Original editor's note: The following article was written three weeks ago. Since then the great battle off the coast of Jutland has been fought. The advantage possessed by the German fleet in the early hours of the engagement bears out the author's contention that Great Britain's near-sighted navy, though master of the sea, is badly handicapped by Germany's mastery of the air above the sea, which gives the German fleet and eighty-mile radius of vision.

There is such a thing as *air power*. When a squadron of German Zeppelins[1] is capable of crossing the 400 odd miles which separate Germany's North Sea coast from English shores, when it can discharge two tons of shells per vessel, ward off British fighting aeroplanes and safely return to port without being seriously interfered with—which is mostly the case—then that airship squadron indubitably proves the existence of air power.

Sea power is chiefly a matter of construction, training, and numbers; so is air power. Only a fleet comprising vessels of all types in due proportion can effectively exercise sea power; the same rule applies to air power. To rely only upon aeroplanes and anti-aircraft guns for fighting Zeppelins is just as contrary to sound military science as it would be to entrust the defense of a maritime country entirely to coast batteries and mosquito craft.

To be sure, air power does not yet impose itself with a overwhelming a force as sea power; but this is due only to circumstances, as aircraft, being still in the initial stage of their development, cannot

---

1 Throughout this article the term Zeppelin is used in a generic sense i. e., meaning a rigid airship, just as the term dreadnaught is employed for describing all-big-gun ship.

Comparative Zeppelin strength of Germany, France and Great Britain at the outbreak of the war. On the left, thirteen German ships in commision and four (in white) building; on the right, above, one French ship built and two building; on the right, below, two British ships building.

yet fully exercise the functions for which they are ultimately intended. Some future day air power will surely dispute sea power and finally become supreme; and there are already indications at hand where air power is beginning to overlap sea power.

By opposing faster and heavier-gunned battle cruisers and a larger number of dreadnaughts to those of Germany, Great Britain has paralyzed German shipping and has bottled up the Kaiser's High Sea Fleet in the Kiel Canal: she thus rules the seas. Still an inferior German battle cruiser squadron succeeded several times in raiding English coast towns, escaping—save once—without being intercepted and forced to fight. Why? Simply because while England rules the seas, Germany rules the air above the seas, or more correctly speaking the air above the North Sea.

Great Britain has no Zeppelins, i.e. rigid airships capable of great endurance, for reconnoitering the North Sea; and as seaplanes do not possess a radius of action sufficient to carry out this duty, Sir John Jellicoe's Grand Fleet has to rely on its 30-knot scout cruisers, whose range of vision is limited to 20 miles, for gathering information about the enemy's whereabouts. Observation balloons and kites offer but poor substitutes for long range airships, whose speed and movements are independent from naval vessels, whereas balloons and kites are anchored to the mother ship and therefore are largely dependent on the latter's speed.

Now turning to the German "system" we find that a fleet escorted by Zeppelins, flying at a height of 5,000 feet and at a speed of about 60 knots, can detect the enemy at a distance of 80 miles, i.e. at a range four times greater than the one possessed by British naval scouts. The enormous tactical advantage gained thereby for the Germans has well been illustrated by the latest naval raid on Lowescroft, where, owing to their scout airships, the Germans were able to keep at a safe margin from the British battle cruiser's ever-watchful "eyes."

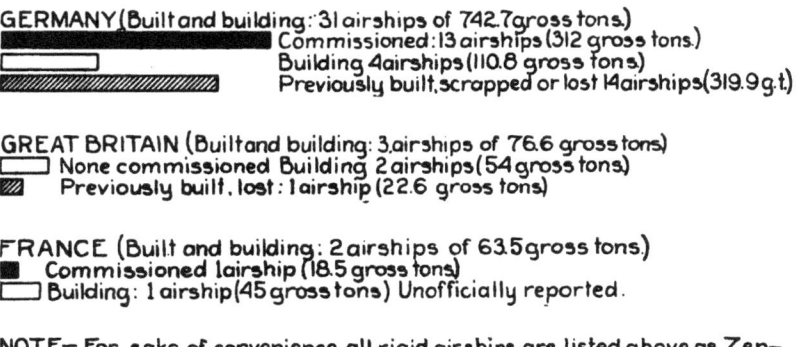

GERMANY (Built and building: 31 airships of 742.7 gross tons.)
▬ Commissioned: 13 airships (312 gross tons.)
☐ Building 4 airships (110.8 gross tons.)
▨ Previously built, scrapped or lost 14 airships (319.9 g.t.)

GREAT BRITAIN (Built and building: 3 airships of 76.6 gross tons.)
☐ None commissioned Building 2 airships (54 gross tons.)
▨ Previously built, lost: 1 airship (22.6 gross tons.)

FRANCE (Built and building: 2 airships of 63.5 gross tons.)
▬ Commissioned 1 airship (18.5 gross tons.)
☐ Building: 1 airship (45 gross tons.) Unofficially reported.

NOTE— For sake of convenience all rigid airships are listed above as Zeppelins; Tonnage, expressed gross or total lift, which furnishes a better basis of comparison than volume.

Table showing comparative strength of the Zeppelin fleets of Germany, Great Britain and France on August 1st, 1914

· *Essays* ·

Such is the influence of air power upon sea power. This extraordinary situation, where a fleet, gun for gun and ship for ship the superior of its foe, cannot prevent the latter—for lack of swift information—from raiding the shores of the country which is topspin the sea, makes it worthwhile to examine the underlying causes which brought about this condition.

For the past ten years the great military nations of Europe were all engaged in building up airship fleets; but it seems, in the light of subsequent events, that Germany alone realized from the beginning the exact nature of the advantages a persistently followed-up airship policy would confer upon her military and naval forces. The nations now forming the Grand Alliance seem chiefly concerned with the development of the aeroplane, convinced as they were that a fleet of such mosquito craft would quickly be able to put out of action any "gasbag" as airships were contemptuously refers to by their detractors.

Still, for some time it looked like France, and, to some extent, Italy too, were determined to meet Germany's steadily growing airship fleet in the only way that might have put them on equal footing with the aerial forces flying the lack-crossed ensign: by matching airship with airship. But if such was their object, both Latin countries were badly handicapped in this realization by a policy of misplaced patriotism, which favored the building of non-rigid and semi-rigid airships exclusively, these types being national products, while it barred vessels of the rigid type of for the sole reason that the latter had been originated in Germany.

The Germans had no such scruples. While Count Zeppelin was exerting every effort to improve his airships, the German army authorities tried to purchase in France one airship each of the semi-rigid Lebaudy and the non-rigid Astra types. Having failed to achieve their object the Germans resolved to copy the vessels they couldn't buy: this is how the Gross-Basenach and Parseval airships came into being. It is but fair to add that, since this "inspired" inception, vessels of the above types have largely developed upon original lines.

The German authorities seem to have been quite aware that in spite of their limitations the non-rigid and semi-rigid airships could fulfill some functions to the satisfaction of their owners—chiefly in conjunction with army operations and harbor defense, where their ease of transportation, low cost and general handiness were greatly appreciated. But the Germans were nonetheless convinced at for strategical reconnaissances and chiefly naval scouting high-speed airships, capable of long endurance, we're required and that these requirements could not be attained by either one of the above mentioned types. This is why, undaunted by countless accidents, many of them tragic, Germany never lost her faith in the Zeppelin and, what is more, even encouraged the development of another type of rigid airship, theSchütte-Lanz. Thus, when the German navy lost their first two

Zeppelins, four new vessels were laid down at once, three of them at the Zeppelin factory and one at the Schütte-Lanz works.

It is infesting to compare this progressive policy—which at the time was cal led adventurous—with the hesitating attitude of the British authorities towards airships in general and Zeppelins in particular.

After having tried and, generally speaking, failed to produce a serviceable lighter-than-air machine of original design, the War Office—which in 1914 was alone in charge of airships—purchased from foreign manufacturers a number of non-rigid and semi-rigid vessels, while the Royal Aircraft Factory furnished some small airships for instruction purposes.

The Admiralty seemed for a short time to be animated by a more progressive spirit. In 1909 an order was placed with the well-known shipbuilding firm of Messrs. Vickers, Sons and Maxim for a 21-ton airship of the Zeppelin type. His vessel, the "Mayfly" was launched two years later, but unfortunately broke up while she was being towed out. Of her shed. As it proved impossible to repair the "Mayfly" and no credit was available for a new construction,the British Navy stopped experimenting with Zeppelins until 1914, when Mr. Winston Churchill became First Lord of the Admiralty. At the insistence of this far-seeing minister, twelve airships were laid down at once, two of which were Zeppelins; but before this building programme could be carried to completion, the great war broke out. By this time Germany had commissioned thirteen Zeppelins and a half a dozen minor airships, while Great Britain possessed but three small non-rigid vessels.

It is rather astonishing that the British naval authorities should not have realized any sooner the value of airships and, particularly, of Zeppelins for naval scouting. In 1909 Sir Percy Scott—many of whose "revolutionary" predictions regarding naval constructions have been vindicated by the great war—wrote, in a preface to Jane's *All the World's Airships*, the following prophetic words: "In gaining information of the locality, strength and disposition of the enemy's fleet and so possibly unmask his strategy … an airship's services would be invaluable, for it might not be possible to obtain the information in any other way."

Twenty-two months of warfare have fully demonstrated the truth of Sir Percy's assertions. Germany has been able to use her Zeppelins with marked success in many diverse functions, about which little has come to light yet. It is noteworthy, however, that one Zeppelin was decorated with the Iron Cross "for coöperation with submarines during a successful attack on three British armored cruisers." Several Zeppelins have also cooperated with German submarines , for enforcing the so-called "submarine blockade" by stopping and occasionally sinking such merchantmen as they could not bring to German port. Other Zeppelins have been engaged in patrolling the German shores from Holland to Denmark to Russia; still others have played an all-important role as fast scouts for such portions of the German fleet as have ventured beyond the range of Heligoland's coastal batteries. Their participation in the latest naval raid on Lowescroft even raises the question, whether the twofold slipping of the British blockade by the German commerce raider "Moewe" may not be attributed to intelligent cooperation between her skipper and one or more Zeppelins. The high speed of these airships, and their faculty to send, as well as receive, wireless messages makes this assumption appear quite plausible.

German official reports seem to omit purposefully all reference to this sort of work done by Zeppelins, while particular emphasis is laid on the destruction achieved by Zeppelin raids against the British Isles. These incursions on undefended shipping and manufacturing towns—however contrary to laws of civilized warfare they be—come well within the German definition of "commerce war," as practiced by German naval forces of several occasions. ("Vide" the raids on Scarborough and Lowescroft, the bombardment of Madras by the "Emden" and that of Papeëte (French Oceania) by Admiral Von Pee's squadron; the latter instance is particularly enlightening, as all the shells were deliberately at the business section of that port.)

From a military viewpoint the Zeppelin raids on England are of comparatively small importance, though some of them may have served the purpose of a "reconnaissance in force," either for ascertaining the whereabouts of Sir John Jellicoe's Grand Fleet or else for reconnoitering the location of English coast defense works. If such really was their purpose, then the dropping of the bombs was successful from e German point of view, as it forced the British to disclose the location of their batteries by firing on the air raiders.

There still is another important function which Zeppelins may fulfill with a fleet: gun-spotting. During the Gallipoli campaign the "Queen Elizabeth" repeatedly fired across the peninsula, hitting targets invisible to her gunners, the correct range being given by seaplanes through wireless.

But seaplanes cannot yet—on account of their short radius of action—cruise with a fleet out to sea; it is true that they might be carried on motherships, but in this case their movements will be dependent on their floating bases, whereas Zeppelins may cover 1,000 nautical miles independently. The advantage then lies obviously with the airship, the more so as the latter might spot the guns while remaining stationary and send, as well as receive, wireless messages—things a seaplane cannot do.

The British Admiralty seems to have at last awakened to the realization that Zeppelins constitute excellent naval scouts and that a lack of them places a fleet in an appreciable handicap against an enemy possessing such airships. The view was frankly voiced by Mr. Balfour, First Lord of the Admiralty, in the House of Commons.

Essays

"It is extremely desirable that we should have lighter-an-air machines in order to supplement the efforts of our fleet by machines which, in many respects and in favorable weather, are far more effective than the swiftest destroyer or the most powerful cruiser. Therefore we have done and are doing our best to develop lighter-than-air machines."

These words are particularly interesting in view of a report which reached here last November, stating that Great Britain contemplated building 50 Zeppelins and other airships within two years, whereafter sufficient vessels would be laid down each year to insure complete mastery of the air. Provided this report is true, it will be interesting to watch the development of Great Britain's bid for aerial supremacy—and Germany's answer.

On the Threshold of the Flying Age.**
An Analysis of Recent Progress in Aviation
By Ladislas d'Orcy.

**(originally published in The Outlook Magazine, 1921)*

Is the flying machine of today a comparatively final type which requires, like the automobile of ten years ago, only detail refinements to become generally adopted for up bid and private uses, or is it merely a stepping-stone toward a fundamentally different kind of aircraft yet to be invented? Is aeronautical engineering developing along lines leading to a clearly visualized goal, or is it merely "marking time" in an endeavor to overcome seemingly insuperable obstacles? Briefly, are we on the threshold of the flying age?

The uninitiate in aeronautics often asks these questions. Ten or twelve years ago a definitely reply would have been hazardous, for considerable doubt existed then as to whether the airplane might not ultimately be us planted by the helicopter or by the ornithopter. Today this doubt is practically a dispelled. The best-informed opinion in the aeronautical world is now agreed that the airplane has not only reached a state of comparative finality, but also that it is likely to remain the principle, if not the only, type of practical flying machine. At the same time it is admitted that the helicopter or direct lift machine has distinct, though limited, possibilities as an improved substitute for the kite balloon.

ORINTHOPTERS NOT PRACTICAL

No such prospect is, however, held out for the orinthopter or wing-flapping machine, which, it should be realized, offers a fundamentally unmechanical solution to the problem of flight. In the animal world propulsion is essentially alternative motion; but man-made vehicles all are. Propelled by rotary motion. The legs of a horse, the fins of a whale, the wings of an eagle, all move alternately—

that is, to and for; the wheels o f an automobile, the propeller, of a steamship, the airscrew of allying machine, all turn around an axis. The main reason for this dissimilarity is that rotary motion affords a much more efficient system of propulsion than would a mechanical reproduction of the alternating propellers of the animal world. In the orinthopter the problem is further complicated by the fact that the Windsor most birds do not merely move up and down; in fact, they describe with their tips something approaching a helical path. Thisitwould be extremely difficult to reproduce mechanically, and the mechanism would be so delicate as to be of doubtful practical value.

In contrast, the airplane represents a singularly simple and mechanical solution. The wings are rigidly fixed to the fuselage and the only moving parts are e control surfaces and the airscrew. With the aid of these the airman an impart a degree of flexibility which, though somewhat short of that possessed by birds, is fully adequate for safe flying.

ADVANTAGES OF HELICOPTERS

The only thing an airplane cannot do is rise from the ground without a preliminary run. While this is not a very serious drawback, there may occur conditions, particularly in warfare, where such a performance would be valuable.

The helicopter offers to solve this problem by rising from a standstill under the impulsive of large lifting screws rotating in a horizontal plane. That such a machine can rise by direct lift has been experimentally proved, but that it also an effect horizontal flight and make a safe landing in case of engine failure has yet to be demonstrated.

The problem is briefly the following: In an airplane, when the engine stops the wings enable the pilot to glide down to a landing, for in gliding flight gravity takes the place of the forward pull which the propeller supplies in

The Berliner Helicopter Undergoing Trials near Washington, D.C.
The two lifting screws, of 13 feet diameter, are driven by an 80 horse-power rotary engine and have lifting power of 900 pounds. The wight of the machine is 620 pounds.

power flight. But in the helicopter both sustentation and propulsion are dependent on the rotation of the propellers. What assurance is there, then, of a safe descent with a disabled engine?

The answer is that the blades of lifting screws may be considered as so many wing surfaces which act under the influence of air resistance exactly as the wings of an airplane. Only, the latter are fixed with respect to the airplane, while the blades of the lifting screw rotate around an axis. If now, in the case of engine failure, we permit the lifting screws to rotate freely under the action of the upward air stream the helicopter encounters in its fall, sustentation is created, whereby the rate of descents slowed down sufficiently to insure a safe landing.

To glide down at an angle with the horizon, instead of descending vertically—which may not be feasible on account of obstacles on the ground—the helicopter requires horizontal control. This may be effected by controlling the inclination of the propellers in combination with elevators such as are used on airplanes. The pilot will then be able to alter the trim of his machine at will and assume the angle of descent required for a safe landing or for horizontal flight.

Experiments with helicopters, though not sufficiently conclusive to disclose their practical merits and drawbacks, appear promising enough to warrant hope for a speedy solution of this question. In the meantime the airplane remains the only practical flying-machine of this day. It is, then, timely to inquire how far this vehicle has progressed on the road of safety and reliability—features that most often interest the layman.

SAFETY IN AIRPLANE FLIGHT

That much-discussed topic, safety in flight, depends chiefly on the reliability of the power plant, protection against fire, and the ability to land in restricted spaces and at a low rate of speed.

While the developments made during the late war advanced aeronautical engineering in a marked degree, they did not fully solve the above-named problems. The importance of getting results in the shortest possible time precluded the evolution of the airplane on the basis of extended scientific investigation. With peace returned, such an opportunistic policy is no longer necessary, and as a result some remarkable strides are now being made in an endeavor to eliminate the remaining shortcomings of the flying-machine.

The aero engines produced during the Great War, developing high power for an extremely low weight (two pounds per horse-power for the Liberty engine), dodo at the cost of reliability. Such a sacrifice is not, however, justified in commercial aviation, where reliability must be the main slogan. Commercial aero engines may have a greater dead-weight than the war types if this goes hand in hand with a more dependable operation and with lower fuel consumption. Such an engine is not only cheaper in production costs, but also cheaper in upkeep, because less specialized materials can be used in its construction. By running such an engine at from eighty to ninety per cent of its maximum power a reliability comparable to that of the automobile or a locomotive could be attained and the life of the power plant would be materially increased.

Present-day aero engines can be operated for some two hundred hours without overhauling, which at 100 miles her hour represent 20,000 flight miles. As to the life of such engines, many of them have functioned satisfactorily for several thousand hours, the corresponding flight mileage running into six figures. This, it will be admitted, is not a bad showing in comparison with automobile performance.

The Damblanc-Lacoin Helicopter, a French machine which combines some of the features of the airplane with those of the helicopter. The two engines which are to drive the lifting screws are missing in this picture.

A WEAK POINT OF THE AERO ENGINE

Probably the weakest point of the aero engine is in its connections—the pipes and joints leading to fuel and oil tanks and to the radiator. Rigid pipes are unsatisfactory as a rule, because the vibration of the engine gradually weakens them until some day they break. The use of flexible connections is therefore preferred, although some fuels eventually dissolve the gasoline-proof lining of these pipes.

The question of secure connections has a very important bearing on the safety of flying, for the gasoline escaping from a broken joint or pipe is likely to be ignited by the backfire of the engine. This is what happened to the luckless imported mail airplane that burned up mid-air last summer. It merely served to emphasize theft that even an all-metal machine is not safe against the fire risk so long as we employ a highly inflammable fuel—gasoline—for it's propulsion. Hence the development of heavier fuels is a vital question in aviation, the more so as the sources of gasoline supply are becoming gradually exhausted. For the latter reason synthetic fuels—mixtures of gasoline, alcohol, and benzol—have recently been developed and successfully used in aero engines. Until less inflammable fuels become available special safeguards have to be provided on flying-machines against the fire risk. Fire-proof bulkheads placed between the engine and the cockpit or the cabin, gasoline tanks capable of being dropped from under the machine or emptied in case of fire, all answer this purpose, and so does the fire-proofing of the entire machine by means of special compounds or "dopes."

The Gastambide-Levasseur variable surface airplane, which was recently put through successful trials in France

The chord (width) of the wings can be increase by the pilot by means of thin sliding panels from 5¼ feet to 10¾ feet. The machine is shown with the panels extended.

THE VALUE OF PARACHUTES

The subject of fire hazard raises the question as to the utility of the parachute. Parachutes have been experimented with successfully and extensively. The only puzzling point about them is that in cases where they would prove most valuable—that is, when the airplane is hopelessly out of control—the nearness of the ground makes it almost impossible for the parachute to function properly. On the other hand, there being always the possibility of righting the airplane at greater heights, it is probable that passengers and crew would stick to the airplane to the last rather than take to the parachute. Interesting experiments have, however, been made with parachutes intended to function near the ground by pulling the occupant clear of the machine, the parachute being shot into the air by an explosive charge.

Where the parachute promises to be really of value, however, is in the case of fire in mid-air, provided the equipment is fire-proofed. For this reason alone it seems likely that in the future the equipping of aircraft with parachutes will be made compulsory, just as life-savers are on ships.

Essays

ABILITY TO LAND IN RESTRICTED PLACES

The third requirement for safe flying is the ability to land in restricted spaces, which means landing at a slow speed and coming to a stop.

The war airplanes have, as a rule, too high a landing speed—about fifty miles per hour—to be satisfactory for commercial uses. Some commercial machines built since the armistice are much more satisfactory in this respect, a landing speed of from thirty-five to forty miles per hour having been attained by several types, while one particular machine actually lands at fifteen miles per hour. The last is a small airplane, it is true, but the mere fact that such a machine exists is a hopeful sign for future improvements.

Progress in this direction may be expected from some recent experiments with wings of variable surface and various camber (curvature), the initial trials of which have been successful. By these means, combined perhaps with reversible propellers, the airplane of tomorrow will be able to land at a very low speed, to come to a stop after rolling ten or twenty yards, and to rise rapidly from the ground after a ferry short run. Restricted landing-places will then have lost their terror for the users of the air.

For large airplanes four-wheel landing gears will probably become current to prevent nosing over in soft ground, and the use of band brakes on the rear wheels will contribute to bringing the machine to a short stop. The substitution of the rubber strands now used as shock-absorbers by a more mechanical device—steel springs, oleo-pneumatic shock-absorbers, etc.—also appears as a necessity in view of increasing the life of the equipment.

COMFORT AND CONVENIENCE

Such are the principle points involved in the safety of flying. But if safety is the main requirement of commercial aviation, comfort is a hardly less important factor in its success.

Great strides have been made in this line by building airplanes with in-closed cabins, where the passengers sit in comfortable armchairs and look upon the ground through curtained windows, being fully protected against e blast produced by the airscrew. Provisos for heating the cabin in the winter and insuring efficient ventilation are not so common and still require much thought. The least progress has been made in suppressing the roar of engine and its vibrations. Unless an efficient silencer is invented, it seems likely that special noise-proof cabins will come into being in which the passengers will be able to converse freely without the use of telephone attachment.

Though a matter of convenience rather than comfort, self-starters are becoming quite common on aero engines. Their generalization will eliminate the source of many accidents which have happened to aviation mechanics in "swinging the prop," and their use should be made compulsory on all flying-machines.

STRIVING FOR IMPROVED PERFORMANCE

While no radical changes in the appearance of the airplanes are likely for some time to come, the monoplane again seems to commie to the fore, at least for machines up to a certain size. This is mainly due to the introduction of very thick wings, which permit internal trussing, or cantilever construction, and thus solve the long-standing problem of how to brace monoplane wings securely without using a maze of wires and struts.

As a monoplane is, for the same wing area, more efficient an a biplane or triplane because of the lack of interference between the wings, and the cantilever construction permits the suppression of resistance-producing truss elements, the thick-wing monoplane marks an important step in improving performance.

Whether the advent of is type of will bring about the rapid generalization of metal in airplane construction is a debatable point. Until the airplane has reached a greater degree of finality in design it will be cheaper to build it of wood than of metal, despite the durability of the latter. If an airplane

The Zeppelin Giant Monoplane, which is noteworthy for the mounting of the engines in the wings.

The great thickness of the wings may be gathered from the size of the men sitting on them. The machine is built of steel and duralumin. This plane is still in the experimental stage, as shown by the fact the landing gear gave way when used at the end of its test flight

becomes obsolete in two or three years because it's performance is no longer up to current standards, it would be foolish to make it so durable that it would be airworthy for ten years. Furthermore, in small machines metal construction is heavier than wood construction and repairs are more expensive and difficult because they require special machinery. "Crashes" also damage a metal plane more severely, for metal has not the resiliency of wood, and severe shocks, transmitted through the entire framework,are likely to terminate the usefulness of a metal wing when a wooden wing may only be locally injured.

Therefore, for the time being, composite types of construction—using, for instance, steel wing spars and longerons with built-up veneer wings—seem most promising.

Resuming, it may be said that the present-day airplane is, despite some minor shortcomings, fully capable of taking are of the demand for extra-rapid transportation of passengers,mails, and express packages. In appearance the single-engine tractor airplane is now probably the nearest to finality, with the monoplane likely to supplant the biplane.

The status of the multi-motored airplane is not quite so certain. The present practice of mounting two engines outboard between the wings seems only a temporary expedient and one which is open to serious criticism. If one of the engines fails, the missing pull of the idle power propeller will tend to pull the airplane into a spin, unless the pilot acts swiftly on the controls. The ideal solute would probably be to have twin propellers driven through the gear shafts by two engines located in a central engine room, with a third engine kept idle for emergencies. Should the main power plant fail, the emergency engine would be meshed in with the propeller gear box and the airplane would continue its flight at a reduced speed until the manpower plant is repaired. This solution would demand the use of variable surface wings, for these would be extended when the less powerful emergency engine has to drive the propellers, and be retracted in normal flight.

That the large passenger carriers of the future will embody some such arrangement seems a foregone conclusion, for only a multiple power plant affords absolute insurance against forced landings, and the twin-engine airplane of today cannot fly with its full load on a horizontal path. It may stretch its glide for many miles; ultimately it must land.

The development of an improved multi-motored airplane offers, therefore, to aeronautical engineers a particularly large field for manifesting their talent.

Is Transport by Air a Success?**

By Ladislas d'Orcy, Editor of 'Aviation and Aircraft Journal'

**(originally published in The Outlook Magazine, December 7, 1921)*

Is transportation by air a success? This is a question thoughtful Americans are asking with growing frequency. United States mails are daily carried on a seventy-two-hour schedule between New York and San Francisco, thus gaining two days on the fastest transcontinental railway service, and last spring the coast-to-coast mail delivery was actually accomplished in 33 1/2 hours from the time the mail was put on board the airplane in San Francisco to the moment it reached Mineola, Long Island. This experimental extra-rapid mail delivery was achieved as a result of an all-nit flight from Cheyenne to Omaha, a distance of some eight hundred miles. It is needless to stress the value of this demonstration; the figures speak for themselves.

But, while the ails are swiftly carried through the air from the Atlantic to the Pacific, the traveler who should wish to take advantage of the Wright brothers' invention for the purpose of cutting down distances will find it impossible to do so in the United States. It is true that he may charter an airplane and fly from New York to San Francisco, following the United States Air Mail route, where he may take advantage of the "ground organization"—air ports, fuel depots, radio stations, emergency fields—provided for the safety of the mail fliers. Outside of this route he will face much greater hazards, as landing-fields are few and far between. And should this traveler inquire into the competency of the pilot and the safety of the plane, he will discover, to his astonishment, at no official standards govern either.

The airplane in question, if built by a reputable firm, probably left the factory embodying all the safety features known to aeronautical engineering; but its maintenance may have been neglected since it was put in service, although this may not be visible under a new coat of varnish or paint, and the traveler has no means of ascertaining the present condition of the machine. The pilot may be known as a first-rate flier with several thousand hours' experience in the air; still, he may suffer from some organic trouble which, thou unimportant in the beginning, might unexpectedly assume serious proportions in the air; again the traveler is unable to determine this.

Such a state of affairs seems almost incredible, considering that before a man can drive an automobile he is compelled to pass an examination, and that buildings, bridges, and seacraft are regularly inspected and licensed by Government and other public authorities. Yet the fact stands that today any person can build and fly any kind of aircraft and take up paying passengers without being compelled by the law to show his qualifications for such an enterprise.

Some States of the Union have passed legislation for the regulation of air navigation and some cities have added sundry ordinances to this incomplete legal apparatus; but these laws and rules are seldom, if ever, enforced. Furthermore, it is not desirable that aviation be regulated by State laws, for the possible existence of forty-eight different aerial codes would prove nothing short of a calamity whose chief result would be to stifle the healthy growth of air transport. To visualize what this would mean, suffice it to remember that in e course of a trip from New York to San Francisco at least ten States have to be flown over in a total time not exceeding thirty-six hours. Aircraft altogether move too fast to be regulated individually by States. In Europe, where the areas of sovereign countries are, as a rule, no larger than that of different States of the Union, the absolute need for a common aerial code found its expression in International Convention for the Regulation of Air Navigation elaborated by the peace Conference, to which all the Allied Powers became signatories. Although the United States signed this Convention, Congress has not so far ratified it, as it is linked up with theLeague of Nations Covenant, nor has it provided any National air legislation. A rapid solution of the resulting "aerial lawlessness" may, however, be expected if Congress passes the bill (S. 2448) which Senator Wadsworth, of New York, has introduced in the Senate, and which provides for the creation of a Bureau of Civil Aeronautics and the appointment of a Commissioner of Civil Aeronautics whose jurisdiction would practically extend over all civil air activities in the United States.

This Commissioner would license the operation of civil aircraft after due inspection of their design and construction in the factory, and would, in addition, maintain a periodical inspection service to ascertain the conditions under which the machines are maintained. He would furthermore issue certificates of competency to aviators qualifying for their duties rough theoretical and practical examinations, and through a medical visit which also would be periodically renewed. Finally, he would foster the development of civil aeronautics by developing e "ground organization" and enforcing the aerial traffic rules required for safe flying.

How urgent the need of such a Federal agency is may be seen from a report, prepared by the Manufacturers Aircraft Association, on the aviation accidents which occurred in the United States from January 1 to June 30, 1921. There are recorded for this period a total of 58accidents for an aggregate flight mileage estimated at 3,250,000, and of this total ten accidents caused fourteen fatalities, twenty accidents were responsible for injury to the occupants, while in eighteen instances there were no casualties. This works out alone fatal accident for every 325,000 miles flown, a ratio which compares favorably with official foreign figures if the estimate of the American flight mileage is substantially correct. In Great Britain, for instance, the number of fatal aviation accidents per miles flown in 1920 was one in 195,000 miles; but it is only fair toads that the English weather, with its frequent fogs, is particularly adverse to flying. Considering this circumstance, the showing made is remarkably good, for the total British flight mileage represents some 62,000 separate aerial journeys, in which 106,712 passengers were carried, so that fatalities among the latter were only one for every 7,750 flights.

On the other hand, the greatest credit is due to American aircraft constructors and pilots for having made such a safe showing despite the lack of Federal air regulation. Had the latter been in existence, the number of accidents would undoubtedly have been less. This appears clearly from the report of the Manufacturers Aircraft Association, which carefully analyzes the causes of accidents. Thus it is shown that seventeen accidents were caused by the pilot, either through incompetence, carelessness, or bad judgement, to which number should be added eight due to "stunting." Although "stunting" is a necessary requirement in aerial fighting and it may in unusual cases prove of great help to civilian pilots finding themselves in a tight corner, the practice of indiscriminately "stunting" civil airplanes is indefensible from the view-point of safety, and it should therefore be prohibited when the Federal Government shall possess the power of doing so. Canada, Great Britain, and France have come to the same conclusion, and heavy penalties, including the suspension of the pilot's certificate, await the offenders against this ruling.

Lack of proper inspection of the airplane prior to the flight as responsible for eleven accidents, while poor landing-fields or a lack of them caused eight mishaps. The remainder of the accidents are apportioned as to their causes between lack of weather forecasting, lack of route directions, collision, and unknown causes. The following is a recapitulation in tabulated form of the civil aviation accidents which occured in the United States from January 1 to June 30, 1921:

Faulty piloting:	17	Faulty engine:	6
Poor field or its lack:	10	Faulty accessory:	2
Lack of weather data:	2	"Stunting":	8
Lack of route data or flying limitations:	2	Collision:	1
No inspection:		Carelessness in the field:	2
Faulty craft:	3	Cause unknown:	5
		Total number of accidents:	58

Essays

With reference to the above statistics, it should be noted that, according to the estimate of the Manufacturers Aircraft Association, some 1,200 aircraft are engaged in commercial flying in the United States today. But, despite this large number, not a single aerial passenger service operates on a regular schedule in this country, chiefly because of the lack of "ground organization" and the absence f Governmental regulation. The 3,250,000 miles flown by civil aircraft during the first six months of this year are almost entirely he result of what may be called "itinerant flying"—that is, operating in the neighborhood of a given locality from a single field. "Joy-riding"—or "beach hoping" in the case of seaplanes—with paying passengers made up the bulk of this business. Intercity flights represent only a small percentage of the total flight mileage.

Therefore, if we wish further to pursue the inquiry whether transport by air is a success, we have to look for information abroad, where regular aerial passenger services are in daily operation. The majority of these air lines are operated by French companies, which are heavily subsidized by their Government. Thus for the fiscal year of 1921 a sum of 20,000,000 francs was ear-marked for subsidies alone out of the civil aviation budget of 185,000,000 francs. The remainder of the appropriation is provided for the maintenance of the Government agency which regulates civil flying, for the development of commercial aircraft types, air ports, etc. The subsidy takes the form of a premium paid in proportion to the number of passengers and pounds of freight carried, in addition to which the Government assumes the obligation to pay the company one-half the construction cost of each new commercial airplane that is added to its fleet.

Critics of this subsidy scheme assert that it is too generous and that it will eventually stifle true commercial air enterprise. The answer to this criticism is that the French Government is determined to build up a commercial air fleet which should sere as a reservoir of trained pilots and auxiliary *matériel* in a time of war. Now to keep this fleet, going on sound business principles a clientele of aerial travelers has to be created first, and to this end the subsidy is large enough to enable the air-transport companies to carry passengers at a rate hardly in excess of that charged by railways or steamships if one considers the time and money saved. This ay be gathered from the follwing table:

Route	Time (hours) Air	Time (hours) Railway & Steamer	Fare (francs) Air	Fare (francs) Railway & Steamer
Paris - London	3	$7^{1/2}$	300	181
Paris - Amsterdam	$4^{1/2}$	13	300	122
Paris - Prague	7	12	500	318
Toulouse - Casablanca	31	99	840	670

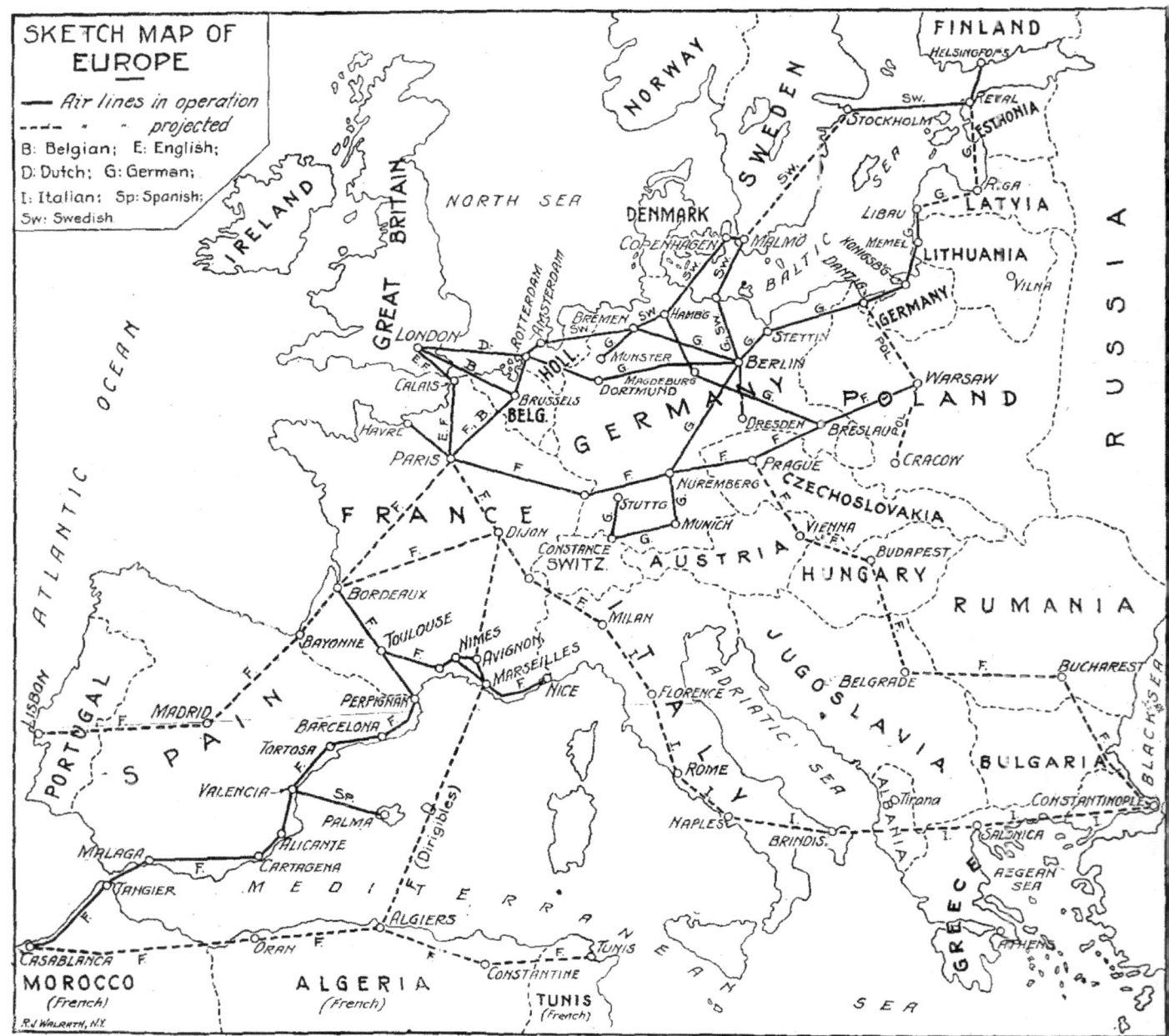

The Growing Network of Air Lines Over Europe

Essays

It is admitted that today the operation on schedule of commercial airplanes is not profitable, and that in most cases it even involves financial loss. The reasons for this situation are, first, that the operating companies are still using a large number of converted war airplanes, which are not the most efficient from the commercial point-of-view; and, second, that, being held to a schedule, the machines often fly with small "pay loads," whereby heir earning capacity s naturally reduced. On the other hand, airplanes purely designed for commercial purposes have proved to be much less costly in operation and maintenance than the converted war craft, so that the gradual weeding out of the latter is bound to prove a boon to the operating companies.

As to the public's response to the appeal of air transport, statistics show a very marked growth in the number of aerial travelers as well as in the amount of merchandise shipped by air. This development seems to justify the contention of the French Air Department that when the public shall have acquired the habit of traveling by air the flying clientele will have assumed such proportions that the air-transport companies will become self-supporting, and so justify a large reduction of the subsidies.

The following table, which is based on data compiled by the French Air Department, shows to what extent commercial aviation has developed in France since September, 1919, when the Government authorized the resumption of civil flying. The figures for 1921 include only the first four months of operation.

Year	1919 [1]	1920	1921 [2]
Number of flights	1,173	4,428	1,625
Number of passengers	729	5,968	1,884
Pounds of merchandise	30,800	271,100	92,900
Pounds in mail	1,025	13,900	4,655

[1] September 1 to December 31 only
[2] January 1 to April 30 only

While the poundage of merchandise carried by airplanes may not seem very impressive in the light of railway or steamship operation, it should be realized that air-borne freight is of a special nature, in which precious articles of small bulk and light weight pre-dominate. During the past year the value of air-borne merchandise imported into and exported from England, mostly clothes and furs, had a total value of £5,000,000. Among the more important shipments there was one of French clothes for women worth £1,500,000, while other merchandise included men's and boy's clothing, watches, electrical appliances, paintings, and motion-picture films. How rapidly this aerial trade is growing may also be seen from the fact that for he last quarter of 1920 the value of British imports and exports carried by aircraft was fur times greater than for the corresponding period in 1919.

It is not only the time-saving feature which prompts a growing percentage of the European business world to take advantage of air transport. High speed by itself cannot introduce a new means of rapid locomotion. It must be seconded by reliability and safety Of the latter we have given exhaustive data in the connection with air transport, but a few words remain to be said with respect to reliability.

Abroad the reliability of the air-transport services varies a good deal according to the operating company. On the Paris-London route, for instance, the French services maintain, as a rule, their schedule better than their British competitors, because the former are penalized for every ten minutes defaulted on departure, the penalty being charged against the subsidy. This system works surprisingly well. On the Toulouse-Casablanca route—the only one for which figures are available—the operating company maintained in 1920 a service efficiency of 96 per cent; that is, it defaulted only 4 per cent of the scheduled flights. This is very remarkable if it is considered that this route runs over large stretches of wild country, mainly in Morocco, and that its total length is 1,200 miles.

Facts such as these speak for themselves. They show that the European business world is realizing that it pays to travel by air if one is in a hurry, and that it equally pays to ship by air certain classes of merchandise which lose much of their value by delays in delivery. Hence they cheerfully pay the comparatively high rates which the air lines are forced to charge until an increasing volume of business will warrant reduction.

OTHER BOOKS BY VertVolta PRESS

Pioneer Days on Puget Sound, by Arthur A. Denny
978-1-60944-051-0, $11.00

Be Vigilant, But Not Afraid: The Farewell Speeches of Barack Obama *44th President of the United State of America and* Michelle Obama *Former First Lady of the United States of America.*
978-1-60944-111-1, $9.00

Anarchism and Other Essays, by Emma Goldman
978-1-60944-113-5, $14.00

Fly to the Assemblies: *Seattle and the Rise of the Resistance*
edited by Marcus Harrison Green
978-1-60944-116-6, $15.99

Emerald Reflections: *A South Seattle Emerald Anthology*
edited by Marcus Harrison Green
978-1-60944-109-8, $17.00

Emerald Reflections 2: *A South Seattle Emerald Anthology*
edited by Marcus Harrison Green
978-1-60944-132-6, $15.99

Vancouver's Discovery of Puget Sound: *Portraits and Biographies of the Men Honored in the Naming of Geographic Features of Northwestern America,* by Edmond S. Meany
978-1-60944-126-5, $16.99

www.ingramcontent.com/pod-product-compliance
Lightning Source LLC
Chambersburg PA
CBHW081427070526
44586CB00020B/2516